The
Destiny of Man

SPREAD THIS GOOD NEWS

From:

To:

Daniel Obikwelu

The
Destiny of Man

NATURAL AND SPIRITUAL

Order this book online at www.trafford.com
or email orders@trafford.com

Most Trafford titles are also available at major online book retailers.

© Copyright 2013 Daniel Obikwelu.

All rights reserved. No part of this publication may be reproduced, stored in a retrieval system, or transmitted, in any form or by any means, electronic, mechanical, photocopying, recording, or otherwise, without the written prior permission of the author.

Printed in the United States of America.

ISBN: 978-1-4669-9415-7 (sc)
ISBN: 978-1-4669-9414-0 (hc)
ISBN: 978-1-4669-9413-3 (e)

Library of Congress Control Number: 2013908441

Trafford rev. 06/14/2013

Trafford Publishing®   www.trafford.com

North America & international
toll-free: 1 888 232 4444 (USA & Canada)
phone: 250 383 6864 ♦ fax: 812 355 4082

This book is dedicated to YOU.

You are created by God and recreated by the same God in the spirit of His Eternal Word who manifested Himself as Christ Jesus. It is the most amazing story that God took flesh and died to redeem human race.

Since God dared to die for man, it means you are so lovely and precious: empowered to defeat and explore the world—to transcend the standard of the natural man to the image of Christ who is the head of all principalities and powers.

'You are a chosen generation, a royal priesthood, a consecrated nation, a people set apart to proclaim the praises of God who called you out of the darkness into His marvellous light. Once you were not a people at all and now you are the people of God; once you were outside the mercy and now you have been given mercy'.

1 Peter 2:9-10

Kudos to my family and my lovely friends who have been there for me in this great journey of my soul; you have helped me so much. Greater praises to the angels of light who ministered these truths to my spirit. May your name be magnified oh God of love and truth that used me to communicate this message and placed this book of destiny in the hand of this my amazing friend!

Contents

Author's Note ix
The Formation Theory 1
The Nature of Man 14
Fallen Angels at Work 31
The Fate of the Natural Man 44
The Spiritual Nature 68
The Divine Visitor 89
The Mystic Voice 103
The Foudation 116
The Triumph of the True God 144
The Only Choice We Have 164
The Destiny of Life is Optional 186
Entering into His Rest 210
Some Biblical Substructure of this Book 225

Author's Note

Isn't the most amazing story about you? To hear that you are not just an earthly being, but rather a missing spiritual being who found himself in the flesh. He is called man, but considering his unique physiology and his angelic appearance, he is called a higher animal—because of his marvellous abilities. Look at the beautiful things he has invented in the world he met in utter darkness; though it is said that the natural man had fallen from the glory of the Garden of Eden to the shadow of reality, yet he has transformed the world tremendously.

In the womb of the morning before the sun rose, man left a place beyond our scientific imaginings and geographical placement to find himself here on earth. What an afflictive episode that the Ancient Father of man took the painful but necessary decision that man must return to the earth, reconcile with Him and start afresh his spiritual formation before his returning.

How can a stranger adapt to a strange land? Only by becoming one with where he finds himself. Therefore the mystical nature of man who left a place had no option than to form flesh, to be able to live on Earth until he is through with his spiritual formations.

When God Himself, who made man, decided to visit the earth for the reconciliation and to remind man that he had left a place, He had no option other than taking flesh as well in order to communicate His message and rapprochement. Though the former may find it very difficult to return because of the cryptic mutations that had taken place, yet he must go because the destiny of his origin bears witness against him that he is a stranger in the material body. God only sent man away to be a higher being made of Himself on his return.

The Destiny of Man is the exploration and the excavation of The New Creation—to fathom the depth of man both in his higher and lower natures. It is theosophical: a consciousness of the eternal truth and codification in the Scripture about man and his great lover—the God of creation. The truth is divulged, and certain mysteries that stand as puzzles are revealed—about the mystical nature of man both in the Garden of Eden and the material world. Yes! The great mystery of the two different natures of man in Adam and Christ Jesus who answered the second Adam is unveiled, so that the eternal life and victorious destiny of man may be achieved if the right choice is made. Whether one lives his life only according to his animal nature or not, going back to spiritual where we come from is a sine qua non.

It is indeed a rapturous spiritual blossoming that kept religion and science in unending squabbles. Of course science and spiritual matters can never agree, since science is the fruit of the intellectual mind of the material nature of man, which has lost the spiritual insight of God and the origin of man. As the Scripture says, 'For what is exalted among men is an abomination in the sight of God.' And another text said, 'My thoughts are not your thoughts, and your ways are not my ways.' (Luke 16:15 and Isaiah 55:8)

Indeed a great thing has happened to the human race in our generation: the understanding that the Scripture, which has two covenants of life and death, is talking to the two spiritual nature of man that determines the fate of one's soul, which has separate destinies of life and death. Perhaps those who are not in the covenant with the manifested Christ will be exposed in the mysteries therein and confessed with us that the Messiah was The Christ born of the Virgin Mary.

As we have said, the message is theosophical: therefore in reading this book one must equip himself with a meditative mind in order to assimilate what the spirit whispered. The message of this book is communicated to the conscious mind from the spiritual realm where the destiny of our world is predetermined. To those who have made themselves available, to the chosen or those who were found on a fertile land—to them, the spirit communicates the hidden mysteries of our being. What they know or teach is beyond their consciousness as human, but is being communicated through them as a medium; so boasting is excluded from any man.

Our spiritual life is a life of faith; of course you must know that fruitful faith is the one that has gone beyond the ordinary to the level of truth of what is invisible, even though you cannot see it. Beyond our sub-consciousness dwells our hidden nature. Pray that God Himself will put your animal nature in check through His mystical power, so your spiritual nature will behold the invisible things that define our stay on earth. The consciousness that this book will ignite in you will prepare you to put up with the powers of your lower nature, so your soul can unite with the spirit of Christ and take you back to where we lost with the first Adam.

The truth of this book is truly a great destiny of man, which is inspired at the right time when the world is in utter confusion about the true nature of man and his orientations. I was in the condition of the complete unknown while writing this book. Even though the mystery was hovering over my head, yet it was totally spiritual, but I was naturally tossed around by all manners of wind, especially when this work was on course; but His right hand was mighty. I was natural so that the Spirit would minister the truth as it is.

Until now, you may not have known who you are; neither have you known the true nature of Christ until you are exposed to the destiny of this book. Go through it and your destiny will change forever. It is my prayer that the words of the Scripture be open to you as you read—for it pleases Christ that it can never remained sealed, for that long-expected enemy is about to be born.

A prophecy said, 'Very soon Christ will tell the world how man and the world were created.' Open your mind as you read and see if Christ has a message for you; because I am certain that His spirit used me to bring about this truth.

What you are about to see in this book will swing you! But relax, for it's taking you to the fertile land where you will experience the depth of His love and the truth of our existence. It is my advice before reading this book to get yourself on level ground and not on the edge lest you drift away, or find yourself standing against Him who puts this book in your hand. For God loves us and want us to come to the full knowledge of the truth. It is the destiny of this book to transform man to the supernatural destiny—making him a participator of the life to come even though he is still in the flesh.

Being a child of the holy mother the church, I therefore surrender the theology and the theosophical cognisance of this book to the supreme authority and the judgement of the church of Christ Jesus, the greatest teacher of all ages.

The SWORD which is a symbol of physical death also has a greater mission to save a soul from spiritual death.

The Formation Theory

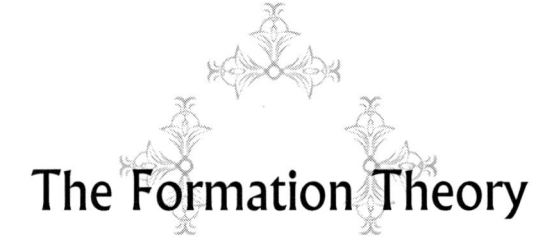

Beloved, consider the content of this book a mystery beyond my contemplation in the ordinary, but rather a silent whisper of the spirit. I adore your Most Holy Spirit 'Oh Eternal Now', the Alfa and Omega. You have truly made a crippled man run; I solicit your mercy through the intercession of the host of heaven that you may open the eyes of my brethren who may be blind, that they may see your wonders and glorify your mercy which is made manifest in the greatest misery of man whom you love so dearly and exalt him to your inheritance.

They have portrayed themselves in different character, claiming to be gods in human form, yet they died like other men, which is opposed to their claims. They claimed to be prophets and seers and some of them proved it with signs and wonders which accompanied them: predictions that later came to pass, which filled people's minds with a sense of wonder. They claimed to be kings ordained by God and were arrayed with the glories projected towards them from men and women of every class; great exploits were achieved by them as well as disastrous failures. Men of great wisdom and intelligence! They have achieved greatness and innovations that changed the world from age to age. Yet many lived but never existed, listened but did not understand; maybe the saying may be applied which says that all fingers are not equal. But were all their claims true? Were they not just as ordinary humans, eventually dying with all their glories vanished away?

Who are you? No clear answer has been given to this question since the two people involved neither understands what one asks nor the answer the other is giving. This question may have millions of responses according to natural man's proud senses, unless one bows down in humility in accord to the mysteries of Christ Jesus who knows the very depth of man—for He is the Word that created all things in the beginning. Christ, knowing the full condition of man's weaknesses, expects man to acknowledge his miseries if he needs liberation. This liberation will eventually exalt man to the full knowledge of the glorious nature he possesses owing to the manifestation of the invisible God as a man in Christ Jesus who gave His life in ransom for many. Truly He is the king, the prophet and the amalgamator of the heavens and earth; He is the peace offering and the reconciliation between God and man. All the prophets and sages were manifested to herald His days. In the canticles of His apostles, He is represented as the fruit of the marriage between heaven and earth, which made it possible for Him to unite both heaven and earth, visible and invisible.

Every other created being knows what they are and accepts their state, but man, because of the multiple identities in his spirit, could not truly define himself. Paradoxically his sub-consciousness is spiritual, and in contradicting his natural consciousness and dispositions confuses the soul about his true identity.

The creator of man in the beginning built man as a house and put him as a spirit or a dweller in that house with one entrance which only He the creator had access to: to commune with the spirit of man that lords over the creations of God. But with time, that house of God called man collapsed and fell, owing to disobedience. After this fall, the intruders who had no access to the spirit of man earlier broke the code and entered the depth of man; they possessed and contaminated the precious spirit of man. This made the nature of man in the Eden Garden incompatible with the nature of God who had made him in His image and likeness. Man has multiple personalities; he defines himself as this today, but tomorrow you will see the same man acting in a way contrary to what you witnessed him confessing yesterday, because his animal nature is fighting to control his hidden nature which is spiritual.

When a house is built, well fenced and secured with doors, no one can enter that house except the owner or whoever is given access to the building. But once the fence and the doors are removed, everything will have access to that building: thieves, lions and all manner of reptiles, because the owner has lost much of the control of the house. This was the condition in which man found himself after the fall; he became very afraid and vulnerable, and that which he was afraid of suddenly invaded him and yoked him into bondage. The Bible said:

'The thief does not enter except to steal and to kill, and to destroy.' (John 10:10)

Any house invaded by this type of thief will never remain the same. It's like when a lion in its prime is looking for a territory. A lion never enters a new territory without first doing two back legs ritual to mark the end of a dynasty and the beginning of another; it goes on to establishing its presence by putting its chemical signature on the ground to set a mark before settling down to claim the territory. In a similar way the reptiles are deadly and territorial; whenever a reptile enters a house, it normally lays eggs in that building, knowing all too well that its presence is not welcomed, so when its eggs are hatched and the young ones are born, it will be almost impossible to eradicate them because they know no other place as a home other than where they were born, just as every living being has a special devotion to the place of their birth.

This was exactly the case of man after the great sin of Adam and Eve—not only that they fell from the glory of God, but that they were also possessed and contaminated by the evil one who defeated them on that tree. Stepping into the most secret place of man, he pitched his tent therein and dwelled there. God who made man with a freedom of choice lost man's complete allegiance; man chose to be a slave rather than a son of God. He chose to obey fallen angels rather than God; therefore God had no choice than to allow man to follow his choice but not without banishment from His dwelling place.

Adam's sin has reduced Adam from spiritual man to a natural man who is nothing but a nature, capable of doing anything that contradicts the spiritual origin of man because of his contaminated nature. Just as his new lord had done, losing his heavenly state, so man also lost his state. Thus after some metaphysical understanding about the nature of man, I refuse to and desist from blaming anyone from any inclination he was born with or into, for we all have natural wounds of all kinds. But heaven frowns on such a person if in pride he refuses to reject that nature and to follow Christ who only manifested himself for all of us, who were the greatest grandchildren of Adam and Eve, contaminated with the wild eggs of the fallen angels to rebel against our origin.

These children of Adam and Eve to whom the spirit of God in the Gospel referred as the old man or natural man must necessarily in an unpleasant manner be vicious with no exceptions or substitute. Because he who defeated and is ruling that nature has nothing to give his subjects other than his poisonous venom which he has in abundance. In the Holy Scripture, he is called the perverse from the beginning and the father of lies.

According to Christ Jesus in His Gospel of Life, everything that comes out of the depth of the old nature of man is not in agreement with the will of God; neither can he obey the laws of God anymore, which is very strange to his new state. Thus He came to give man a new nature, which is able to fulfil the reason that God created man to have fellowship with him.

... ...

Natural man is a selfish being, who enjoys doing his own thing—which is sometimes offensive to God, who made man to behave like Himself, The Holy One. This is the answer to the primary question about who we are indeed. After the knowledge of self, if a natural man, the true fruit of Adam and Eve, failed to recognise himself as a being who is capable of doing anything evil, even as he sees in the lives of his fellow men despite the grace of God, the same is a deceiver and a dreamer: he is someone who may not have had the true examination and knowledge of who he is—just like one who forgets what he looks like after seeing himself in the mirror. Bring to your mind the Gospel call, which says, 'Deny yourself if you want to follow me.' The spirit that controls the natural man is full of misery thus Christ never wanted that nature to follow Him—for it is in vain that a wise man showers a pig, which must return to where it belongs.

Man is called humus or earth. Because the origin and anthropology of the chemistry of man was from the earth from where the creator picked him in the beginning and exalted him with the breath of Himself, giving him soul and spirit to live among the hosts of heaven. No matter how black, brown or white the nature of the old man may claim to be, he must find his colour in the soil for I have done good meditations with the different colours of sand and have emerged with this knowledge: that every colour of man has the same type of soil, which goes in agreement with man's colour. Thus after life on earth, that man must return back to the mother earth, which must be its final destination. The animal nature of man is truly some portion of the sand activated by the breath of God.

Adam had no stages of formation when he was first made; he was just a complete man who had the same image as the one who made him. His maker visits him; he sees God and even hears His footsteps in the garden whenever he arrives. (Compare Genesis 3:8.) Then, he had one will with his maker; he had no instinct of animal nature as we all have now after his disobedience and the subsequent fall. He was just a spiritual being a little lower than the angels, who were in the spiritual kingdom and not in the animal kingdom.

Most times, when we talk about the fall of Adam and Eve, people always think they had the kind of nature that we have now, or have always dwelled in this material world. But it's not true. Adam was an exalted being who had flesh but had full consciousness of spirit; he was far more of spirit which made him live as if he did not have flesh, just as most of us now live with less consciousness of our spiritual nature and some do not even know or believe that man is a spirit in flesh.

Because of this full consciousness of the spirit, Adam and Eve were able to see and commune with God who made them have a cordial relationship as His lower creatures less than the Angels; also they related with the Angels as comrades and companions, though the Angels were fiery spirits and of higher nature. They were in flesh but the flesh was spiritual and had no dominion at all over them because it had less or no function; it was just their encasement, which they could move about without any barrier, in the same manner in which we see a tortoise move its shell about: a shell that, even though it's part of the creature and grows with it, is dead. Even so Adam was truly spirit in the orphic flesh. It was their sin that activated Adam's and Eve's flesh, which was just like a tortoise shell, and they got stuck with it and began to live like animals as they found themselves where we are now. They used to be naked and did not realise it until they sinned against God, which robbed them of the spiritual nature they had. Then they realised that they were naked and started hiding because of shame and discomfort; they started feeling temperature, and instantly they saw themselves in the material world, being of a different nature from what they were before.

The Garden of Eden is a spiritual realm higher than where we are now, called Earth, which was made for animals. Even if angels would come down here to live, they too would become like animals; thus they always levitate when they appear, though acting as if they stand solidly, but it is not so for they obey that rule. Since Adam and Eve realised they were naked after the fall and started feeling differently, it showed that they were in a realm where their flesh had no life. This garden was a spiritual abode of a spiritual nature of Adam before his fall to this place where we found ourselves. Thus the Scripture said that they started tilling the soil and ate its fruit. (compare Genesis 3:23)

To think that this garden was part of the ancient world or the world destroyed by the flood is to be carnally minded. In the scripture, it is said that God placed a cherubim at the east of the garden with a flaming sword. (Compare Genesis 3:24.)

In Ezekiel 28, 13-16, we read how the man of that garden defiled his splendour and was cast out. No human mind can even contemplate beyond this cherub, not to mention talk of a physical approach, because it is entirely spiritual.

In vain the natural man uses the scientific approach to fathom the spiritual things because the nature of man formed outside the Garden of Eden has little to do with God, for the creator needs the spiritual man back in His presence. We will explain more on this in subsequent chapters as we explore some certain verses in Genesis.

St Irenaeus said, 'Though Eve had Adam for a husband and companion, yet she was still a virgin.' We do not know exactly how long the two were in this state before their fall, but the fact remains that God wanted them to increase and subdue the world in a more exalted manner than how it was later fulfilled. (The natural man is only capable of increasing in the world but can never subdue it until the supernatural man is recreated in Christ.)

Man was meant to will good things that they desire and it would have come to pass had he stood firm in the garden; they can reproduce that which looked like them in just the same way as they were formed because, being spirits, they were enveloped in mystical love—for the life which was in them was the spirit which can increase. Remember that their nature knows but one will: to do only good because their creator and His angels are always good. Everything we now do on Earth is strange to heaven except when love is elevated beyond physical attraction and human instincts. (If the natural man could use the insemination to procreate, what about the spiritual Adam who was created in the image of God with the power of increase?)

Remember what God said about man during the destruction of the tower of Babel, when man decided to build a tower up to heaven to meet the creator.

'Nothing that they purposed to do will be withheld from them.' (Genesis 11: 6)

And from there God scattered them abroad over the whole face of the earth. Without this great wisdom of God to destroy man's one language and put an end to that structure, children of men would have built that tower to heaven, for there is the nature of God in man even though he had fallen.

The truth we are establishing here is that Adam and Eve were of a superior nature than what we are now in possession of, which is more that of an animal. A nature which was beyond death because the flesh that can die, as it were, had no life, consciousness or control over the spirit; because the fruits of that garden are mystical, and cannot and did not feed the flesh. Therefore the part of man that was earthly remained lifeless. Yes! Death entered into them because there was a kind of mutation immediately they ate the forbidden fruit.

It is true that the Creator formed them from the dust, but He extoled them with His breath to the level of spiritual beings. In other words, God's Spirit exalted the moulded dust to exist at a higher level, just as gold is dug and refined in the fire to look good and can never be what it used to be; it was from dust but is no longer dust. Remember what the Psalm said: 'Taking His Spirit he returned to the dust from where he was made.'

At a certain time in his life, Adam was flooded with memories of his formal glory, he remembered who he was, and there were tears when he was sharing his stories with his children as were retained in his memory. He remembered how he enjoyed the company of the heavenly beings, how his spirit was as free as the air that we breathe, and how there was not much gap between him and the angels. He remembered the days when all animals gathered around him in homage to the image of their God because both Adam and Eve were radiating the glory of God that they truly represented. They were spectacles for the rest of the creations, both the angels and all the earthly creatures. When they fell, they became the arch-enemies of the earthly creatures for depriving them of the glory of God they used to worship in them. He was truly not an ordinary man in the sense that we think, as he had no inclination of sin and possessed the nature of God at the lower level. God was truly his father and friend: as St Luke Gospel called him, 'Adam the son of God' (Luke 3:38), because He made them to enjoy them prospering and ruling the lower creatures.

In fact, addressing the creator as God began with the history of sin. As they lost their place, horror of Him entered into them. God, which means mystery and terror, becomes His name to the old nature of man, while the new man knows Him as a loving father. In relationship with God, He must treat you as son and you in turn must feel it, otherwise you are still in your old nature that can never be accepted as a son; to the old nature He is God and to the new nature He is truly a Father. When Christ appeared, He answered the son; through the incarnation He entered human nature so that through His flesh, which He commanded us to eat, we could receive His nature. In us He dwells, making His home within us, and we become one with the host of heaven: children of one great ancestor who is The Lord of all creation.

As we have it today, the old nature of man thinks that he is still ruling the world as the Almighty made it in the beginning—to be in control of both the animals in the sea and the birds of the air. But all those authorities were lost with that nature of man losing his formal state. How could man have been the lord of the creatures if he was not created more of a spirit who has no barrier? How could he have had the ability to rule the flying birds? How was it possible for him to control the sea creatures if he was not made to exist in both the sea and dry land as we see in some species of animals? Some birds can fly, adapting to the water and also to dry land. Man was more of a spirit who can adapt both aquatically and otherwise; he can be anywhere, even though his abode was the Garden of Eden until his fall, thus he had dominion over the beings in the air, sea and land. How would it have been possible for him to dominate if he was in this state as we have it now? You must accept the truth that Adam was in charge of all the lower creatures because he was truly in a higher state, but when he chose to heed the fallen angels, God did nothing but cast him down to the level of animals, though he maintains leadership but not without difficulties and fear, and according to the principles of the fallen angels who rule him.

Though the fall of Adam is seen as the beginning of sorrow, it is indeed necessary so that man may fully take the position vacated by the fallen angels.

It is somehow obvious that Adam will fall to the craftiness of the fallen angels because they are higher than him, considering also the fact that man was made of the dust while the tempters are of a higher element. God allowed the evil one to defeat the earth-man Adam so that the heaven-man, the products of Christ, may be created without anything earthly. We may be saying that the devil deceived man but truly it was God Himself who deceived the devil. Yes! He outdoes the devil in craftiness to be able to recreate man in the image of His son who is The Eternal Life.

The church rightly puts it in this glorious canticle of the Easter proclamation,

'Father, how wonderful you care for us! How boundless your merciful love! To ransom a slave you gave away your son. Oh blessed fault! Oh necessary sin of Adam which gained for us so great a redeemer!'

This whole mystery will be understood when your consciousness is rooted to the basic fact of man's existence: that the creator came down to earth and moulded an image of man that looked like Him, and that man became spiritual immediately God breathed upon him. The breath of God in man was his ability to ascend into a spiritual realm because God who animated him is purely a spirit. But man descended again with his contaminated spirit back to his origin after the eating of the forbidden fruit, because the fruit he ate transformed his spiritual being into a material being that was incompatible to the spiritual nature of their creator.

When Christ was teaching on the issue of being born again, He said that this new nature of man is like the wind that blows wherever it wishes. We see some extraordinary phenomena in the lives of some certain people who have the gifts of levitation, flight, bio-locations and many other difficult-to-explain events in the lives of people who were exalted in the mystery of Christ.

In our own understanding, we know that God made man in the beginning to live forever in the Garden of Eden—beholding His glory in the fellowship of the divine worship and exalted in the spirit. There couldn't have been old age, sickness or death, because the flesh that suffers all these was covered with the glory of God. But because of sin, his destiny changed and he was cast away to the place where he began a new history of sorrow; suffering and pain entered because their spirit instantly dematerialised into their body as the glory of God left them. Quest and cares for their material nature started, including building a shelter for their dwelling. Man, finding himself more of the flesh, thinks that his existence is limited to what he can see; this is the reason why people do not know that they are truly spirit in body until one goes deeper in the spiritual life of prayer in the mysteries of Christ. This can only be attained when one's understanding in Christ is lifted above materialism, which is the archenemy of the spiritual life.

... ...

This fruit they ate, which brought death, did not really made them wise as the serpent promised them, but rather it brought shame as they lost that glory, and thus realised they were completely naked just like the rest of animals; their uniqueness had been that glory which they once had, which had glorified their nature making them live as if they had no flesh.

Did you not notice that among all the earthly beings, man is the only animal who needs clothing in order to adapt to unfavourable conditions? Other animals have no need of this, because originally this is the abode created for animals.

God did not entirely leave man in the animal state in which he found himself; rather he promised a redemption and recreation in and with the fruit of a woman. It was truly an end of history and the beginning of a sad episode because that intimate relationship between God, all the heavenly beings and man ended, and another began. Just like a once good and happy family is torn apart when there is a big rift, so the family of God was torn apart by man's disobedience; it remained so until the mercy of God was born out of that great marriage between God and man which reconciled them as they used to be.

Before the coming of Christ, all man's struggles to restore the relationship with God were just labouring in vain. He had no choice than to accept his new state as an earthly being because his sacrifice could not bring any remedy or lift him higher; he must die! For the justice had been decreed against him. God is too holy to accept a defiled nature; you must die and regenerate another nature when the fullness of time comes. Thus the judgement of God was made, though it seemed to be very difficult, but still it was in the favour of man who must suffer captivity in the hand of the fallen angels who defeated him until the fullness of time.

In acts of war, once a nation is defeated, its sovereignty is lost to the nation who had defeated her. This is exactly what happened between man and Satan, who defeated the old man in that garden and that old man lost his control over his entire self, even though God commanded him not to eat that fruit for 'surely you shall die the day you eat it'. As I said earlier, man was built like a house, and the spirit called man was placed therein through the breath of God; now, after this lost battle, the devil who also understood the basic structure of man entered into man after the seal of God was broken by disobedience, putting his own seal as a mark of ownership on man, as a territory which he has prevailed to place his step on, just the way a country puts its flags and effigies on any country under its rule. In the same manner some world power countries placed their effigies on the moon, space, and poles; even so the depth of old man becomes the territory where fallen angels trade.

The fallen angels of darkness who conquered man are the most wicked and horrible beings, owing to the eternal punishment of God who placed a curse on them. What seal did they put on man? As we know, you can only give what you have; so did these fallen beasts lay eggs of rebellion in the spirit of Adam to counter the principles of God. Adam was not that bad after his fall, but he was contaminated, and as time runs his offspring will manifest different kinds of inclinations against the origin of man, which will grow worse as long as man exists on earth. Thus it's very difficult for that nature of man to please God, no matter how hard it tries. And the Bible said:

'They honour me with their lips, but their hearts are very far from me and in vain they worship me.' (Mathew 15: 8-9)

The fact is that this old nature of man had a holy zeal to adore his maker because the original instinct of that union he had with God is indelibly inscribed as a seal on man's soul, but the poisonous seal of the evil one is also stamped on his spirit; his mouth is full of praise but his heart is full of doubt, because that spirit dwelling in him is already contaminated and must respond to the power of him who controls him, to ensure that he goes against whatever he wants to do in order to please God. Therefore the fate and the destiny of the old nature becomes the one heading downwards to inherit whatever awaits him who contaminated man.

Make this confession:

Truly we are new creation in Christ Jesus! With Him we are exalted far above all principalities and powers that control the natural man. Everything lost in Adam has been replaced in Christ who has made us sons and daughters of God. Amen.

The Nature of Man

As there are two covenants in the Scripture, even so man has two spiritual natures in him, which respond to each covenant for the eternal destiny of his soul.

'God dug a vineyard and planted on it the best vine. He expected it to bring forth good grapes, but instead it brought forth wild grapes. In retribution, He took away its hedge and it was burnt; and broke down its wall, and it was trampled down.' (Isaiah 5: 1-5)

Isn't it a marvellous thing that this mystical episode of that great garden did not escape the contemplative minds of the prophets? Through them God revealed both the beginning and the end of man's stay in this valley of tears. It is truly the sad event of man's fall and its consequences; the glory of the natural man was shattered and trampled underfoot. His sanctuary was truly defiled with impurity.

The highest slavery and the punishment of the old nature of man is that he was reduced to the animal nature with less spiritual consciousness—just the opposite of what he was in the beginning. As we said earlier, man was more spiritual, thus Adam and Eve were not much aware of the condition of their earthly nature until they ate the forbidden fruit.

This is the reason why atheists and people who are not yet grafted into the full nature of Christ believe that man lacks spiritual nature and has a mode of behaviour typical of the animal. The truth is that we all have this animal nature with its instinct that we inherited from Adam and Eve. But the good news is that there is a new creation, which God accomplished when He took the flesh of a virgin to appear as a man, for the restoration of man to his lost glory, and the glory of this later man is far glorious than the former.

It is so marvellous that as it pleased The Lord to dwell spiritually in the Ark of Covenant as a shadow of things to come in the Old Testament, so it pleased Him in the fullness of time to create a living Ark of Covenant from where His Word took flesh and lived as a man—recreating all the offspring of Adam who come to Him. Like his maker, these new creations are immortals and exist in the realm of the spirits even though they are in flesh; they are holy and sinless because they are begotten by God Himself. Truly they are sons and daughters of God; and God in turn is their father, as the Scripture says through the mouth of Prophet Haggai who prophesied about these later children of grace, saying that 'the glory of this latter temple shall be greater than the former', as the Lord of hosts says. (Haggai 2: 9)

There are two natures of man living in one temple called man: the old nature of man which is the product of Adam and Eve, and the new nature of man which was given birth in baptism by the mystery of Christ through the water and Holy Spirit. I am talking specifically about a baptised Christian. These two natures that are spirits must coexist in one man all the days of his life and they are opposed to each other. Between these two spirits, one must control the soul of a man who survives the body after death. (After the sin of Adam and Eve, though they fell from their former glory, God did not condemn their souls, but He did condemn their spirit in the flesh. When Christ came, through baptism He creates another spirit of man destined to save the soul of man if he is willing to obey.)

The old nature of man is the nature that is born at any natural birth, controlled by the same spirit in fallen Adam and Eve, which they pass to their offspring from one generation to the next. As I said in The New Creation, 'The whole nature of man both spiritual and physical combines together to procreate.' This spirit is always alive, working actively in all the children of men so far as natural birth is concerned. Thus we have this experience that the soul always battles to please God because this spirit who is superior to soul will always work against man, as the devil is in control of that spirit who is deeply seated in the nature inherited from Adam. This was the reason why the souls of the just men were held in a state until Christ the giver of the new spirit and the eternal life came and died and entered that state to preach and to make them reborn—purging them with His blood because upon Him were laid the iniquities and the punishments of all humanity both before and after His death.

This same spirit that is the true nature of man after the fall is still in full control of a man until after baptism, which gives birth to the new spirit. The contention will now start between the two spirits over the soul of man. The old spirit, having already been contaminated and banished forever, releases its venom to the soul making him live more as if his life started on the earth and will end on the earth. Such a soul, though it may claim to love God, can never please Him having been blinded by the spirit of the world.

...   .

Dwelling in the epistemological knowledge of Christ the second Adam, St Paul said, 'Nothing good dwells within me.' (Romans 7: 18)

This is exactly what we will look into about the nature of the old man. Everyone who dwells in the spirit of truth of Christ's message will confess truly that there is nothing eternally good about the natural man. Of course the Scripture has already concluded that even his good deeds are like filthy rags, which we will explain further in due course. Only a few things are temporally good about the nature of Adam which we all possess and all those goodness start here and must end here—for he receives all his rewards here on the planet earth, as his goods do not go beyond with him, even as the Scripture said.

This nature of Adam inherited by all of us is earthly, and can never live above the standard of the world to the level of godliness.

Having been left in a state of dilemma, he is capable of doing anything, both good in the temporal order and also the most disgusting things leading to eternal death. We must remember that our old nature, having been condemned in Adam, was born unto servitude of the covenant of Mount Sinai to certify that great truth that no one is good as the Scripture says. Therefore it is a call to all of us to have a change in attitude and mentality, after reading this book, that nobody should be killed, condemned or persecuted for any natural inclination passed onto him through Adam's nature which is not his or her personal sin but rather his or her inherited disorder over which he or she have no control over. Thus we all need Christ because He only appeared to give us a second birth, as our first nature has been contaminated and nobody is exempted unless such a person is ignorant and overshadowed by the spirit of pride. He who dares to say that the natural man is perfect does not understand the message of Christ, neither does he understand God who made man in His own image and likeness—for man must act like God if he is truly perfect and the image of God as Adam was before his fall.

It is a proof beyond doubt that a human being is an animal. Whether he is called high or low, he is an animal and must act like one. Every human who needs salvation must accept and confess this truth; that God knows that the later state of man is not fitting for man, that's the reason for sending His son to die and pay for man's sins against God and to free man from captivity. Because the imagination of man's heart is evil continuously, we breathe out sin as the fruits of our thoughts; thus we do things we never meant to do—for the compelling force within us is anti-divine.

This is the complete nature of man. If anyone dares to say that he is good or has no part in the list of things we do that make us lower man with the inclination of sin, he is an angel; and Christ did not die for him. If one who calls himself a Christian does not sometimes find himself struggling with the deadly instinct of our old spirit through which the devil ministers hate to God, he is the most pitiable daydreaming Christian—for a Christian is a sinner on the process of salvation until the final separation of his old spirit battling to claim the soul. John the Evangelist said that 'if we say we have not sinned, we make Him a liar, and truth does not dwell in us'. (1 John 1: 8-10)

This is the confession of the truth I am making for the freedom of many. First, to be a natural human being is to be a sinner as the Scripture says that 'we all like sheep have gone astray; we have turned, everyone to his own way'. All of us descended from Adam; without being a sinner, you will not acknowledge nor understand who God is—Holiness and Righteousness Himself. On the level of self-knowledge, the saints understood and confessed that they were the most miserable in their lower nature. Not just for the sake of saying so but from the depth of their hearts, because the power of the truth was pushing them to confess the truth they realised out of experience in their animal natures. For this reason, God is not ashamed to raise them up from these animal natures into the divine nature of His son and call them sons and daughters. They have come very close to Christ and have seen their selves through the light of Christ; but when one is still very far away from Christ, he might think that he is good, boasting for nothing because he is very far away from the marvellous light. Maybe because he may claim to be good, as the result today is just because he is not doing any harm to people, and foolishly he says, 'I don't need Christ to be a good person.' God who came to save us knows that evil imaginations are our nature and daily bread, thus He loves us to the point of dying for us even when we are still living in that sin which our nature craves.

We fail to understand the true meaning of this scripture: 'Christ died for us while we were still sinners.' (Romans 5: 8) It means that when Christ was dying over two thousand years ago, He loved you today even as you are, with all your genetic codes and disorders so that by dying to that nature, you will become a child of God. The Scripture goes on to say: 'if He loves you to the point of dying for you when you are still a sinner, what will happen when you forsake them?' All the sin one is committing is his nature, because it's the character of the old nature to enjoy sin in its fullness. In a nutshell, to be sinful is part of being human. You must understand what I am saying very well because I am talking about the old nature of man which we all possess, which loves and enjoys sins, and confesses, 'It is my life, and no one tells me how to run it; I am doing my own thing.' What is this old nature of man professing? He is professing that sin is his own life, which is what he is all about: a contaminated nature, and an earthly creature that has fallen and will never return. Despite the grace of God, evil and lust are already dwelling in us equally both in the life of the saints: all it takes is one finding oneself in a negative environment, saying or hearing negative words and it will be triggered. Once it's provoked, it takes the grace of God for one to resist—for it has the destiny of giving birth to sin.

The person we all know as the tempter is not far away, but rather he has something in every human being born naturally as the seed of Adam; only the Virgin Mary was created completely free from his seal and venoms, so that through her God will bring about the new creation by taken her flesh.

The Scripture has been saying about this nature which has nothing else to give but just what he has become. His attitudes and character which appear in his physicality through his actions are his deeds; they are not controlled by man, but by these forces I am talking about which are superior to the human soul: in just the same manner as man was ruling the rest of the creatures, the same manner in which the fallen angels are now in control of the old nature of man. For the fallen angels are spirits while the natural man is spiritually dead. The Scripture, in defining this old nature, said,

> 'He is dead in trespasses because he is walking according to the course of this world, and the prince and powers of the air, this spirit work in the sons of disobedience.' (Ephesians 2: 1-3)

It goes on to say that man was a child of wrath by nature because he conducts himself in the lust of the flesh, fulfilling the desires of the flesh and mind. The spirituality of this book is that the old nature of man must not agree with the nature of God because he is operating from captivity. When Christ appeared, His message was that man's captivity was over. Thinking that they were free, they defied the teaching of the Wisdom Incarnate, reasoning that being the children of holy Abraham made them free. They did not realise that Abraham himself cried so much for the day of Christ, who is the freedom of all the children of Adam, and yet did not see it in the flesh.

Do not think that we are entirely against the old nature; we are not saying that our old nature is entirely bad. No. Though this old man had failed, there is still something good about him because God created him and He is still making use of him to accomplish His work of the new creation. Just as the seed is valued, yet the farmer must sow it in the ground or as it were throw it away full of hope that, though it decays, it will produce a better one. So God also throws our animal nature away to die and to produce a divine man through Christ. Natural man must increase and multiply so that the new nature may also increase and multiply; without its multiplication, it is impossible to have the new creation. Therefore the fall of Adam was indeed necessary for the glorious nature of man. The old man is the one who must give birth to the natural man upon the water and the Holy Spirit will give a new nature. But you must understand and accept that everything good that proceeds from the old nature of man, no matter how precious it may look, is just temporal and must end on this passing world even the nature he took outside the garden with its natural endowment; all his adventures and innovations do not go beyond. A generation built and says it's fantastic; another generation arises and says that it's outdated and pulls it down. What shall it profit a man to labour for the perishable things and lose his precious soul for which Christ died?

After the fall of man, when any human being is born, it's just the birth of an animal nature of man. When God started making a way for the redemption and recreation of man through Abraham, He started through circumcision, which is a type of baptism to make Abraham's children unique among all the sons of men. One of my teachers said to me, 'Tell me how you are not an animal and I will tell you how you are the first class animal.'

Indeed the old nature of man that coexists with the new nature is not much different from other animals, even though it claims to be a higher animal because of the nature it had before his fall. What does it do differently? Man has organs and faculties just like other animals; it procreates like other mammals, and it feeds and defecates like other animals. Other animals labour for foods and build houses for safety even as humans do; the animal nature of man discriminates and hates just as we see in other animals, we are territorial just like predators in the wild, and we even go to the extreme of being brutal against our fellow human beings in defending our borders. We live and die just as other animals; to crown it all, he has proven himself as a homosexual animal and the world leaders are striving so hard now to promulgate this as human right laws because it's an indisputable fact beyond doubt about the children of Adam. It is true because the deeper knowledge to which my spirit had been introduced has opened my understanding that owing to the sin of Adam, his products are capable of doing anything because that is the level they were reduced to. Since the nature of man had fallen into the pit of destruction, there is an apparent need for another version of spiritual nature of man who must accomplish the mission of the first man who failed out of the Garden of Eden and started procreating like other animals, which God had never planned for him.

Trust this wisdom when it said that the manner in which man procreates now is not really the manner originally intended for man; after all, other animals procreate in a likewise manner. There was a unique manner of which the sin of Adam had deprived him; remember, as punishment they were told, 'In pain you shall bring forth children.' (Genesis 3:16)

When the second Eve appeared, she gave birth without losing her virginity and stayed virgin afterwards to fulfil that original intention of God, so that the new creations would also be able to fulfil the original procreative manner intended by God from the beginning through baptism. Also he must subdue and defeat the world to prove himself to be an offspring of God, as the Scripture says. (1 John 5: 4)

... ...

When Christ the Eternal Word of God made flesh appeared through the virgin birth, He declared as it were at the top of His voice that anybody who wanted to have eternal life must be reborn. This is to say he must be recreated because the nature of man who has been waiting for the Messiah is contaminated by the fallen demons that control him. This is the meaning of the Scripture when it says that, 'Christ came to His own and His own did not accept Him.' (John 1: 11)

Yes! The old nature of man can't simply accept Him because the man who left the Garden of Eden is not the same man Christ met in the world. That man has lost spiritual connection, having stayed too long in captivity. Therefore He must create the version of the spiritual man who must accept his creator and God. Think about what the Scripture says again about the nature of Christ and man:

'Jesus did not trust Himself to them because He knew all men and had no need of anyone to offer testimony about the nature of man. For He knew what was within a man.' (John 2: 24-25)

The true nature of man before the holy baptism is full of decadence, irrespective of the level of holiness he pretends to. I have come to understand that nothing pretends and claims to know God in the manner in which the old nature of man claims. Thus the Holy Spirit abhors him so highly because of his hypocritical nature, which makes him proud just like his master. This hypocrisy made that nature to pray, long for and offer lots of sacrifices for the coming of the Messiah. But what did he do when Christ finally appeared? He tried to kill Him as a baby, completely rejected His personality and His message of life during His public ministry, and eventually killed Him who came to give new life through the ministry of the baptism, His flesh and blood.

This is the hypothesis of the new creation: that when a human being is born, he is just like every other animal until he is reborn in the holy baptism which makes him truly the image of God as the spiritual Adam was.

The truth is that the animal nature of man cannot fulfil the law of righteousness of God as it is said that a bird that drinks from the river can never feel satisfied anymore with the drops of the dew that forms water on the tree leaves. The Bible says:

'The mind of flesh is enmity against God; for it is not subject to the law of God, nor would ever be.' (Rom. 8: 7)

Every human being has this inborn instinct of animal, which has a way of doing things on his own, according to the responses of his faculties and organs within him. So there is a tendency that he must act according to his nature; no matter what he does, he must remain where he is, because he who conquered him is mightier than him; he has a rope on his neck just as humans use rope to control their animals, which does not prevent that animal from portraying its characteristics as an animal whenever it gets the chance; but the owner subjects it to his control because any animal with a leash around its neck has lost its freedom. This is exactly what the devil that conquered the old man did to him. He wants to do well but could not, because he is in shackles by the wicked spirits—trying to do the will of God under captivity, which is impossible.

The theory and practice that defined the character of the baptised human being is that he has the nature of Adam and the nature of Christ in him. This is how the Scripture summed up the nature of man.

'As the first man Adam became a living being, even so Christ Jesus the last Adam became A Live Given Spirit. We bore the image of the man of dust and we also bear the image of the heavenly man.' (Compare 1 Corinthians 15: 45-49)

The animal nature of Adam born at every natural birth and the divine nature of man born in baptism must necessarily live together until man is done with his assignment on earth. The more the soul cooperates with Christ, the more his new nature grows and the old nature loses its strength until he become Christ-like. The same is the opposite if he rejects Christ; he is left with no option than to celebrate the inheritance that Adam left for him. At the end of every life, God who knows where the two natures joined together will separate the new man from the old, and He will dry up every deadly fluid inherited from the old man because these two natures have separate destiny of death and life, which they will receive at last. Truly during this separation of old spirit from the soul, there is a great battle between the angels and the demons; the soul is the battleground. This is where purgation comes in, according to the theology of the ancient church kerygma; the soul will experience fire at this point because we are so attached to our old spirit, being truly part of us from birth. This is the reason why everyone professes that heaven is our home but nonetheless doesn't want to die because of this attachment to the spirit of the world. The devil himself will try through that spirit to claim a soul, especially one that is so attached to it and through it has sold himself to the demons. Pray hard to stand firm especially at the hour of death—for truly it's a great battle to save a soul! As I said before, this old nature has few good things to offer which are on the temporal level; but the new man is all-round good because his nature is to fulfil the divine doctrine according to the instructions of the Holy Spirit.

This new baby who emanated through the mystical union of water and Spirit is the one who feeds on the body and blood of Christ, who hears the word of God and keeps it; he spends all his days on earth doing good and keeping all the ordinances in the eternal Gospel while waiting for his rewards in heaven. But the old nature of man may do good sometimes but only with a view towards receiving his full reward of praise here on Earth, based on his proud nature, so all his good deeds are polluted by the demons that hold him in bondage.

The truth is that God who condemned the natural man in Genesis did not do that for any other reason than just because He knew too well that the state into which man degenerated could not avoid being evil and must play against His will in everything.

The Destiny of Man

If God must achieve His eternal plan for man, there must be a need for a new man, and He justified His actions by sending man out of that paradise without any regret. During the Incarnation, this loving father had no other way to prove the depth of His love towards man other than to humble Himself to become man—not only the higher nature of man that Adam was, but also descending as low as the animal nature to which sin had reduced man. The truth is that God fell down just like a fallen man to redeem man, in the same manner one dives into the river in search of a drowned man; even so Christ dived into the same river that drowned man to be able to save man, staying in the same water yet not drowning, to save us.

When Christ was born in the cave of Bethlehem in the midst of animals, it was not only to symbolise the poverty He chose, as we always know; it was truly to prove that man is not much better than the animals in whose world he found himself. Therefore, He must be born in the midst of animals too, though He is God, so that He can recreate the lowest natural man who acts just like the animals.

... ...

In Genesis, man was the product of waters on which the spirit of God was hovering; this spirit of God and the water He created were the course of the conception of the creations, which were later separated from this water. When He destroyed the first world, it was to this same water that He returned all the livings by causing water to fall both from heaven and under the world because the world was hanging on the same water after He declared 'Let the dry land appear.' (Compare Genesis 1: 9, and Psalm 22: 2.) When Christ was instituting the rites of baptism, He used this same water formula and the same spirit He gave as the beginning of the new life by invoking the three persons in one God: the same God who said in Genesis, 'Let us create man.' And Peter said, 'Water now saves us, which is baptism, for the answer of good conscience towards God.' (1 Peter 3: 21). Therefore in the same way water was the source of creation of the failed man, He also used it in recreation of the spiritual man.

Moses the saviour whom God used to accomplish deliverance in the old covenant also figuratively experienced a rebirth through water; for the mother said with faith, 'My son shall surely live.' When she was no longer able to hide him, she wove a basket with bulrushes, and smeared it with pitch as well as tar. She placed the baby Moses inside and laid it in the reeds by the riverbank. When Moses was found, the Pharaoh's daughter named him Moses, saying, 'Because I drew him out of the water.' (Compare Exodus 2: 3-10) So Moses himself as a baby, symbolically by divine mystery, was baptised before he was used mightily by God.

The true reason for baptism is regeneration. If baptism makes us children of God and members of Christ, it means that before baptism or without baptism, as it were, we might rightly say that one does not belongs to God, because he can never please God no matter what he does. This is the reason why the early Christians baptised their new-borns in their baby stage to make the child a true child of God overshadowed by the divine grace; for it is the best thing for one to be pursued by the grace of God rather than chasing the grace of God, which can never be met up with, as is the case with unbaptized people.

It is also very important to remind us that a confession of Christ as our lord and saviour is not enough to claim that we are new creatures. No! You must be grafted into the mystery of His body and blood, which is your new life: food and drink indeed that keeps His subjects spiritually alive. (Compare John 6)

This communion is the true life of the new nature you received in baptism; without it that new nature cannot grow, as we explained in 'The New Creation'. Confessing Christ without grafting into the true principles of new life is like when the bat is saying that it's not a bird but it flies; it says that it's not an animal but gives birth just like mammals.

The greatest confession of a baptised person should be that he is a new creation in the true image of God! The animal nature of man is not the true image of God, but the nature born in baptism, which is the same nature that was in Adam before his fall is truly the image of God. Only that nature can fulfil the law of God and keep the divine doctrine, being the citizen of heaven. You may now ask why people do not observe or experience this new nature within themselves early in their infancy.

There is indeed the new creation through baptism; but how can life manifest itself or grow when no attention is given to it? The bitter truth is that after baptism, we attend more to the animal nature of man with little or no attention to the spiritual nature. From infancy, we are connected to learning more about our environments and social functions than we are to the mystery of Christ, which introduces us to our spiritual nature and routes. So in this case, our animal nature grows taller or to its maturity before some of us starts feeding the spiritual nature which at this point suffers much to grow because we are used to the animal nature, which is equally spirit.

However, this is the mystery of God and the manifestation of His wisdom in allowing us to develop fully as human beings, knowing the wisdom of this world through learning and failures though He has given us a new nature that is the opposite. During this process, our nature and self is developed to its fullness, so that through self-denial grace will be imparted to our soul—for the new life is truly grace over nature.

This truth is seen in the lives of the saints because most of them have very strong Christian backgrounds with highly religious parents, who not only went to church often but also spent their daily lives in prayer and in deeper communion with God. When a child is brought up in such a family, there is a tendency that he will grow up rooted in the doctrine of godliness to obey the spirit of grace, even though some may later fall out of this; but the unique identity of Christ stamped in their spirit will continue to convince them of the truth, as in the case of St Augustine of Hippo. Even in the old covenant, those who came close to God have this same strong background of being able to encounter the spirit of prophecy. Consider also the life of young Samuel who not only had religious parents but himself grew up in the temple.

Today, we only go to church on Sundays and spend the rest of the days doing our own thing and labouring for the food that only serves the material needs; how then can we grow in spirit? Even though our material needs are very important, they must come second; we must, like Mary the sister to Lazarus, choose the better part, which is staying very close to Christ in order to know what this life is all about.

During Christ's ministry He said, 'Do not labour for the food which perishes, but food which endures to the everlasting life.' (John 6: 27)

This principle is not possible at all for the old nature of man but it is for the new nature, which does not belong to this world. That's why you will believe with the saints that Christ did not minister His blessings to the old nature of man, but to the new man because the old nature works directly or indirectly against eternal life even when it seems to be doing well. How can He minister His blessings to the nature of Adam since He is the new Adam who came to liberate the soul from the spirit of the old Adam? He only raised a sword in the new nature against the old man.

Because our animal nature is old, and cannot fulfil all the principles required of us, let everyone accept this Christ Jesus who has come to give us life in abundance: Jews, Gentiles, Moslems and atheists, for there can never be another who can give his life for his subjects in the manner in which Christ sacrificed Himself. He is truly God among His people! Thus the Scripture says, 'He who is in Christ is a new creation.' What other miracle would another Christ or Messiah achieve to compete or equate with the recreating ministry of Christ Jesus? What compassion will amount to the one He gave to the prodigal son, the adulterer and a convicted criminal? What freedom could another give a natural man who is enslaved by the devils and the law? And the populace in His days asked, 'When another Christ comes, will he do more signs than these which this man has done?' (John 7: 31)

The conclusion is that He is God in the flesh who accomplished what no other person could do except the infinite Himself, who can do all things to save His own. He laid down His life for the freedom of the whole human family who believes in Him.

Confession—

With Christ Jesus I am a divine generation! I am no longer an earth-man for God Himself has recreated me to live as a spiritual being even though am still in flesh.

'Let he who has no SWORD sell his garment and buy one.'
Luke 22:38

Fallen Angels at Work

When that ancient serpent defied the authority of God in heaven, it was as if all the angelic spirits were tempted and moved by the action of this prince, and some of them who could not stand the test lost their abode permanently before the presence of God and were cast out of heaven with eternal damnation as their inheritance—for it is impossible for them to return to heaven, as there is no room for mercy to any angel who sinned against the truth imprinted in their nature.

In her mystical song in praise of the Angels St Maria Faustina said, 'Then the faithful spirits cried, Glory to God's mercy! And they stood firm in spite of their fiery test.' (Diary, p. 615, no. 101)

When these fallen angels lost their place in heaven, their prince also entered the Garden of Eden and tempted man into eating the forbidden fruit, in just the same way as he tempted and seduced some angels who followed his path of rebelliousness. In the same way the angels sinned and lost their true nature and abode; in the same manner man also sinned and lost his true nature and abode. After their fall, these fallen angels who have no physical body depend on the body of Adam's offspring to perpetuate their mission towards destroying man. He possesses and obsesses man to offend God because he has control over that old nature of man. But their greatest surprise and hatred for man was that God was able to forgive man, gave him a second chance even to the level of promising him a new nature, but that He did not forgive them even when some of them craved to go back. This is the reason why the greatest weapon of the devil against man is to project into him that God will not forgive him whenever man falls into sin, especially sin that leads to death, thereby holding him in bondage to continue in sin. But the good news is that the greater the sin and the miseries of man, the greater the mercy of God upon a repentant soul—for God truly takes pleasure in forgiving sins.

Yes, when both man and fallen angels were cast out of the divine presence, the fallen angels retained their spiritual nature while man lost his. These God did because He foreordained that He would create another spiritual nature of man in the incarnation of Christ, while the fallen angels who retained theirs were eternally condemned because they were spirits.

These fallen angels have different characters and functions according to the positions they used to occupy in heaven—for everything God created has a unique function, which is quite different from another. After their fall, the angels turned these beautiful gifts into evil towards destroying man. This is the reason why man has different natures and inclinations that were never found in the soul of man from the beginning; neither are these acceptable to God, who loves man so dearly because a loving father does not hate his son. As man increases on the face of the earth, even so these fallen angels were taking up position in the depths of man; for already they had put their seal on the depth of Adam and Eve who were the parents of all the living.

The first major sin after the fall of man was murder. Cain, having been possessed by the fallen angel that hates God, could not value God anymore to offer to Him a worthy sacrifice; in jealousy, this spirit induced him to kill Abel even though God warned him. (Compare Genesis 4: 6-7) Through his sin and subsequent punishment, man's condition continued to get worse because it is sin that attracts suffering.

Even though these fallen angels had brought man down to the nature of animals, that wasn't enough for them; they entered into the sexuality of humans to ensure that natural man was as close as possible to an animal. We will see in subsequent chapters how the egg of the fallen angels in the depth of Adam altered the sexuality of the fallen man, as men increased and drifted further apart from the nature of God. Having become a homosexual and bisexual animal, sex becomes the most important thing to a natural man because this is the quest of the fallen angels in creating their own order of ruling which must be anti-divine. Consequentially, these fallen legions started manifesting all manner of evil in man whom God had made so good from the beginning. The prince of the fallen angels is the demon responsible for idolatry, which is the highest crime against God: 'wickedness, covetousness, maliciousness, full of envy, murder, strife, deceit, haters of God, and violent, proud, inventors of evil things, disobedience to parents, untrustworthy, unloving, unforgiving and unmerciful.' (Compare Romans 1: 29-31) Spiritually speaking, all manner of sin is traced and found rooted in the depth of Adam in whose nature was laid the egg of sin. Therefore all the children of Adam necessarily must be sinners. (These natures of fallen legions induced into Adam become the nature and tradition of the fallen man, which the law invaded upon in the days of Moses.)

When God was preparing the nation of Israel with the holy Law and the fiery message of the prophets, the fallen legions were busy settling in the hearts of the rest of men to whom the Jews referred as the Gentiles, in other to establish their own kingdom and empire because they had claimed man and the world that used to be under man's control. Their intention was to use man to fight the principles of the righteousness of God, because they pushed the natural man in any direction they chose, even though they were unwelcome guests in the depth of man, yet they controlled the spirit of man. If man had stood firm in the beginning, those fallen angels would have lost their mission against man, but because man failed, he lives in no knowledge of his spiritual concept and his inheritance and freedom were lost.

Seeing that they have prevailed in introducing their own doctrine in man's spirit, they started to manifest themselves as gods in imitation of the Almighty God. As spirits, they began to dwell not only in man but also in the trees, rocks, rivers, mountains, and even in animals—making man venerate and worship them as gods. It is easy for man to worship them because there is a sense of adoration in the heart of man, and also they have sown their nature in animal man, and their nature in man must in turn pay them homage to gain them more strength to rule man.

By showing portents and signs, they made themselves gods and even started to demand a certain amount of good behaviour and purity from man. All the unique attributes of God, these demons copied to act truly as gods. Thus all the ancient gods of Egypt, Greek, Rome and other parts of the world acted as if they were protecting their people while all of them were demons. The fact is that all the gods that the world ever worshipped or venerated were fallen angels. Their original intention in heaven was to be like God, but since they could not they came down to earth with the same intention; having conquered and dethroned man, they established their thrones as gods.

As the Bible said, 'There is no peace for the wicked.' That same rebellion was still working among them, as some of them could not even obey their prince who led them to disobedience. With time these gods could not unite anymore; having become territorial according to their ranks, they started clashing with each other over some certain control over man. This is when some of them began to act as good spirits in the pretence that they loved man, in order to gain more of man's allegiance and territory. One inflicted sickness and another healed it. They started teaching men how to make weapons and instruments for war, teaching them the skills and acts of war, possessing them and making some of them the lords of war, and with them invading another kingdom of men in showing himself superior to their god. Men for their part sacrificed human blood to them in order to be in control and also in imitation of the prides of these gods; men proclaimed themselves as gods and even demanded worship. Man worshipping his fellow man, because the prince of the fallen angels himself had taken place in his depth.

… … …

In the mythology of gods, we see these evil spirits acting and playing gods in all corners of the world and cultures. The sun god, the moon goddess, the fertility god, the sea goddess and their like: all of them are demons who transformed themselves as helpers of man, even some of them the anger of God had banished into the underworld beyond the reach of living man who controlled only the realm of death before the coming of Christ. Though they may have claimed to help in war, agriculture, fertility and so-called protection, they were all accursed spirits. In imitation of God, they played some kind of justice, inducing people to perpetuate evil and also punishing them, but it was all fake for they were in a confusing mission towards the destruction of earth-man.

As the Almighty God was choosing priests among the Jews, as we will see later, so were these fallen angels choosing priests and priestesses whom they held totally in bondage to make both human and animal sacrifices for them. Virgins and pregnant women were sacrificed on demand from the priest as an act of god for some certain favour. Some of these deities even demanded the most horrible manner of sexual immoralities from their priests in the shrine as a kind of ritual and sacrifice.

Because these fallen angels had different offices and functions before their fall, they used those functions in a negative manner against the godly principles. As they had made themselves gods of the earth, the manner with which men approached their offices varied, some demanding human sacrifices, some demanding animal sacrifices, and some demanding music, dancing and incantations. Yet they were all misleading spirits with the destiny of eternal destruction who offered no future for man.

When God created the sun and the other constellations, it was just for the benefits of man and to honour man. But as man deteriorated, the demons started using these heavenly bodies against him by decreeing false things; through their wicked potions they invented magic and all manner of necromancy to get the spirit and soul of man far away from the truth of God. The use of certain stars and different evil practices in secret places proliferated. Men developed more interest in the beauty of the sun and stars instead of its maker; the worship of the sun and the rest of the constellations spread. It did not end there; men also engaged in the use of the circle of animals (Zodiac) and reading of palms to study their future, becoming more superstitious in their beliefs instead of supernatural. These were the aims of the fallen angels—to turn the heart of man away from invisible realities and focus only on things he can see and prove with common sense. Seeing all this use of constellations against man, God declared in a Psalm, 'The sun shall not smite you by the day or the moon in the night.' (Psalm 121: 6)

After the fall of the tower of Babel and the spread of men all over the face of the earth, man drifted even further from God as colour and racial prejudice began. As God scattered man, so the gods were scattered as they followed man to wherever he went, inspiring in them the building of shrines for these deities even up to present. Due to the wickedness of man and the prevalence of evil and abominations, some men were deformed in a severe punishment to look less like ordinary known man. Some even looked horrible to behold; some were transformed into half-man and half-animal or fish, and were forced to live in the wild or in the sea. (Upon the remains of some of these species of man hangs the later claim of evolution, because these fallen angels will forever dwell in the old nature of man to work against the truth of God to the detriment of man.)

Though these wicked spirits were exercising the height of their wickedness upon man, the Almighty God did not allow some of them freedom anymore as we mentioned earlier, lest they bring about a complete destruction of man's nature. He invaded them with His war-faring angels who had earlier thrown them out of heaven as the book of Revelation recorded, binding some of these wicked spirits with chains and fetters of iron. The one who received the praises as God, the one who sowed the seed of denial of the existence of God in man, and the one who destroyed human sexuality and such like were caged, to be released towards the end of the history of man on earth before the great day of judgement. And the Bible said, 'For God did not spare the angels who sinned, but cast them down to hell and delivered them into chains of darkness, to be reserved for judgement.' (2 Peter 2: 4) Today there is evidence that some of these caged spirits have been released against man, since some of us deny the existence of God, refusing to adore Him. Such men are left on their own to be proud of what they should be ashamed of: living their lives as if they don't have souls, comparing themselves as ordinary animals. (Compare Romans 1: 20-30)

But even as these spirits of error born in man continue to torture man, so God also continues to come to the assistance of those who struggle to seek their origins, for through these struggles God knows His true children.

To be a fruitful Christian, one must therefore know and understand that there are gods whose mission is to destroy man and keep him in the animal nature, which can never do anything good to please God. But how could one understand this when he denies the existence of God? How is it possible when people who confess Christ barely know Christ or have a relationship with the one whom they confess as God? Therefore no man will understand the gods and their evil mission unless his faith goes beyond ordinary faith—to the level of truth into his sub-consciousness that there is truly a God. Because as the saying has it, 'it is only when one has a true friend that he would know that those he used to have may be enemies who posed to be friends.' Knowledge of the true God exposes the worships of gods and the demons that exist in the depths of a natural man.

Every nation under the sun has gods that they worship, even though they may not realise it, as these gods always hide themselves under the masks of culture and tradition. So far culture has not accepted Christ who is the manifestation of God, though that culture may be proclaiming the Almighty God, yet they may not know that most of their principles are rooted in the gods who live among them and within them. There is a necessity of acculturation whenever Christ entered any culture: to purify and exalt it to the doctrine of the true God. Remember, as we said, that the old nature of man always wants to please God even though he is in captivity; so this culture in captivity is what the Gospel of Christ liberates and frees from contamination when we truly open our hearts to Christ.

But especially in our days the populace hates Christ; they do not even want to hear His name invoked, as if He is the enemy of the human happiness. This is a typical example of the presence of a fallen angel in the soul. Until this contrary spirit has left the soul, such a person will always stand against God and thereby lose his soul. The only crime this loving saviour committed is that He humbled Himself and became part of condemned humanity, only to take us back to the spiritual nature which we lost in Adam. Look at His gaze as He appears in the pictures; it is the gaze of one who meant peace and not war. The lasting truth is that, whether or not we want to get stocked in animal nature, we must all return to spiritual nature when we rise above this temple called flesh. It is better to battle with the gods dwelling within us, and to follow Christ so that our souls will be free from all the anger of God, which awaits the gods who destroyed the world.

Looking at the Scripture, you will see that The Ten Commandments acknowledged the existence of gods when it says, 'Thou shall not have any other gods besides me.' The scripture goes further to show gods in action in the nations when He invaded Egypt with His Angels: 'I will cross through the land of Egypt that night, I will strike down the entire first born of their land, from man even to the cattle. And I will bring judgements against all the gods of Egypt. I AM THE LORD.' (Exodus 12: 12)

These judgements upon the gods are because they were invisibly responsible for all the evil that sprang from the culture of Egypt, which enslaved the Israelites. Through all the years the Almighty has dealt directly with the Israelites, it has been always a relationship which forbids them an intimate relationship with all the surrounding nations because of the contaminating presence of the gods they worship. When Moses' staff turned into a snake in the Pharaoh's presence, did the priests of the gods of Egypt not turn their own staffs into snakes as well? All through the Old Testament writings, it is all about God liberating His people from the control of gods.

      ...   .

This was the complete nature of man when, out of love and mercy, God called worried Abram, because the whole family of men had completely forgotten their origins and had turned to the fallen angels who had made a deification of themselves as gods, paying them homage that they should have given to God. The fact is that, apart from Abraham, the whole family of man were worshipping idols inspired by these fallen angels. Thus the Scripture says, 'All the gods of the Gentiles are demons.' (Psalm 96: 5)

From the first day He called Abraham, God never failed to warn him about the strange gods that were worshipped by the children of men. When Abraham left his father's house with his servants and Lot's family, only he knew that the God of creation they heard about as children in the moonlight story was real.

This is similar to the way we were told fairy tales about some things that sounded real but later, when we grew up, we discovered they were stories without evidence and we quickly got them off our mind. The same was the experience of all the children in Abraham's childhood time. They were told stories about God and Adam, all His manifestations, how He destroyed the world in the days of Noah, the destruction of the Tower of Babel and the likes; the same happened to them when they grew up—because of no concrete evidence, they disregarded the stories as folklore because they saw that their fathers who told them these stories were worshipping visible images as their gods: a different picture of the Living God they told them about in the stories. That is how God kept His story as folklore in their mouths until Abraham started seeking for Him who truly lives and eventually heard His voice and decided to leave his father's house in search of Him.

Throughout all the land as they passed through searching for God, Abraham saw the inhabitants practicing this idol worship just as it was in his father's land. This created lots of doubt for him and also hardened the hearts of his followers; they didn't know whether to believe in Abraham's newly found God, which had no image. But they continued to follow him, not because they believed in his God, but because of his charisma and his skills in the acts of war; his God was dragging them along to alleviate the troubles of His beloved Abraham. God who knows the depth of the heart of man knows that the idolatry spirit of the companions of Abraham was so great; He did not allow them to settle finally with Abraham. He settled them in separate lands to enable the flow of His Holy Spirit to work in Abraham for the future salvation of the entire humanity. This idolatry nature of man was the reason why the descendants of Lot later returned back to their vomit; despite all the exploits of Lot to establish the true worship of God, the Moabites, his posterity, became a pagan nation and so were all the descendants of other people who left UR of Chaldean in search of the God of Abraham.

Because of the nature of the old man, which we all possess, no one is completely free from the manipulations of these gods and demons: both the children of Abraham through physical descent. In spite of all the love, signs and wonders performed by God before their very eyes, that nature in them which will always hate God rebelled against God and returned to his origins in worshiping Idol—the god that he can see and touch, even though God had separated them from among all children of men to be a holy people to Himself. Even in today's world, you can still see the worship of such gods in different religions and also the incorporation of these idol worships in some cultures and traditions as the way of life. This is because that ancient serpent truly laid an egg in Adam. The uniqueness of the snake is that it is venomously poisonous. It is obvious that the snake that deceived Adam and Eve may have bitten them as well, so that death will truly run and manifest itself in their natures eternally.

This mystery of the venom of the devil in man was the reason why Christ in His teaching said shortly before His passion that, 'The ruler of this world is coming, and he has nothing in me.' (John 14: 30) What Christ is saying here is a confirmation of His divinity and the new nature of man He is: not only Him but also the Virgin Mary who gave birth to Him and remained a perpetual virgin in her flesh, spirit, senses and all her faculties, which exalted her far above all virgins and all generations of men. This is why Christ and Virgin Mary lived above sin. As I said in The New Creation, there is nothing of Adam and Eve in them.

In all the temptations of Christ, it is impossible that He will fall because there is no instinct of fallen man in Him that can respond to the projections of the devil; therefore all the arrows of the Satan to hunt Him return back to Satan's destruction because it cannot trigger sin in Him to act against the truth He is. Understand me in this manner; can a remote control made for a Panasonic product work on a Sony product? It cannot, because they do not have a matching censor that can respond. Even so Christ and His mother, the new Eve, did not respond to all the persuasions of the devils; for it was impossible for them to sin or act against God and His grace which dwelled fully in their spirits. As the new Adam and Eve, they were of the same spiritual level which Adam and Eve was before their fall, and was tempted even more but they stood firm.

Christ is a mystical nature of man who does not deserve death, thus His death and resurrection became the life of all the children of Eve who have inherited death from Adam, because Christ Himself who died sacrificed His righteousness and stood as a condemned Adam before His father. This is the highest truth the kingdom of darkness fears against any offspring of Christ. Upon this truth hangs the true life which the body and blood of Christ gives to all who obeys Him and feed on Him, if possible daily.

The devil is not called the ruler of the world in vain; he is a crafty spirit who masterminded the fall of man and how to hold him in bondage; to do this he must have a portion of man. He has a censor like in the old nature of man through which he gets into the soul, especially those who neglect the nature of Christ. He acts, lives and also speaks in the old nature of man without man's control or without man noticing, unless you are rooted deeply in Christ. Even when you are rooted in Christ, sometimes you find yourself in bitter struggle with the devil, trying to act or speak.

But He turned and said to Peter, 'Get behind me, Satan! You are an offence to me, for you are not mindful of the things of God, but the things of men.' (Mathew 16: 23) This was the word of Christ to Peter who was trying to prevent his master from dying because the devil was speaking through him. In the right sense of man Peter was right, but God who knows all says that the devil is speaking. How many times have we stood against God in this kind of scenario to defend ourselves against the will of God? This will induce you to understand the Scripture when it said that it is hard for man to enter heaven if he does not deny himself in following Christ. Truly the ancient enemy rules the old man, and through him he establishes his kingdom to torment the saints who are passing through. For instance, in the church and in religious life, people who refuse to deny their old nature become the instrument of torture and hardship for those who truly want to follow Christ. They stand against the progress of the church and become the enemy within—trying to establish their own self instead of asking for the grace of self-denial. This is the mystery of Christ, though; He allows this for the purification of the souls.

What we are talking about here is the mystery of the ubiquitous nature of the devil. Sometimes people ask, 'Why is he everywhere?' It is because he is living in the natural man he defeated and through it manipulates the soul to act for him. He ceases to know the soul or being everywhere when the soul connects to the spirit of Christ to live as a new nature; he ceases to know or understand even the language of the soul because in difficult times the soul groans, which can only be interpreted by the divine spirit. For God to dwell in man at this level, Christ must have overthrown the prince of the world not only geographically but also in the depth of man in order to set his soul towards the destiny of true nature of man.

Confession and Prayer

Christ Jesus! Come in your fullness and live in me. Destroy the rules of darkness in my spirit and soul; let the power of thy Gospel destroys the counsels of gods in the depth of my being. Amen.

The Fate of the Natural Man

What is the heart of our saying? Are we saying things that are rooted in imagination? Far from it! Rather we are predicating the fruits of meditations, the consciousness which streamed into our spirit because the hour is at hand. We are excavating the depths of man, to place the gods of the world and the nature of the old man which they have conquered in their right positions in the exaltation of the Almighty God who truly created man, loved him and placed him in His presence to have communion with him. This message is theosophical; for the most ancient spirit has poured out His spirit mightily in our days to unearth the truth destined to save the soul of any man who humbles himself through the power of His grace.

The Biblical theory of heaven is the absolute presence of God—where God is beheld as He is. Heaven is also the place where the pure spirits that comprise both the angels and saints unite as one family to enjoy the presence of the fountain of the Lord of all spirits. This is where Adam used to be even though his kingdom is called the Garden of Eden, yet it was a complete presence of God and a formal position of man among every other created beings until he was driven out of it and he found himself in the strange place where there are lots of troubles and discomforts leading to necessary death.

If you are a comrade of St Paul who confessed that we are the citizens of heaven, you must believe with me that this place is not a complete place of joy because for the eagle not to fly but to be kept in bondage under the pretence of domesticating it is a tragedy—for the eagle is meant to soar in the highest air and make the choice of where it goes or what it eats.

My spirit strongly compels me to say that it is a paradox when man, after receiving the new nature of Christ, does not work and longs for heaven; because being in Christ is to live a tradition of heaven whose citizen you are though on exiled earth which has different traditions. Of course I have never seen a man dwelling in a strange land who does not miss home and therefore longs for it, knowing that even the wild animals do not lost the sense of the smell of their birthplace, though they may have left there and travelled far away for long periods of time in search for the green pasture, yet they must go back to feel the touch of home.

Generally it is true to say that all men are strangers here, whether or not one believes in God. I have not seen any man who is comfortable on Earth regardless of what he professes. Even the most solitary person on earth is not an exception, for trouble always makes its way to that person, even to their hibernations. For God who loves man though He chased him out of His complete presence does not as it were want man to feel comfortable where he found himself lest he forget his origin completely. Therefore we may say some anxieties are necessary for man in the world so that being uncomfortable, he may look for comfort which the presence of God alone can give, even as He said, 'Come to me all you who labour and are heavily laden, and I will give you rest.' (Mathew 11: 28)

Apart from the consequences of sin and the devastations which the fallen angels have caused, the soul of man, which is so tender and vulnerable based on the love of God and His angels which he used to enjoy in fullness, does not feel complete within the fleshly image of man, therefore it continues to long for freedom, love and that completeness which he has lost. Hence the reason for these discomforts within man, whether in riches or in poverty, because the spirit is imprisoned in the flesh. Even in married life, which is the climax of human love, man does not own himself but rather belongs to his or her partner, because marriage is a kind of self-denial to be able to live as new but one person.

Do weather conditions favour man? Most times we may say yes but our inner craving and body systems have the answer. In winter we moan and cry about the severe cold, which is cruel indeed and ever-ready to take life away. We see man and other animals crying to God for the summer, which is blessed with sunshine. But are we comfortable with the sun when it finally appears? The answer is no, because even in the summer sometimes we see God's judgement on the old nature of man manifesting itself through the heat of the sun, reminding man that even though the earth may look habitable God has a better place for him. In extremely hot weather, for those in the tropical regions or tropical rain forest, we see them crying out for rain, and even when it comes sometimes it becomes unfavourable. In all these contradictions and discomforts with what we call the natural law, we see the judgement and language of God which reminds us that we are strangers here—that God Himself did not will the earth to be a habitable and permanent place for the same man He created for pleasure in the Garden of Eden, even though man had taken another form; for the soul of man will never be comfortable or feel at home until it finds itself back in the presence of God where it was before.

Who will blame man? Trying to make the world more habitable, he made it worse and triggered climate change. The Psalmist said, 'Even as the deer yearns for the running streams, so my soul is yearning for you, my God.' (Psalm 40: 1-2)

Oh son of man! Tell me how possible it is for this thirsting deer to live without water? Tell me what happiness is, if man does not find himself back in the presence of God just as the aquatic animals are unsafe until they return back to the water?

At this point, we bring to your consciousness that the first nature of man, which is the direct or indirect product of Adam and Eve, has been condemned and banished from the presence of God. This is not as strong as it sounds, because He who created this man loves him and could not stand the abhorrent presence which disobedience had caused. Therefore He chased him out in order to bring him back in the fullness of time as a true son with the spirit of Christ. As we see in the incarnation, Christ took the same form of man who was sent out of that mystic garden to till the ground, so that He might recreate him and be the way for he who wants to go back to the most ancient father.

During the celebration of the sacred mystery, the officiating minister always proclaims in a very loud voice that, 'In love God created man, in justice He condemned him and in mercy He redeemed him.'

In this proclamation, the church reminds us about this great truth—the fall of man and his rising, the spirit of old man which is condemned being contaminated by the fallen angels, and the spirit of the new man which is created in the image of Christ Jesus.

The condemnation in this sense means complete disapproval, of something unfit for use. In this sense whatever that is condemned must decay with time, just as we condemn our properties which are no longer useful.

Before we proceed further, there is need for us to understand in greater depth that man's soul is a spirit. He also has a spirit, which elevates and connects him to the nature of Him who made him. This spirit is the true strength of the soul, connecting him to God and keeping him in union with all the ministering spirits, including the Angels of light. Without its spirit, the soul cannot do anything; in other words it is responsible for all the actions of the soul and can determine the destiny of the soul. After the creation of man out of the dust, it was this spirit which exalted man into the paradise that God had made for him. During the temptation and the fall of man, it was through this spirit, which directs and controls the soul, that man was tempted—because it is a door to the soul, as we may put it. This spirit of man, having been deceived and contaminated by the devil, could not withstand the presence of heaven anymore and was cast out of paradise; because the soul can do nothing without its spirit, he found himself with his spirit back to where it came from, because man's spirit is the director. Therefore, because the love of God is irrevocable, He did not condemn the precious soul of man which He so much loved; rather his spirit was condemned and his environment was cursed to make man's sojourn on earth difficult.

When the appointed time came for God to bring man back, He did the most amazing work by creating another spirit for man so that the soul of man, by bending his ear to the new spirit, will find his way back to God. This spirit of man, which the Scripture referred as the old man, is the one that has been cast out with the demons who have conquered him, and he can never return any soul back to God irrespective of the soul's efforts through it.

These two spirits through the cooperation of the soul will determine the final destination of every soul. It is the choice of the soul to follow the principles of this old spirit to death or to follow the new spirit which is the product of the Holy Trinity through the water and the spirit to have eternal life in returning back to the garden of the Lord, as the verdict has been decreed that 'a soul that sins shall die'. The final destination and the destiny of every soul depend on the spirit he chooses to obey, Adam's or Christ's.

Beloved! What I want you to understand clearly is this—that man is truly the soul, body and spirit. After the fall of man, the spirit which connected soul to God which made man more of the spirit, dematerialised into the flesh; being under the control of the devil, he held the soul in bondage. In vain most times does the soul under the control of this spirit try to connect back to God; in vain the soul dares to please God because it depends on its spirit to do well. In baptism, Christ creates another spirit for the soul of man to earn eternal salvation. A soul who rejects his old spirit and clings to his new spirit during his sojourn on earth will, through the same spirit, be returned back to God when his exile is over. A soul that does not reject his old spirit but is rather enslaved by it will go down, both soul and the already condemned spirit which he obeyed. This is why Christ is called THE SAVIOUR and THE REDEEMER. Give this most sacred title given to Christ a deeper meditation.

You may ask now, 'what about other religions, who do not acknowledge Christ but believe in God? Let this truth be implanted into your soul that Christ is the salvation of God for the whole world for those who believe in Him. We dwell in the confessions of the Apostles that there is no other name under heaven given to men through whom man must be saved.' (Acts 4: 12) There is no compromise to this, irrespective of what the modern theologians may be teaching. This is our faith rooted in the mind of the Holy Spirit, not on human eloquence and intelligence; not even the minds of the intellectuals can comprehend or compromise on this. This is what we heard from Christ Himself that, 'he who does not believe in Him shall be condemned.' (John 3: 18) After His death and Resurrection, He sent His Apostles to go and minister His salvation to the whole world, and He repeated the same utterance again that he who does not believe in Him is condemned. (Compare Mark 16: 16.) Because only in believing in Him and receiving a second birth shall this new spirit of eternal life be given.

Because we lack understanding in the mystery of the appearance of Christ, we think somehow that Christ came to establish a religion just as other prophets or seers did; consequently people thought that they could attain the righteousness of God through any religion they chose, as long as they believed in God. This is because man has not clearly understood the nature of man before his fall and the condemnation that followed the natural man after the fall. Christ is far more than the prophecies of the prophets; in fact the mind of the prophets did not even contemplate Him fully. The Scripture insists that righteousness is not attained by keeping of the Law and the ministry of the prophets, as the law was to hold the condemned children of Adam in further bondage. Accept this truth: that Christ is the God of all the prophets and the King of all the religions, and the completeness of all that fallen children of Adam and Eve need to return to God. This is what the Scripture meant when it said that God has given us adoption through Christ. This adoption is made possible only through the spirit born in us by Christ during the holy baptism; thus it is said in Romans 8: 15 that 'we have received the spirit of adoption of sons, by which we cry, "Abba Father".' And this spirit of adoption was received through Christ Jesus to God Himself. (Compare Ephesians 1: 5.)

It is said also that all humanity is subservient to the influences of the spirit of the world. But at the completeness of the time, Christ was born so that the adoption may only be received through the same Christ. Therefore since the spirit of adoption comes only through the mystery of Christ, we exalt the mystery of our faith in Christ Jesus beyond every contradiction, every doctrine, every affirmation and domination—to declare without wavering that eternal life is only achieved through Jesus Christ, who is the Word of God formed in the womb of Virgin and sinless Mary, who is the Holy Spirit defined in the church and in the hearts of the saints above all contradictions as the new Eve.

When we read about the fall of man and the justice of God that followed it, we may not grasp the full meaning and its magnitude until our spirit is exalted in the first condition which Christ pronounced as a must-do for anyone who wishes to follow Him. 'Deny yourself! Deny yourself if you wish to follow me.'

... ...

This is what He who condemned man in Genesis said to the same man as an invitation back to his former glory when He became part of the banishment as man. The Eternal Word of God humbled Himself to become man—ministered to the children of Eve so that His own would hear Him and follow Him. Therefore because of this mystery of self-denial which He practised first, in which He became a new nature although most ancient, there is need that the new man who is the product of God in the divinity and humanity of christ must find himself on the same neutral ground where Christ also found Himself. There, humanity is divinised through self-denial, and God Himself in Christ is humanised through self-denial. There, man and God become one; and man, being able to do the will of God, becomes truly the adopted son of God.

When the spirit of God is dealing with a man, He does not tell him everything at once; rather He reveals everything slowly to him as they walk along together. The Scripture says, 'I have many things to tell you but you cannot bear them now. However, when the Spirit of truth has come, He will guide you to all truth.' Therefore following Christ in truth and in spirit will reveal the mystery of self-denial slowly until its depth is revealed to the apogee: that the nature of man as we have it now is contrary to what God made him from the beginning. There is no doubt that Christ Jesus is a Deity Incarnate as His church continue to profess in all ages and His teachings are spirit just as He Himself is spirit though in human flesh. It is time for humanity to wake up from slumber and take a different approach to this divine invitation of Christ: 'Deny yourself if you want to follow me.'

First, what is the reason behind people denying themselves? Maybe because someone has done something wrong and is afraid of the just punishment, it may be that his identity provokes fear or something more horrible. People deny their identities because such revelations mean death; for example, in medieval times and beyond, people who had the spirit of witchcraft hid and avoided being made a public spectacle of, through the cruellest deaths. Yet many deny who they are to avoid discrimination and all manner of fear. In acts of justice people deny who they are or their actions due to the fact that a death sentence or severe punishment is reserved for whoever admits to such identity or crime. So why must I deny myself to be accepted? May be I am disgusting or not worthy, or maybe I will be sentenced to death by justice, and therefore being afraid of death I must deny myself and live.

The architect of the whole universe had already warned Adam that he must surely die on the day he dared to eat the forbidden fruit. Consequently death started working within him and Eve from the day they ate the fruit and were cast out of the garden. Outside the garden their joys were turned into pain; in sorrow of death they found their food and bore children. Procreation for man was meant to be mystical, but as we have it, the judgement was made against Eve. 'I will greatly multiply your sorrow and your conception; in pain you shall bring forth children.' (Genesis 3: 16) Natural man was condemned all round, both in finding his food and in procreation. Thus when the Virgin Mary appeared, she gave birth to Christ mystically in an exalted manner; by becoming her children, the new creation can achieve the eternal plan of God by co-operating with God in creating a new nature of man within the old nature through baptism. And anyone can give this new life even to the dying person who has not known Christ. Apparently for this new nature to grow, he must deny the old one that has the sentence of death working in him. This death working in him is this seal of the fallen angels incised in every natural man.

A man left his father's land and settled in a strange land; for certain reasons he could not go back to his father's land because there had been a big quarrel that had led to his departure. So he found a wife in his new land and raised a family, for he said 'I shall not be a stranger forever; raising a family is the best thing I need to do which will enable me to forget my father's land.' When his children were of age, he told them his story. He was so rich in the tradition of his fathers that he transferred his entire heritage to them, even given them a tribal mark that he himself had on his face. After his death, the fourth generation upheld that tradition of maintaining this tribal mark. One day, one of them came in contact with a man with the same tribal mark riding on a horse; he was a king, with all his followers having the same mark. When he and the king saw each other, they stopped briefly; after a familiar mutual look, they passed by without comment. When the young man got home, he told his father of how he had seen a group of people who looked like them, with the same tribal mark. 'There is a festival of the kings from various kingdoms taking place in the city hall,' said his father. 'They must be one of the far kingdoms taking part in the festival.' They quickly got ready to proceed to the event, as his father believed they must be people of their great-grandfather. When they got there, the father saw everything just as the son had told him; their tradition was the richest of all the traditions present.

After sharing their story with the king, they requested if they could be reunited with them and follow them back to his kingdom—for they had been longing for a day like that. The king turned down their request, saying, 'Even though your great-grandfather was our son, yet you have stayed too long in a strange land. Now we have nothing in common with you despite the mark on you; you are now a stranger and no stranger or foreigner is allowed a foot in our kingdom for we are royals, the symbol of which you have on your face. You can come back to our land again and enjoy your royalties, but one of us must stay with you for a number of years and teach you all our traditions. Only after this will you become one of us. In our kingdom, we have no rules and laws, only our tradition and language, which is our guide and which you don't have.'

After careful thought, he concluded: 'I must follow this instruction given to me and return to my root, for what I have now is not mine except this mark on my face, which makes me unique. To be truly myself is to follow the destiny of this mark, which is indelible for it bears witness against me in this land that I am a stranger no matter how free I claim to be. I must deny this culture though it is very difficult, because I have found the reason why our fathers inscribed this kingdom on our face.'

This is the same thing a man must do: deny the tradition he is used to and cling to the one whose mark he has in the depth of his being even though it's very difficult. For from one generation to the next the soul of man continues to bear witness within, that he is from God and a stranger in the world indeed.

We have used this little story to explain what reality about human existence in the world is, and what he must do to return to his origin. Does an Asian with origins in Europe change his traits and colour to that of Europeans simply because he has been there for five generations? He will change in culture and language but his physical appearance and attributes bear witness to the fact that he has left a place. For him to recover that identity and natural inheritance, he must trace back to his roots.

A man who finds himself in another country and still wants to carry on with the traditions of his origin must maintain his culture, knowing too well that a day will come when he must go back to his home otherwise he will become a stranger and unacceptable. Therefore lots of denial is needed so that he will not get used to a strange culture. Not only did man come from God, he also came from a different realm; thus he must deny where he found himself in order to be able to go back to his former state. How can one do this unless he discovers that man left a state and place? How can one discover this state if he is so comfortable with the shadows of reality? For everything in the world are shadows of the truth. Thus the Scripture says that the world and all contained therein is passing away.

Accept this truth that this mystery is the mind of Christ when He said, deny yourself.' Where man is now is not his state at all, thus every flesh must experience death which is a complete transformation into the spiritual realm and the original nature of man which St Paul called spiritual body—having the same form or shape but a pure spirit like the wind.

Was man not banished from the presence of God? Were they not punished by He who multiplied their sorrows and cursed their environment? Therefore when He came in flesh, there was need for Him to create another within. It is in mercy that He asks us to deny the nature of Adam in us, which has so many troubles not only that he is punished by God but also that he who has conquered him is ruling him, manipulating even his good deeds. So far man still has the animal nature that was as a result of the event of which took place in the garden; the consequences continue with that nature. You who shoot for heaven must deny this nature because he has failed. Denying the spirit of Adam that has become worldly is the only option a soul has for him to be able to cling to the new spirit, which is created by Christ. This new man God loves and treats as a son because his spirit is the spirit of Christ Himself. He is a free nature and the demons are so afraid of him having nothing in him because he is a citizen of heaven—speaking the language of heaven, which no one understands except his comrades and God who gave it. When the trouble like Great River invaded a soul who is striving for salvation, the soul may not be able to pray; a cloud of darkness that comes through his animal nature, tears and sorrow, becomes his outward prayer because of the questions the accuser of soul projects onto him, which he lost words to defend himself. It is at this level that the new man in him groans and speaks that mystical language known alone by heaven, and it liberates quickly restoring the soul that has already despaired of life.

... ...

The Bible testifies that those in flesh (natural man) cannot please God. (Romans 8: 8) Natural man is that nature which was chased out of that mystical garden to go and till the ground; he is the true nature of human being. He is expert in dichotomy, full of envy, his interest is only in things he can see and prove with his senses, he obeys the commands of his animal nature and thereby continues to be a slave—building high edifices in the world as the only home, not looking back to hear the voice of his true Lord calling him home. He cannot please God, says the voice of the spirit, because he was conceived and born like an animal and therefore must live and die like one. This is not what God wills for man, though every man must die even as all food is seasoned with salt; but the true child of God is dying with his soul filled with the sense of joy that he is passing away from exile into the glorious liberty of being born of the spirit of Christ. He is uplifted with the word of Christ in the Gospel, which says, 'I am the resurrection and the life; whoever believes in me though he may die, he shall live.' (John 11: 25) This is the greatest joy of the soul departing the body into reality. Contrary to this joy is everlasting sorrow—for the greatest tragedy is for man to live and die just like the animal nature into which he was born.

When the true knowledge of self is done and the true nature of man is identified, the next thing for the soul who needs salvation is to deny; because the result of the findings must not be any other than the nature and character of animal which is born whenever a woman conceives. Since we are called to deny self, we must deny all the negative characteristics of this animal nature and use its positive ones upon which Christ stood to recreate. Since it is a denial, it means you are taking another nature which is not earthly, but of God. Do not be offended to hear that we are born just like the animals, for it is proven both scientifically and biologically. We think that natural man is highly exalted when we see man as a monopoly of wisdom and knowledge. But animals are also very intelligent within their own capacity; they calculate their gestation period when they are pregnant; birds of the air know well when they are due to lay eggs and begin to make their nests, and their calculations are accurate. They also know how to gather their food during the time of plenty. Other animals in the wild know when to cry to God for their food, and He gives it to them to keep them alive.

Make no mistake about this or misunderstand this mystery; there is the nature of Adam and nature of Christ Jesus. These two natures are two opposite parts of man and necessarily must coexist in every baptised soul. The destiny of the former is to descend because he has been judged and cast down with his offspring, while the latter has the destiny of ascending because he is free from condemnation and all the negative elements of the world; for He who created him is from above. Thus the ministry of the Holy Spirit through the Apostles from the day of Pentecost ministers Christ not only as God, Messiah or prophet, but also as the second Adam. (Compare Roman 5: 19; 1 Corinthians 15: 45.)

The exalted voice of the Holy Spirit strongly told us to put off, concerning our former conducts, the old man who grows corrupt, and to be renewed in the spirit of our mind: to put on the new man who was created according to God in righteousness and true holiness. (Ephesians 4: 22-24)

The natural man, as we will see in the next chapters, has many wounds which are incurable, unless a soul through the grace of Christ clings on the nature of Christ and works hard for his salvation. For as long as the old spirit is working in man, death and justice of God in Genesis Chapter 3 is at work with his rebellion and its consequences. Only by so doing will his old nature, which is spirit, start losing control over his soul until the new nature takes control—taking the soul back to his origin, and at this level a soul will start to see things truly the way they are, having been in utter darkness with the spirit of the world which rules the children of Adam.

To celebrate or live a life under the control of the spirit of the world is the greatest risk a human will take over his precious soul—living a basic principle of the world without considering that his soul is a stranger both in his flesh and in the world. Job in his days made a prophetic utterance concerning the condition of a natural man, 'that man born into the world is born to trouble'. (Job 5: 7)

Trying to do good he is nonetheless enslaved in a strange nature which makes it impossible for him, having been chased away to a place where he will eat more of the fruit that decays, to alienate himself further from the nature of spirit that was once a greater part of him. As it were, the old man has chosen a place and a state for which God did not make him, nor can he adapt to it; therefore both his nature and the relationship with God are altered.

When a creature created to inhabit in a specific place or region finds itself in another region, not only its natural appearance will change but there will also be a metamorphosis in its original character and attributes, for it to be adaptable in the new place. To retain its original nature or do things the way it used to in the former abode is impossible, neither would the things and place it has left behind change to accommodate these changes. This is a typical analogy and is the situation of man when he found himself outside the Garden of Eden; anthropologically and morphologically life must not be the same for man outside the

Garden of Eden; and his relationship with heaven will never be the same either, neither would heaven change to accommodate his strange natural instincts. He began to dig the ground and eat its fruits, and so he became more earthly—becoming more natural and active in flesh than in his spirit; since he chose natural fruit to activate his flesh in the enslavement of his soul and spirit, the Lord of the garden did not hesitate to chase him away to a place where he must be necessarily negative to the nature of himself and God.

The animal nature we have now on the planet earth is what was hidden in the Garden of Eden; and what we had in that garden became our hidden nature along with God and His angels who are spirits. All spiritual existence became a hidden thing from any natural man; but a man who trains himself to become mystical is allowed a glimpse of what we have lost in paradise—thus the Christian mystics exist on another level of being human.

In the garden, his food was the mystical fruits of the Garden of Eden, the place of heavenly delight until he dared to eat that fruit. Yet all the efforts of man to adapt to where he found himself were in vain, because his soul was a spirit; looking unto heaven from the cave of the earth where disobedience had placed him, Adam cried unto the Lord for mercy to return to His presence, seeing that he was under the bondage of a strange spirit. God heard his and Eve's cry, and through His help they started to evolve and to explore the earth because they were higher beings and not meant for beneath. Take a good look at the kind of flesh He formed; is it not quite different from other animals, though they all feed from the same fruits of the earth?

In the world there is a spirit that as it were claims ownership of the world and controls it. This spirit is very strange to the soul and the true nature of man, and no one will understand this mystery until he has the spirit and the nature of Christ; it is called the spirit of the world. It works in the flesh, which is enslaved to it to keep the soul of man in bondage, focusing on the life of the flesh and never thinking about his origin. Thus Christ cried, 'What shall it profit a man to gain the whole world and lose his soul.'

For one to live above the concupiscence of his nature and all its desire to obey the status quo, he must yield his soul to the spirit of Christ, which is the complete opposite. This spirit of the world is the controlling force, a standard set up by the invisible forces, and most times they do this through natural man they rules. It is a kind of covenant between the two, which the weaker must abide by as a law coterminous with the state in which he finds himself. It makes man human and natural, to keep his soul in everlasting slavery to the flesh—to fulfil all the deeds of the flesh. At most times this spirit is in pari passu with the nature of man, which Christ described as the tradition of man in His Gospel. For a man to resist this spirit, he must experience what is called death through the power of the gospel in order to receive the spirit of God which spiritualises his senses and mentality—making him lose himself and cling to the divine nature created by Christ. Yes! You must lose your senses to be true followers of Christ; the world, your friends and your loved ones will tell you, and even you yourself will know that you have lost them because of Christ.

In the Gospel of John Chapter 8, Christ openly called the populace 'the children of the devil, who only want to fulfil the desire of their father', because they refused to accept His teaching. This is in line with a similar statement made by His forerunner John the Baptist, who called them 'broods of vipers', because strange spirits which were not of God were working in them.

Christ concluded by saying that they refused to accept Him because they are not of God. Remember that this people He was talking to had already believed in Him but could not accept Him. What a paradox that people professing to be the children of God were addressed by the same God as the children of the devil because of metaphysical chromosomal mutations. Simply they were not the same man He had placed in His garden, who was a spiritual being though made of dust. Thus you must accept this truth and spirituality that man needs the new nature of Christ to be able to say yes to God with Christ Jesus in order to obtain all the promises of God.

In 1 Corinthians 2: 12, we are reminded that we have been freed from the spirit of the world and are now given the spirit who is from God, that we might know the truth of God. Whoever has this new giving spirit, and adheres to its voice, ceases to be a natural man: doing what God would always do, loving what God would always love and abhorring things that heaven abhors. God Himself, seeing this spirit of His son in man, rejoices to call him son or daughter for the spirit himself knows no other father but God of heaven; thus He taught them in prayer to call God 'Our Father'. St John the Apostle goes deeper in explaining this when warning that a believer should not love the things in the world (that is, attaching one's soul to them) because such a person has no love of the father in him, being carried away with the lust of flesh, eyes and pride of a life which has nothing to do with God but is a natural character of man. Can man worship God if not in and through his spirit? Could he come to Him in truth if he has not been given the spirit of truth from God which reveals and convinces of this truth hidden from the reach of a natural man who sees the things of God as most foolish things—whose faculties the gods of this age have darkened?

Blessed is the creative mystery fulfilled in Christ that exalts man above the standard of his nature and the basic principles of the world. This mystery was what enveloped Peter and Paul, moving them to chant hymns of praise glorifying the Father of our Lord Jesus Christ who transfers man from utter darkness to His marvellous light, making man a heavenly being on earth, a royal priesthood, a holy nation consecrated to God. A marvellous light indeed that man will be on earth and get grafted into the nature of God as the greatest love of Christ, yet the children of men could not accept this salvation because of the passing pleasures of sin, and the glories of the world which pass with time.

Have this great truth in the very centre of your mind: that when the Bible said that man was made in the image and likeness of God, it did not mean this nature as we have it now but rather a nature which Adam had in paradise before his fall. We will talk more about this nature in subsequent chapters—the glorious nature which Christ has recreated in man, which we see in its fullness when He died and resurrected with a glorified body. Therefore, let our mentality and confessions change; because we have been baptised into the nature of Christ, address yourself no more as a child of Eve but instead boldly proclaim at the top of your voice that you are a child of Virgin Mary, the new Eve, a brother or a sister of Christ; for so it pleases God who gave us Christ because truly old things had passed away and are decaying. This is what the spirits want to hear, both the spirit of the old man and the spirit of the law, so that the ministry of death established through Moses will lose its grip on your soul and you may worship God as a son or daughter and not as a slave. For the accusations, negatively inherited inclinations, handwritings and coded signs against man's soul begin to lose their energy on man the day this great mystery is confessed from the depth of his being. Because just as Adam and Eve were our first parents through natural birth, even so Christ and Virgin Mary become our supernatural parents through baptism.

Never again should anyone who aspires to go to heaven refer to himself as the poor banished children of Eve. For that old Eve and her offspring will never return to that glorious kingdom from where they were banished. (This consciousness does not mean that Adam and Eve are in hell)

... ...

The message is that the birth of any man is a birth of a nature with a natural inclination that must rebel against God notwithstanding the innocent look of the child or the holiness of the parents. No matter how gently a child poses, there is an inclination against God aimed towards him, which will manifest itself when the time is due. It differs in individuals as some have more wounds in them than others, both physical and spiritual. Human beings are born with all manner of inclinations, genetic sicknesses, and hereditary disorders in sexuality, mentality and genetic codes. Thus the ministry of Christ brings the new beginning—making old things a thing of past, and giving the nature a new nomenclature and a start to a new life, no matter how wounded the nature might be.

The early Christians knew and lived by the true meaning of baptism, giving more attention to the day they were reborn into the nature of Christ than to that of their natural birth, which has many contaminations and contradictions spiritually and towards God. If baptism truly saves, as 1 Peter 3: 21 says, the church sums up her teaching in this manner by saying that baptism makes us the children of God. By implication, there was something going on within the depth of man with the destiny of eternal separation from God before the baptism, which introduces one into the saving ministry of Christ Jesus. Of what benefit it is to celebrate the birth of a nature that has no destiny of life towards God? A pitiable nature, which has many accusations and condemnations chasing it? Thus it is only man's newborn baby that cries at birth, among all mammals. What is the fruit of celebrating the birth of a nature that the author of life asks me to deny? Is it not a blessed and just thing for me to celebrate with joy the day God has begotten me through Christ as the day of my birth?

I did not say that you should not celebrate your birthday; you who are born with royal blood or a perfect nature that do not need Christ's nature. But the bitter truth is that no one is born with a perfect nature, for we are all the product of the failed nature of man called Adam. Otherwise one is standing indirectly against the scripture and the appearance of Christ who took upon Himself the sins of our old nature—making God a liar.

It is better for us as Christians to celebrate the day of our baptism more than the day of natural birth if we truly want our old nature to let go of our soul. This statement may sound extreme to some ears; but it was the same when it was first communicated to my spirit. Yes! Because my old nature immediately resisted it, even as you may be doing now because you are also a carrier of this old nature that wants to control the soul. But let the Holy Spirit calm you down, so you may look beyond. How can you look the truth in the eyes without bowing your head? Relax, for the Holy

Spirit is not in haste to convince anyone. Do not attack or reject this salvific message immediately, but like Virgin Mary let us learn how to be calm and ponder this and other mysteries of salvation in our hearts, and see how the Spirit of the truth will convince us with His truth that sets us free. Remember it's still your birthday, irrespective of the day it is being celebrated.

We are what we celebrate; just as one who wins a trophy or achieves something great celebrates and derives joy and happiness from that which he celebrates, so one who celebrates his natural birth celebrates his birth and all the destinies attached to it. Remember that the Scripture said of the Christians that we used to be in darkness but we are now being in Christ; we have been transferred into His marvellous light. Now, in sincerity, is it better to celebrate the birth that without baptism makes one dwell in darkness or the birth of the marvellous light? Is it better to celebrate the natural man who cannot discern spiritual things and the destiny of his soul, or to celebrate the spiritual man created in the nature of Christ for heavenly inheritance? May God help you in doing the arithmetic to arrive at the right point in this delicate topic. We all know through the Scripture that Adam and Eve have changed the destiny of their posterity. When a natural man born with a specific disorder celebrates his natural birth, is it not to exalt these contradictions that pollute his soul and keep him in bondage?

It is time for us to stop and think about this. The worst is that we renew this ritual every year and by so doing ignite the fire of concupiscence in us; thus it is very hard for us to die to old self and live the new life of Christ because in ignorance we are celebrating that which we are denying. What we are saying now is what Job foresaw in his days and started invoking curse on the day he was born. (Job 3: 3)

To him that day was not worth celebrating after he experienced the true knowledge of self through all his experiences, which exposed the depth of human miseries. The cry of Jeremiah was the same; as a prophet he was prophesying against the old nature of man for the spirit in him was convincing him that the day of

Christ would bring about the new nature of man who would be free from the troubles of natural man—otherwise he would not have invoked a curse of such a magnitude on himself. (Jeremiah 20: 14-18)

We are yet to uncover the fullness of the reason why Christ was manifested, for His Spirit is doing marvellous work these last days to define some hidden mysteries for a last evangelisation.

What you need to do now is apply humility of heart and deeper meditation to the word of God, even though we all have been celebrating our natural births without calling to mind the mystery of our faith in Christ who for this same reason was not only called the Messiah, but also the new Adam. If old Adam begot children, the Second Adam has a similar destiny in a higher order of having mystical children.

Today is still a very new day to say no to the things of yore and to celebrate truly that exalted nature which Christ has given us—for that day worth celebrating, to be in agreement with what we have been confessing. What a confusing and foxy theology that a Christian confesses that he is a new creation while he celebrates the birth of his old nature without calling to mind the day he was reborn? Of what gain is it to celebrate the nature destined for corruption that can never ascend but must descend with he who rules him? To celebrate our birth in Christ is a blessed devotion indeed, which disarms the greatest enemy of man.

Having said all this, we still need to thank God on the day of our natural birth for the gift of life and for our old nature which still has a lot to do with the glory of God and the exaltation of our new nature. Our old nature, as we have said, is not entirely bad, but this mystery is revealed for the salvation of our souls, which we must try our very best to salvage from any poison that runs from the ancestry of Adam which we celebrate on the birth of animal nature. Upon this hangs our destiny of making it to heaven, which no one in his right mind should gamble with.

Oh, the bitterness of the soul that rejects his salvation, which is costlier than the creation of fallen man! Oh, the torture of Christ to redeem man! That God Himself shed tears of blood and cried bitterly for help and eventually died to be able to save many—not even all. Do you not want to be that part of many—to escape damnation? What is it that man cannot let go to save his precious soul seeing that he found himself temporarily on earth?

I am not speaking out of human thinking on this issue, therefore it's not easy to accept or digest this without His grace. This same mystery is the kerygma of the liturgical celebration found in the church. Have you ever asked yourself a question or considered the reason why the old liturgy of the Christian church, both east and west, celebrates only the birth of Christ, Virgin Mary and John the Baptist? This is the work of the Holy Spirit sending a message to convince us that their births were the only births free from Adam's spirit. John the Baptist was the only lucky fruit of Adam who was baptised in the womb by the Holy Spirit—giving him a new nature above anyone born of a woman, as Christ confirmed in His teaching. Yes! John the Baptist was a man with an angelic soul.

Truly we have been saved and purchased by the most precious blood of Christ, as 1 Peter 1: 19 confessed. In mercy the Almighty God has indeed shown Himself a father by giving His son as a prize to ransom man. It is like the story of a man who had a sheep that he loved and cherished so much, he kept it in his garden with provision of varieties of food that it need not stray from his owner's territory. One day the sheep entered a forbidden forest, ate grass there, and was captured by the enemy who not only hated sheep but also could not provide the sheep with good food. Having stayed for many years with its captor the animal became worthless and gaunt. Because its former owner could not see or love any other animal the way he loved his lost sheep, he embarked on a journey searching for it. His heart was so sorrowful when he eventually found the sheep, yet he was not without joy. He was sorrowful because his sheep could not recognise him and he himself could hardly recognise the sheep, if it were not for the seal of ownership he had set on it, which remained indelible, connecting both together. 'This sheep belongs to me,' he insisted to the captor, who in turn replied, 'But it is mine now and as you can see it is no longer the same sheep that left your garden, having lost the look it once had when it was yours to the yoke of my own kingdom.' Even though this sheep looked very strange and could not recognise its owner any more, the owner demanded to have it back even though it would cost him his life.

This is the extent to which God had gone in order to redeem man. Though man has grieved God, and consequently became a slave of Satan, yet He embarked on a journey into that dungeon—giving up His only son to die the death of man, so man might be free to come back to Him and enjoy the nature and glory of which God has made him. But natural man prefers blindly to remain with the greatest enemy of his freedom, who convinces him that the way home is too far and too difficult, therefore he decides to remain a slave even though his Lord had died for him and with His blood purchased him in convincing him that his captivity was over. How far away is the home that a man will not strive to return after great exploit, no matter how dark the night is?

It is true that the road back to our heavenly home is not easy, but let your soul be strengthened because God has truly begotten you—giving you a new nature that is glorified far above the nature that was enslaved. Let His promise sink into your depth, for He said, 'Fear not! I will be with you till the end of time.' The consciousness of His ever presence is the highest weapon and victory ahead of you even in the utter darkness, because He is ever faithful to His word. Be encouraged by the power of the Holy Spirit because you are a purchase of God! Every baptised Christian by the virtue of the chrism oil upon his soul is destined and empowered to defeat the world and the devils if only he is willing to obey and pray. God is not strict, as our old rebellious nature always tries to impress on us; wickedness is not in His holy nature. Not at all! It's just that He loves and owns man; we are from Him and He is trying His best to get us back to that nature in which He made us, which is fitting to His spiritual presence. He does this with all carefulness, almost afraid of hurting us, for He is not ready to risk losing us. Because Christ who has adopted us, being life Himself, has experienced the death of those to whom He gave life.

Confession and Meditation:

I am a new creation of God! Purchased by the precious blood of Christ Jesus.

The Spiritual Nature

From the beginning man was created a spiritual being with the flesh but his flesh was completely hidden, in the sense that he never knew he had flesh until he ate the fruit and it became the opposite; his spiritual nature hid. After death we will regain the full consciousness of what we have lost. May God always be with man and aid him who is enslaved to the flesh to fulfil all that is required spiritually so he will not be alienated from the true nature of man at the end of this exile.

To understand and believe that man is a spirit in the flesh is a great beginning for a natural man to ask himself: where did I come from? Why am I entrapped in the flesh? This consciousness indeed is a kind of deliverance and freedom just as the scripture says that the fear of God is the beginning of wisdom. The spiritual nature of man is more real than the physicality of man but because of a lack of wisdom owing to the corruptions in our flesh, most men lose this reality or may not even know the source of their being a living being—which is also a fundamental activating principle determining one's character.

In Psalm 102 it is said, 'You send forth your spirit and they are created. You take back your spirit and they die, returning to the dust from which they came.' The physical nature of a human being would not have been able to do anything without his hidden nature which animated him—using all his organs to see, hear, talk and walk. This true nature of man does everything, and it moves his physical body wherever he wishes. When a living being in the flesh is making locomotion, his spiritual nature is the part that inspires, orders and makes these movements; even as he moves his physical body, man's spirit goes before him like a shadow dragging him to his destination, thus sometimes some people who are more sensitive sense events or occurrences ahead. This is not imagination but truth and consciousness, because I know for certain that some people are gifted in seeing the soul just like a shadow moving ahead of the living man. It is very simple to understand this reality when you recall a scenario where on your way you remember a friend or acquaintance and suddenly you bump into him. This is not a mere coincidence, but rather because your soul is ahead of you, connecting you to the person who approaches; you were able to sense it because you have stayed recollected, for it is impossible to experience this without being recollected.

The spirit is life even as life itself is spirit and keeps our body alive, making the blood circulate. Thus the body dies once the spirit is separated. We see the flesh becoming heavier than it was when it was alive because the spiritual nature is gone. The mystery of life in the body can be compared with what we see in technology and electrical gadgets, which function whenever they are connected to power but cease to respond as soon as they are disconnected. As an electric current empowers gadgets to function, so the spirit soul of man activates the flesh to be alive. Whenever it is withdrawn, the body also becomes useless and melts away.

As we have said, man was created as a spiritual being made of earth to be free as spirit but because of sin he was enslaved to body to live his life on earth where he found himself in bondage, although we may not grasp the fullness of this mystery now until we are exalted in certain mystical experiences.

Who knows if he will live well for the number of years he must dwell in that prison before he returns to his formal state or is banished forever? Enslavement of the spiritual nature of man in the body may be seen as part of the punishment for the disobedience of man, considering that God gave him dominion over all visible creatures, to rule them according to his desire. As it were, how can this type of natural man achieve this great task if he cannot first have dominion over his body? Was it not said that charity begins at home?

Let us not drift away from reality even though we are in flesh. The true nature of man is irrevocable, irrespective of the conscious state of the human mind; just as the blood circulates in the human body, one cannot deny it simply because he is ignorant of it, the same way this truth stands. The Creator Himself made man in His own image, to participate in His immortality, thus the invisible aspects of man retained this nature regardless of whether he believes it or not.

God is infinitely great and wise in His actions. We have dreams and some people are gifted in trance, yet many people did not see this as the mystery of the spiritual nature of man through which God communicates to man that there is still existence preceding the life in flesh. Dreams, trances and such like are the activities of the spirit which can only be manifested when the physical nature is subjected to weakness, or when the soul is exalted above natural inclinations to see what ordinary eyes cannot see.

You who do not understand how man is a spirit, have you ever asked yourself why man dreams and sees himself hundreds of miles away from where his body is lying unconscious? It's not just a mental image or imaginative thoughts but rather the activities of the spiritual nature of man whenever the senses are less active. It is the physical aspect of man who becomes unconscious during sleep, while the spirit never sleeps. Immediately man falls asleep, his invisible nature will begin its own activities upon which hangs the destiny of each soul, because those spiritual activities sometimes determine the entire life of a soul both present and future. Therefore it is a wise thing to be sufficiently alert to recollect the activities of the spirit and, with full consciousness through the power of God, engage in battle through prayer, balancing any manipulation sensed by your spirit who goes before you both in your conscious and unconscious states.

Some people are deceived through dreams due to lack of understanding or misinterpretations; many people have been exalted through dream because it is a language of the spirit. God Himself has achieved numerous communions with man and deliverance through dreams and trance, as in the case of Jacob whose spirit was exposed to the angels of ascending and descending which the ordinary eyes of flesh cannot see. Those that are gifted with visions and trance will attest to the fact that their ordinary eyes do not see beyond. So be wise in the activities of the spirit shown in the dream for even though God uses it yet it can be manipulated by the devil; for he too can project dreams onto the soul through the old spirit of man which is under his control. Thus sometimes in the dream of the night one may see oneself doing what is contrary to one's beliefs or what one confesses. Sometimes dreams may come through whatever spirit you are connected to or the desire of a soul as well, but be wise in discerning your dreams.

In John 6: 63, it is said, 'It is the spirit who gives life; the flesh profits nothing.' Christ Jesus who is the master of all creations declared this. We may say that the flesh is the means by which the spirit can carry out its functions; it uses the eyes to see, its legs to walk, its mouth to speak and it can speak without opening his mouth, and can visualise what was seen before even when it is out of the reach of the eyes. Therefore it's a true saying indeed that the flesh profits nothing. Sometimes when we decide to do something, our spirit is willing as it inspires the thoughts, but we see the body out of weakness may not be responsive. It becomes active once the spirit imposes its force on it, and it must respond to the pull, as it has no option.

Truly the flesh is the greatest enemy of our spiritual nature, thus we cannot do what we wish because the two are always in bitter struggle, the former always willing but the latter always weak. Therefore you must agree with me that the spiritual nature of man was indeed punished in the flesh as long as he lives in the world.

Sometimes, our spiritual nature is somehow allowed a freedom to practise its nature; for example, it can race round to twenty or more different places in a few minutes and come back to where its complete nature is. Sometimes somebody may be standing with you, but not really there with you, which we call absent-mindedness. Ask what you said a few minutes earlier, and the person has no clue because he was not really right there. Through the transport of their spirit, people who are very strong and more conscious of the power of their spirit can act in a different manner, far from where they are. They can minister to an acquaintance very far away. Thus a close relation may be very far away from you and suddenly you have the strong feeling of his presence; it is because his spirit is around you. The great difference between the angels and human is that angels appear immediately where they will in less than a moment but the human cannot because he is in bondage of the flesh.

In the Gospel, Christ compared His new creations with the wind, which goes wherever it wishes, because they have been born of the spirit. It is the case of handling spiritual things with the spiritual—for whoever that is born of the spirit must strive with all possible vigour through the gifts of the Holy Spirit to act in the invisible, enjoying the freedom of the sons of God because he has no barrier. It was seen in the lives of certain people who experienced levitation, bio-location and flight, and with little experience, I can attest that this is truth. This extraordinary phenomenon is what Christ manifested in His saints and mystics to prove that this new nature of man is not of the earthly origin but divine, just like Himself. During the life of St Padre Pio, the stigmatic priest, a man was wondering how the saint managed to be on his two feet throughout the time of celebration of liturgy, having on his feet the wounds of Christ which bled occasionally. The saintly man simply declared, 'I am hanging.'

... ...

The ministry of Christ and His Holy Spirit is a process of transforming natural man into the supernatural existence, which is totally spiritual. Looking into the lives of the Apostles in the Scripture, especially the Acts of the Apostles, we see these transmutations from their weaknesses in the Gospel to their boldness and courageousness in the Acts of the Apostles after the coming of the Holy Spirit. 'Pray and tarry in Jerusalem until you are endowed with the Holy Spirit.' This was the word of Christ to them—knowing that the Holy Spirit is coming upon them to exalt their spirit mystically for signs and wonders. This Holy Spirit has nothing to do with the flesh, thus Christ says to them, 'Wait and pray until the coming of the Spirit.' The Apostles roasted themselves in the fire of prayer until the Holy Spirit was poured upon them. As we said, this Divine visitor does not compromise with the flesh; He only works through their spirit to detach their soul from the slavery of the flesh, giving them the power to subject their animal instinct to the obedience to the spiritual principles of God.

With the Holy Spirit upon the Apostles, we see Apostles who used to be afraid, changing to the firebrand men empowered to change the world; they were just like ordinary men, but were more of the spirit. People started seeing them as gods even as St Paul was addressed in Lycaonia. (Compare Acts 14: 11)

Their lives as a new nature kept up the crescendo until it reached the climactic stage. Thus they were able to do marvels, their shadows and presence manifested as healings just like their master. We read the account of some of the Apostles, who were freed from prison without much understanding of what actually took place.

It was the manifestation of the highest concentration of the nature of Christ alive in them. Their spirit took over their human inclinations completely, and exalted them to act in the invisible, to connect with the ever-present angels of God—to escape the danger of death. At that level they were able to see beyond human vision and to see the angels who were assigned for their deliverance. The Scripture said that the Angels of God always encamp around those who revere the Lord to rescue them. (Psalm 34: 8)

These Angels are ever-present even in our lives today but being able to see them depends on how we respond to that great call of Christ to deny ourselves—for this self-denial is the only way back into the spiritual existence which man lost in the Garden of Eden.

We can only see things the way God made them, when we are exalted in the truth of the mysteries of our salvation and are ready to tell ourselves the truth. This is the truth that sets us free indeed. 'That to be in the flesh is to be exiled from God.' (2 Corinthians 5: 6)

This saying sums up this great mystery of the spiritual nature of man. This reason is why having faith is so important in the lives of the children of heaven who are exiled in the flesh. This faith is absolutely the life of our spiritual nature that senses that great beyond though trapped in the body. Thus the Scripture says that without faith no one can please God. The natural man depends on what he sees, touches or proves. But the spiritual man exists only by faith, knowing and dwelling in the truth, which contradicts his natural mentality and strives to keep it. Eventually, we must all depart from this earthly house; only the truth as known through faith survives, because the flesh and all its deceit are temporal.

Since we are going to account before Christ all that we did in the flesh, it is therefore essential for a soul in the body to strive to be in control of the poisons of the flesh through the truth of God as revealed in the Scripture and in His church, knowing that all the knowledge of the human natural mentality is just like a shadow which is not real. Know you also that all the deeds of man, whether good or evil as compelled by the flesh or faith, must be accounted for because it is the action of the inhabitant called the soul no matter the spirit that influences him.

Life of the spirit is when one allows his spirit to connect to reality. To the Lord of that garden of delights that was lost through disobedience. When this is done, the final result is the soul living the life of heaven on earth because he allowed his spirit to lead the way. The truth is that God speaks when the nature of man keeps silent, as He said: 'Be still and know that I am God.'

This is where the soul adopted by the Spirit of Christ connects to the tradition of heaven where he truly belongs. Such a soul in the flesh is the one whom Christ addressed as being in the world but not of the world; because he unites with the Spirit of Christ to live above the standard of his human nature to the fullness of heavenly nature. In this Our Lord's Prayer is fulfilled: 'Thy will be done on earth as it is in heaven.'

When a soul starts to act in this manner—depending on what it can prove to be truth—such a soul is already alienating itself from the doctrine of godliness because life itself is a mystery beyond human grasping. To get the depth of this mystery, it is good for us to go back to Genesis. There we ask ourselves: How it all did start? Where do we come from? Where do we find ourselves? Where are we going?

I am so tempted to compare man to a sheep when he was in the Garden of Eden, but man in that garden was never like sheep to God—The Great Ancestor. Rather he was seen as the son of God. (Thus Christ answered The Son of God when He appeared in human form so that through Him we can regain the lost status of man.) Now on earth, we are being referred to as the sheep of the Lord because we are passing through a process, and when that is fulfilled, the sheep will cease to be fed with grass, having become complete, and we will be placed back in that garden as sons.

... ...

The Garden of Eden is a spiritual reality beyond our geographical placement, which exists just as the earth exists. It is a wonderful thing that our science has proven that there are existences beyond our solar system, which are all the marvellous works of our God. To think that this great garden is somewhere within the planet earth cannot be truth, because the nature of man in that garden was completely different from the nature in which man found himself on the planet earth. If this garden was part of the world elsewhere, the flood of Noah must have wiped away everything, which will make it impossible to trace its geographical position; but it was never a material world.

As we have said, man was an earthly substance that was exalted by the breath of God into the Garden of God, to enjoy the presence of God with the fiery spirits called the Angels. According to the book of Genesis, God formed man from the dust and breathed upon him and he began to live. This breath of God is spirit, which not only animated Adam, but also made him a spiritual being. This spirit made him more than an earthly being while the origin of his encasement made him less than other heavenly beings. So we may say that he was enjoying the divine nature of God merited out of the love of God.

When this breath entered him, it exalted him from earth to that spiritual garden and realm not only to be in communion with heaven but also to rule all the earthly beings that were formed from the same earth. After the devil chose to disobey God and lost his place, he did not go out without trying to lure man into disobedience as he had already lured some angels into following him. When man chose to do what the devil suggested instead of God, he was immediately robbed off his eternal life and he found himself back to the earth in one moment as soon as he was cast out.

The Scripture said, 'Therefore the Lord God sent him out of the Garden of Eden to till the ground from which he was taken.' (Genesis 3: 23) This is a clear statement that spiritual Adam was cast out of a place to another where he became natural Adam. He who cast him out did not necessarily send him to the world, but as men found themselves in animal form, the best option and a suitable place was the earth, which is the only place where their new natures could adapt because originally they were the product of the earth.

Planet earth is so beautiful and full of life, but it was not really made for the spiritual Adam and Eve from the beginning, but rather for the animals and the sea creatures ruled by man. Did God place man on the earth to explore it? The Scripture said that man was chased out of the Eden Garden. I have not seen a man who chased a recalcitrant fellow out and yet provided another place for him. Such a person must go out and find a suitable place for himself. We must consider this fact—that God created things in pairs: Heaven and Earth, spiritual and physical. The same way we have our earth with beautiful fruits and plants, so the Garden of Eden is a spiritual nature of earth with beautiful trees and plants. (Compare Genesis 2:8-9)

When man was no longer found worthy of that spiritual paradise, he was forced to descend to where he is now. That paradise is what Christ referred to when He promised that lucky thief, 'Today you shall be with me in paradise.'

Let us consider this story. A man, after building a massive business empire, put his son in the position of managing it. But instead of building it up, the son chose to squander the treasure laid in his hand. His angry father cast him out of all his properties, telling him to go and fend for himself. He who cast out the son did not give him another choice of survival; rather the young man went his way to choose his own living. This is the kind of scenario that happened between our first parents with their God, but in their case God showed His eternal love by giving them tunics as coverings for their flesh, to get them ready for the new version of relationship.

If they were not like spirits who existed elsewhere before their fall, of what need were they in need to be covered after the fall?

Though God created on earth herbs and trees which yield foods for man, as Genesis 1: 29 said; yet He planted a garden which was a version of the earth, with a good food bearing trees pleasant to sight. (Compare Genesis 2: 8-9)

Therefore it is an established fact in the Scripture that the earth and the Garden of Eden were two different places. God formed man out of the earth and told him that the fruits of the earth are his food, but He did not allow man to dwell on earth. Out of His love for His image and likeness, He exalted man into His garden, which is a spiritual abode. Meditate on what the Scripture said: 'And the Lord God formed man out of the dust of the ground, and breathed into his nostrils the breath of life; and man became a living being.' (Genesis 2: 7) Subsequently a garden was mentioned. In this garden God placed man after He exalted him with His breath to enjoy the beautiful food and fruit plants in it.

Indeed the spiritual nature of man feeds mystically because he had a spiritual body. As it is recorded, those pleasant fruits of the garden were his food. After the fall of man he started to feed on the earthly food, which made him completely earth-man since he was no longer in the high garden to eat the fruits meant for his mystical nature. Though he became earth-man, his spiritual nature was still alive, but hidden. Do we not eat in the dream in which God keeps reminding us that we have a spiritual nature that survives the flesh? If Christ who is complete man and the image in which we are recreated ate in His earthly life, even after His resurrection, there may be a possibility of such things beyond here. Remember that the mission of Christ is to take us back to our spiritual existence because God did not create such a place in vain. Christ assured His apostles that He would not drink from the fruit of the vine until the kingdom of God arrived. (Compare Mathew 22: 18)

Throughout the Scripture, we see the mention of this mystical food; He rained down manna for them from heaven; Elijah the Tishbite was fed with bread by angel; Christ Himself was referred to as the bread of Angels and of heaven. In the book of Revelation 2: 7 it is said, 'To him who overcomes I will give to eat from the tree of life, which is in the midst of the paradise of God.'

This is the same tree of life mentioned in the book of Genesis beside which God placed a mighty cherubic angel with a sword, after He chased man out. Do you think that God created this tree in vain? No! He created it for the final exaltation of man whom He formed out of the dust and spiritualised him. As God Himself said, 'Behold, the man has become like one of us, knowing good and evil. Therefore the Lord God sent him out of the garden of Eden, lest he put out his hand and eat also from the tree of life, and live forever.' (Genesis 3: 22-23)

Meditating deeply about this tree, it seemed that spiritual Adam himself had not reached the complete nature that God meant for him; rather he was still on the process before his fall. As we have said, he was formed from the earth, as precious as he was; God planted a garden and put him very close to Himself knowing that the day of his final test would come which would have exalted him more had he stood firm. I am quite convinced that God who loves man so much would have completed His great work in Adam had he been able to defeat the devil. God would have given him that tree of life from which to eat and he would live forever, not only in the garden but in the complete presence of God.

When that mighty angel who used to be so bright had it in mind to revolt against God, the omniscient nature of God had already started a plan to use Adam and his offspring to fill the gap that He knew those angels would vacate, being blown away into their destiny. Because Adam failed, God did not allow him to complete his formation; He did not punish him forever either, but instead cast him away back to where he was formed to start afresh. Indeed it is more difficult now for man in the flesh to climb back to that formal glory, thus God gave him Christ Jesus and His Spirit to be with man through man's great journey back to God. The righteous that would prevail will enter back into that paradise, and feed from this great tree for that final exaltation into the complete mystery and nature of God, beholding Him as He is truly is, God who filled all His creations. The second death will by no means have power over the saints who shall feed on this tree of life which Christ the Eternal Life will give. (Revelation 2: 11)

The mystical mind of the apostles understands the depth of this mystery very clearly when the Scripture said, 'Now we are children of God: and it has not yet been revealed what we shall be, but we know that when He is revealed, we shall be like Him, for we shall see him as He is.' (1 John 3: 2) Yes! Because we are not limited to the level of sons of God only, but we are going to be more than sons in His glory because we are created in the image of His son who made us one with His father.

... ...

Thinking so deeply about the positive and negative things we experience in our world where we find ourselves should trigger in every living being a zeal to make this place a better place, though it is very difficult because of the unseen forces working against man. But a wise man who builds his house on rock must persevere to the end knowing that any soul born on the planet earth must strive to get himself back to that precious garden of the Lord—for outside it, man has no rest because that's where God intends man, who is so precious to Him, to be.

It is very essential to look into the movement of the soul; where did it come from? Was every individual soul created separately in the spirit before their incarnation or is it the product of Adam? Looking back to the account of the creation, we understand that the creator Himself created all things so good and declared them to be so beautiful. He also made them complete, giving them the power to reproduce and perpetuate themselves.

After creating everything in six days, He rested from all the work He had been doing. This means that He has indeed finished all He has done, relaxing to rest and watch His work as it displays the wisdom of He who made them. This is one of the greatest things God enjoys, just as man who achieves great things enjoys and admires his work.

After the fall of Adam, God did not change this nature in Adam but rather it continues. Remember this great command: 'Be fruitful and multiply; fill the earth and subdue it.' (Genesis 1: 28) Male and Female, He created them and planted the destiny of their offspring into their depth; thus when a couple comes together in sexual intercourse, they reproduce their image and likeness through their spirit, soul and body. They do not necessarily need God directly to do this because already He had created them to function in that manner. Thus there are changes in the human body once a child reaches the age of puberty.

Immediately the male sperm enters the ovary, the birth of the soul is taken place and it begins to form flesh and blood. Do we not see this great truth in the Scripture when the Virgin Mary who was only three days' pregnant was addressed as a mother because Christ who was a few days old in her virginal womb was already a human being, although He was still in the process of forming flesh? (Thus the spirits treats even a day-old abortion as first-class murder.)

Therefore our first nature is truly the product of Adam and Eve in their spirit, body and soul. It is a great misunderstanding of the formation of man to say that souls were lined up in heaven waiting for their turn to be born on earth. Souls were not created in the spirit somewhere before taking flesh; God created all humanity in Adam. If the souls pre-existed outside their parents before taking flesh, the effects of the sins of Adam would not have continued since they would have been created pure outside Adam's nature. God who is love did not create man to lose or win salvation; the spiritual protocol made it that children of Adam must inherit whatever is in the depth of Adam.

It is an insufficient understanding of the mystery of Christ, and a contradiction, to believe that God creates a soul in the spirit and sends it into the flesh; this does not reflect God as the loving father He is. God knows each soul before its existence in the body and this does not mean that the soul pre-existed somewhere outside the parents before birth. Before the creation of man, there was nothing like the soul of Adam; instead he became a living being, spirit, soul and body on the same day he was made. Though he had a kind of mystical body, yet he was immortal because he had the nature of his creator. This immortality was what he lost; therefore there was the need for the new Adam for restoration. If the soul pre-existed before the formation in the flesh, God who is love would not have the need to send the soul into the body only to condemn him later knowing fully that he must sin as a result of the corruptions of the human nature. Flesh itself is the epitome and fountain of the sins the soul commits. Take away the flesh, and the soul automatically becomes mystical and beyond trouble for it is a spirit. We must always remember this great truth: that Adam was in the realm of spirit, even though he had flesh, yet he fulfilled all the principles of the spirit because his flesh was less active and was activated by the forbidden fruit.

In the Gospel of John 1: 12-13, the mystery of the new creation is revealed. The message of the Scripture is very clear in this verse: that everyone born into this world is just the product of the parents who gave birth to them. If God created a soul pure in the spirit outside the parents, why should He have made him a child of Adam through natural birth, thereby condemning him even when the child is still unconscious of sin? Because the soul suffers the effects of the original sin from the first moment he exists, for the eternal condemnation in Adam follows all his fruits. At least we are all born naked just as Adam and Eve found themselves naked when they sinned.

St John proclaimed in his epistle that eternal life was manifested in the flesh, which was lost in Adam. Accept this truth that all the creations of God were created with ability to self-perpetuating; and also that God's first creation was through Adam to all living. Though Adam was cast out, yet he continued regenerating and perpetuating because God who made him was resting from His work and had sent His Christ and the Holy Spirit who hovers around the water of baptism, giving new birth to the offspring of Adam, who would humble themselves and accept Christ as the ancient God of creation in flesh.

Who is that child born into the world who is perfect? Some are born with physical defects, while others are born with one spiritual disorder or the other. The more we deny it, the more real it becomes because of the poison injected in Adam. When we see children born with all manner of physical disabilities, we should know that the same can happen to another child in the manner in which his senses and faculties function. Most people do not realise this, being ignorant about the true nature of man; they live only according to what they can see and observe. Seeing all these disabilities, sometimes they try to convince us that it's how God created such persons.

It is not the will of God that any human being should be born with any defect, mentally, physically or otherwise. It is these same wounds that already exist in the foundation of man. This is all the more reason for you to understand that God no longer creates but looks after His creations as they reproduce. Is it possible that God will create one to be imbecilic, blind, crippled, a conjoined twin, or with mental problems or all manners of troubles in human sexuality? The answer is no, because it contradicts God who is the fountain of all love and perfection. This is the reason why His Christ was manifested, making a clarion call to all humanity to come to Him all you that are heavily laden, for a complete rest.

Search the entirety of the ministry of Christ in the Scripture; Christ has never seen a natural disability and left it unhealed, but rather He made them whole because God did not create anything to be abnormal. All this He did in the glorification of God, to prove that God is not responsible for any defects or disorder but rather it is the work of the fallen angels manipulating the foundation of the fallen man.

We all are carrying this heavy laden both spiritual and physical; the smaller you think your own is, the heavier it becomes until you bring it to Christ. Every human being needs this Christ who loves us not just because we are good but because we are wounded in so many ways, and He wanted to unleash His healing power upon natural man, the offspring of Adam.

For man to live with his spiritual nature, he must get himself grafted into the nature of Christ as a son. Trying to understand or to live a spiritual life with the nature of Adam is just like dreaming because natural man has lost the power of spiritual discipline. This is the reason why the existence of God can never be proven through scientific intelligence; neither can its findings and proof about human formation from lower to higher animal be truth, since science itself does not believe in the spirit.

Being a spiritual being, man's existence started from a place beyond scientific discovery; he must return there when the exile life on earth is over. If God is spirit, and gave that same spiritual nature to man from the beginning, how is it possible that ordinary and natural man can fathom the depth of God who is purely a spirit? How can it prove the creation and formation of man who is the most exalted visible creation of God? Does it make sense that man who was chased out of the heavenly garden started to trace his origin from mere wild animals instead of his spiritual route? The Scripture said, 'What is highly esteemed before the natural man is an abomination in the sight of God.' (Luke 16: 18) In another text, He said, 'My thoughts are not your thoughts, nor are your ways my ways, says the Lord.' (Isaiah 55: 8) This means that the mental ability of a natural man cannot discern the things of God nor spiritual things, which are not all about what can be proven but how they are. It is what must be for it has been there before us and we must exist within its laws. This helps man to understand that the best way to live in the flesh is to live as the spirit we are—exalting one's spirit above the instinct of animal.

…   …   …

Be elevated in this understanding that there are two natures of man: Adam and Christ Jesus. As we said, all baptised Christians have these two in them; the nature of Adam is for natural life, which includes marriage, raising family and all the things a natural human being can do to live a happy life here on earth. The nature of Christ is the one who through Christ connects back to God and will be able to observe all the spiritual disciplines and live like a spirit. When one wants to serve God and has not gone beyond his natural senses to supernatural, seeing things the way God and His angels see it, which most times contradicts natural sense, he needs a rethink. Consider that a natural human being is born through sexual intercourse and by the will of a couple who decided to make this union, and also consider that Christ who gave us the supernatural nature is a product of virgin birth and therefore is a spiritual man and the Lord from heaven; as St Paul said in (1 Corinthians 15: 45-47) the whole truth will be planted in our spirit. Then its mystery will make man surrender his natural inclinations to the things pertaining to the nature, and to connect his soul to the grace of Christ and master his flesh, which wants him to live as if it all ends here. Think about your parents who decided to give birth to you; think about yourself who keep the same tradition. Think about the Virgin Mary who conceived and gave birth to Christ by the power of the Holy Spirit without losing her virginity.

When all these are well meditated and a deep meditation is made on the nature of Christ who was conceived spiritually and was born mystically, yet is the fullness of God and Man, one will be able to follow His spirit born in us for the total liberation of our soul from the bondage of the flesh and the world. Only at this level would one be able to live like a spirit even though he is the flesh. This Christ Jesus indeed is completely different from Adam, He is that eternal life which Adam would have had, had he endured and eaten from that tree of life in the garden; thus the Scripture declared Christ as The Life-Giving Spirit. (1 Corinthians 15:45)

To think that Adam was just like us in our natural senses in the Garden of Eden is to think like a natural man who has no spiritual background. First, we must know that God is a spirit. For Adam to behold His presence means that Adam himself was more like spirit, because spirit can only commune with a spirit. Those who are lucky to have heard from the Lord or the divine spirit will attest to this, that it is the spirit of man who hears whenever a spirit speaks. So also it was spiritual Adam who communed with the Lord, and this later became natural. When Christ came, man was raised up through the sufferings of Christ. This new man is far more glorious than the former because through Christ, the fruit of man and God, the new man truly become immortal—not able to fall again because he is not only a creation, but also an offspring of God himself who entered into marriage with humanity to raise one inseparable family—angel and man united, God and man becomes one, because the earth is no longer part of the nature of the new man as it was in Adam. Instead he is the same mystical body and the nature of Christ formed in the womb of Virgin Mary who herself was the final product of the law.

This is the final salvation of man—becoming mystical and exalted in the mystery of God. The wave and the spirit of the world will never blow him away, 'and the rain descended, the floods came, and the winds blew and beat on him; and it did not fall.' (Luke 7: 25) His strength is God Himself though he is in flesh but he is a son of God. He is participating in all the inheritance of heaven. This is the end product of the prophecy of Ezekiel 36: 26-27: 'I will give you a new heart and put a new spirit within you; I will take a heart of stone out of your flesh and give you a heart of flesh. I will put my spirit within you and cause you to walk in my statutes, and you will keep my judgement and do them.'

When the soul of a baptised is fulfilled in this manner, there is no longer a difference between him and heavenly saints—for he is the offspring of God born by the spirit of Christ. In him the Father and the Son dwells as the Gospel said. (John 14: 23)

We want you to understand that the fullness of the new nature is to become the dwelling place of God. Though no one has seen God, this new nature not only hears the father's voice, but also can see God because he is born of God, as we have seen in the lives of certain mystics. A clear example is St Stephen. He was in the flesh when he saw God Himself with His Christ standing at His right hand. The same God whom the scripture proclaims that no one can see and live, he saw. He saw Him and proclaimed it loudly as a witness to the truth because he was a new creation who had celebrated the death of his Adam's nature. St Paul himself experienced uncountable beatific visions; in one of them he was taken to heaven to behold a vision beyond unapproachable light. Before his death, his spirit and soul bore witness that he was going to heaven, for which he had so laboured, having poured away his natural life and all its demands as a libation as he confessed in 2 Timothy 4: 6.

The martyrs themselves with the same boldness challenged death with the highest courage, beyond the strength of mortals, because they were no longer humans as it were, for their humanity had been divinised to the nature of Christ who is the Lord of all spirits. When a soul finally traces his spiritual nature and perseveres in that standard, the commandments of God, which are life and spirit, become possible to him. To the core natural man, it has no meaning; it is foolishness to him because it's beyond his nature; he is just a citizen of the world and must celebrate his identity.

The glory of the days to come is that the life of the soul in the flesh has duration, and that a great separation will take place; the soul and the spirit which he obeyed, whether the old or the new spirit, will depart for her reward, either in the marvellous light or in the utter darkness. These are the final ends of our spiritual nature. Understand well these teachings by meditating on this saying of Christ about the resurrection of the just: 'They will be like angels in heaven.' (Mark 12: 25)

How can one be like angels in heaven when one has lived a strange life on earth far from the angelic? By His grace through His Holy Spirit, we will live like the exiled lower angels we are in the flesh—fulfilling our destiny, knowing that He who created us in the flesh is ever-present with us. He knows very well, too, that the material flesh contradicts the nature of the spiritual man who is meant to keep the traditions of the spirit; therefore He is always with us in honour of His great name, Emmanuel.

Confession and Meditation

The flesh profits nothing; it is the spirit that gives life.

'Put on salvation as your helmet and the word of God as SWORD of the spirit.' Ephesians 6:17

The Divine Visitor

This supreme Deity, who manifested Himself as a burning fire to Moses on the Mount of Sinai, who introduced Himself as I AM was the Eternal Word of God. Many years earlier, He introduced Himself to Father Abraham as The Lord. This Supreme Being is the Lord of the whole universe and all spirits. He has been following man, making a way for total reconciliation even though He was the one who cast man out of paradise. He never wants to let go of man so that man will lose complete connection with Him, which would have been the result if He did not use the Law and the prophets to keep in contact with man until the day of His Christ.

Even though God did not leave man on his own completely after the sin of Adam, the fallen legions that possessed man were controlling him as strong wine controls a drunkard. When God could not bear the wickedness of man any longer, having exalted Noah to a certain level, He destroyed the ancient world because its sin had gone up to a superlative level. After the great flood, in His mercy He continued His process of reconciliation with Noah and his posterity who were also prophets. But it was still the same animal nature that must prefer his own way rather than God's will. Did Noah's youngest son Ham not make jest of his father's nakedness, which attracted for him and his descendants a curse from his father? A continuation of the ministry of death, which suppresses one and kept another under bondage even to a generation that is supposed to be free from the guilt.

God's wisdom in His long patience allowed the fullness of the manifestation of the different horrible natures of fallen angels of darkness upon man whom they have taken into slavery before He sent the prophets, who came through Abraham after the holy covenant God made with Abraham.

All the fullness of the characters of the fallen angels in the children of Adam and Eve brought down the Law, who was the Divine visitor from heaven and the prophets the seeds of Abraham who were circumcised, a type of baptism to impose and enforce that law to this particular chosen nation called Israel for the salvation of the whole world. After the coming of this law, God reduced His actions as it were from other children of men and focused more on this holy nation to achieve the highest level of holiness possible from the seed of Adam. It was at this level that the new Eve was created. Through her His Word took flesh and appeared as man: not only for the Jews but also for the rest of the children of Adam to whom the Israelites referred as the Gentiles. These Gentiles were left behind by God to make way for the salvation of the whole human race through the Jews. So boasting is excluded on the side of the Jews, the prince of the humanity—for the Almighty as we may say sacrificed the rest of the world in order to use Israel for the later world's salvation through Christ.

God did not choose the Jews because they were holy or because they were better than the rest of humanity, but because He chose to do so. The fact is that they were one of the weakest of the family of man; they were incomparable with the philosophical ideas of the ancient Greeks, nor with the military might of ancient Egypt and Rome. Yet the Almighty used them to spread His salvation because with the weak He pulls down the mighty. The Israelites, as it were, were people to whom belongs adoption as sons but rejecting Christ because of the same hidden gods which is deeply ingrained in all humanity as well as in them; salvation was transferred to the Gentiles. The same way God used them to deliver the whole world, the same manner in which He will use the Gentiles to bring them to the full knowledge of the truth: humbling them that they are no better than the rest of human family. In reminding the children of Israel of this great truth, Moses said:

'The Lord did not set His love on you nor choose you because you were more in number than all other nation, for you were the least of all peoples. But because He loves you.' (Deuteronomy 7: 7-8)

But the whole world owes Israel homage and prayers even as the Psalm said. Yes, they deserve homage and love. What a nation with a zealous heart of sacrifice! Full of hope and anticipation about the coming of Christ, they dedicated their young daughters from highly devoted families to the temple as virgins for prayers and sacrifice, knowing that the Messiah was to be born of a virgin. In the fullness of time, the most holy and perfect virgin of Nazareth was created, who was blessed of all generations of men.

... ...

The prevailing Biblical attitude towards the law communicates its message as a gift of God and the uniqueness of the invisible and loving father. In the right sense and according to the witnesses to the righteousness of God, the exaltation of the law was the sole mission of Christ who was and is the same Word of God who gave those commandments to Moses. During His earthly ministry, His hearers were filled with great confusion and doubt because of the charisma of this new prophet who seemed as if he was saying something new. Knowing the thoughts in everyman's heart, He said unto them: 'Do you think that I came to destroy the Law and the prophets?' Being confused about the question and how to answer Him, they kept mute. In conclusion, He proclaimed at the top of His voice, 'I did not come to destroy the law but to fulfil it.' (Compare Mathew 5: 17)

He went on to say that every aspect of the law must be fulfilled and made known to people. Let us tell ourselves the truth: when you are making efforts to live according to the principles of righteousness, you must at a certain point come to this difficult knot when your nature will engage into serious battle with the

Pentateuch, and no matter how you battle to pass with your nature the more narrow that door becomes, and the more you say I am no longer under the law, the more the law stands before you and will always be ahead of you until you decide to live the whole principles of Christ, which are the fullness and fulfilment of the law; in other words, allowing the spirit of Christ to be in control. Then the old spirit of man that is supposed to keep the law ceases to control you.

This nature I am talking about here is the old nature of man which goes about with every man; the more you deny it, the more it accuses you and strives with you until you work out how to reason with it through much prayer and knowledge of the word of God, sitting him down with the divine decree. This is the point you need to know the word of God, otherwise he will control you for the rest of your life while you proclaim to be a new creation. This is the point which many Christians reach and become more confused than a wonderer. At this level, many people come up with different ideas because the spirit of self rebels against God with the highest concentration; for this is where the Holy Spirit wants to cripple him, so he must fight with the whole might of his lord—the fallen angels. If he prevails, this is when the child of God who should have persevered will proudly link his defeat with the word of God which says that 'the just shall live by faith', forgetting that which proves and makes your faith alive is justness.

Being just is being upright in the principles of righteousness or conforming to high moral standards. Therefore being just can be truly defined as the visible character of a natural man, which proves the faith that is the invisible nature of the new man.

Let us at this point remember that Christ said, 'Be perfect just as your father in heaven is perfect.' To persevere at this point is best, because here is where you have reached your last strength and Christ expects you to wait there with your struggles until His grace, which is made manifest in weakness, is manifested for your next level of perfection when He takes over your cross. Because from this point on your strength has gone completely and your whole life will now depend on the grace of God.

This is a level in the journey of the faith; perseverance and confession of truth helps one so much to pass over and once you have prevailed, that animal nature will become a slave to your new nature; with self-mortification and constant prayer and communion in the blood of Christ, you will be able to dry up his venom whenever he releases it. The bitter truth is that it is the spirit of the old nature who you were before the new man was born in baptism; he, too, wants to have the best part of you of which the new man is depriving him so the battle continues.

Now the question is: who is this law and what is its mission? Who was this man whose shadow appeared as a future glory? Now if the law was given to Moses as eternal testimony of the living God and was ministered by the prophets and scribes as a glorious covenant of life, it means that the law is eternal life, as Christ said. (John 12: 50)

This law that was given in the Old Testament was truly that same Word of God that later took flesh. Thus when Mary kept it to its standard, He took her flesh to live as man. Before the incarnation, His intention was to live among man, but because of the old nature which man had, He had no place in their hearts to dwell and take flesh, thus He manifested His back to them as a shadow.

This is the mystery behind the mystical meeting of blessed Moses with God in that great tabernacle of meeting. 'You shall not see my face; for no man shall see me, and live,' God said to Moses. During the same meeting, God later passed with His glory, having covered the face of Moses. He passed and removed His hand and Moses could only see His back. (Compare Exodus 33: 20-23)

This people of the old covenant could not see the true face of the law or its true character because of their old nature, for these two cannot agree. The spirit nature of man is the one who communes with God, but in their case their spirit nature, which is enslaved, cannot agree with God. Because of the instinct of this old nature, the whole relationship with God in the old covenant was one of utter fear: not because they loved Him so much but because that animal nature was so repulsive to God, and they were in constant fear of death before God. Eventually, when He appeared in human flesh, He decreed this death upon this old nature, which has been the cause of his fear since he left the Garden of Eden. 'He who wants to follow me must deny himself.' This longstanding fear of the old man has finally come to pass because following Christ is the death of the old nature of man, indeed, because his deeds do not please God for he has lost the destiny of life unto salvation.

When a true follower has experienced the death and life in the great adventure that his faith puts him through, the final result must be the true knowledge of who God is, both in His law, the prophets and His Anointed Christ—who was not so different from who He was in the law as a spirit and Law Incarnate. The former was only a spirit showing his back; the old nature continued to search for his face but never found it. But the latter is flesh and blood with the very face of a human, who through His mystery of baptism gives birth to the new nature that can behold His face and live; for he who is begotten and He who begets are one.

Christ Jesus is truly the Law incarnate. Indeed, we have seen His face and believe firmly that He is the new life for which the old nature of the just men of old had been searching and could not see. They also longed for His message but could not hear it because of their contradicting nature. Though this Law Incarnate came with human face, many people from the day of His appearance till today could never see it because they could not rise up from the deadly inclinations of the old nature and thereby remained in the shadows, which was worse than when He was showing only His back.

If through the law they could see God's back and His glory, even when they were in the glory of the old man, then the law is good. This was what St Paul was saying, who himself was establishing the law, having surrendered his old nature to the law and died so new man would follow Christ, as the new Adam who gave birth to him.

Let me send this message across very clearly. The law which God gave in the old covenant is still alive and will continue to live so long as man possesses this animal nature that contradicts his spiritual nature. This law was given to keep the old nature of man in bondage forever as long as we are still in flesh. As a Christian, whether one believes it or not, this law will continue to rule your old nature until the final separation of your soul. When one is living a double life, this law will remain alive until, through the grace of God, he decides to live the whole principle of Christ; only then the law will die. The scripture says:

'The commandment, which was to bring life, I found to bring death.' (Romans 7: 10)

The death meant by St Paul here is that of the old nature of man, because the old nature is expected to die once one realises there is new nature in him. But the fact that we are more of the flesh at the very first time makes it hard for us to embrace the principles of the new nature; therefore the law stays with that old nature which refused to give way. The Scripture says, 'Know this, that our old man with its body of sin was crucified with Christ.' (Romans 6: 6)

All the deeds of the old man and his natural inclinations are indeed the life and spirit that are contrary to God, so God Himself willingly left the law with that nature to rule it so long as he lives. If the law prevailed over that nature both would die, but if it did not, both would continue with status—quo, and this is the situation in most cases. 'With the mind, I myself serve the Law of God, but with the flesh, the law of sin.' (Romans 7: 25)

The law was given to prepare the heart of man for the coming of Christ. God does not intend to keep it alive after the death of Christ, but it was sin and the old nature of man that kept it alive because it refused to die.

It is very a wise thing, though, that the law lives with the old nature because it complements the whole message of Christ; God who canonised it into the New Covenant Scripture is wiser than all. Though He has given us the new nature in Christ, still He allows us to grow and understand Him through the corruptions of our old nature; so too He left the law to nurture it. The mission of the law is nothing but to kill the old nature of man completely so that 'we may serve in the newness of the spirit and not in the oldness of the spirit.' (Romans 7: 6)

The good news is that the law arrived to revive the fullness of our old nature and to kill it as well, so that the new nature, whose life is the commandment of God which is also the divine life, will live its nature which is no longer ruled by the law but as it were has taken over and begun to live while the former is dying. It is the mystery of God's wisdom to allow the Jews to carry on with their old covenant laid down by God through Moses, though it is said that it was because of the stubbornness of their hearts. It pleased God to keep that covenant alive in them until there is a universal acceptance of Christ, the giver of both the law and the grace. Then there will be the fullness of the New Jerusalem, which the Jews will proclaim with tears of joy—truly the Messiah was Christ, Jesus the fruit of the Virgin Mary's womb!

The message of the law and people's understanding of it has been a subject of debate and some kind of misinterpretation from people who are intellectually proud. The entirety of the Christian Scripture complements the law, because it is the beginning of man's salvation, which the Grace in the New Testament accomplished. Everything with beginning must have an end. Without the beginning, one cannot jump into the end, and without the end, the beginning will continue. The law is the beginner who started the work which grace will finish; he who desires salvation must dwell in both until grace takes over, when one's old self must have wrestled with the law to the point of defeat in the favour of the law. Because the law must defeat our old nature if we truly want to follow Christ in the grace He has given.

The law and the grace are two twin brothers who must get along with each other because they have a separate mission regarding the two natures of man: to kill and to make alive. The grace is working in the soul through the new spirit of man, which is Christ's, while the law is working in the old spirit of man, which is Adam's—which dematerialised in the flesh to hold the soul in bondage to death. This is the reason why St Paul says that 'the deeds of the Law cannot justify or make one holy.' Because the old man is bound to act like the animal he is reduced to. Therefore the law cannot take him to heaven but keeps him in check to allow the new nature, which is created for heaven, to grow. Without the law of 'Thou shall not', the old man will not die but lives, and as long as he lives, the grace will not work in the soul. This is the reason why the ministry of the prophets would have been in vain if Christ had not come. Because the old nature of man they ministered to can never please God. That old man is destined to death for he cannot repent nor can he submit to the divine law and traditions. He must be a wonderer till the end—pretending to love God and whoever gets stuck in it shall never see life.

If the entire scripture complements the Law, how is it that people sometimes contradict St Paul's Epistles? Is it not the same spirit in the law, the Prophets, and the Gospel, and in the other apostles working in Paul? The truth is that one will not grasp the message of St Paul if one is not rooted in the divine doctrine of Christ. This is still the work of the fallen angels, misguiding people into understanding the scripture, thus we have lots of error and false teachings, and some people will say, 'That's how I understand it.' No! The spirit of man does not interpret the scripture, but the spirit of God does! You must bow your head to the kerygma, which the Holy Spirit laid down for His church; though we have different and unique minds and souls, yet it is the same Holy Spirit who teaches the truth as we also have one way to heaven.

The law which Christ in the Apostolic tradition erased was the old rituals: the sacrifices, purifications of all manner, law of circumcision, the washing of body, dishes and all additional Jewish-made laws which they included to keep people in bondage as some of them are contained in Talmud, Mishnah, and Halakah. You can see in the Gospel where Christ was crying against these laws and those who made them: 'Woe to you experts in the law! For you load men with burdens hard to bear, but you yourself do not touch the burdens with one of your fingers.' (Luke 11: 46)

The holy Law of righteousness is exalted, because this is what keeps man in a good relationship with God and his fellow man. The Ten Commandments and all the principles of the holiness of life and true love of one's neighbour, as laid down by Moses, were all the love of God which He gave as a guide for man's life which Christ manifested to establish, excelling above it with the spirit of Christ makes us adopted children of God.

In the Gospel of John, it is said that, 'The law was given through Moses, but grace and the truth came through Jesus Christ.' Here, in the mind of the Gospel, both Moses and Christ were the accomplishers of salvation, of which both of them are important in attaining salvation, for one cannot do without either. When one says 'I am of Moses and go to Moses', Moses will quickly remind that person what he said about Christ in the Scripture: 'God will send you another prophet like me, to Him you must listen.' And another will say, 'I have faith in Christ, and it's enough for me'; going to Christ, He will cast him and his old nature away back to the law of Moses to surrender his old nature to the complete rule of law, just as the apostles did before they could fulfil the law of Christ. The fact is that no one will get this close to Christ without surrendering his old nature to the Ten Commandments for the death of his old man.

Let this truth be important in establishing your spirituality: that even though the deeds of the law cannot take one to heaven, yet without it ruling man's old nature, the soul of man must be condemned to the underworld along with that old man who resisted the rule of the holy law. In the same manner in which the law and prophets point to Christ, so must it prepare the heart of man for the grace of God.

In understanding the law and commandments, we must humble ourselves to the sayings of Christ the Law incarnate in the holy Gospel. When the experts in the law tested Him with a question of the greatest commandment in the law, He said to them, 'You must love the Lord your God with all your heart, with all your soul and with your entire mind. You must love your neighbour as yourself.' In conclusion He said, 'On these two commandments hang all the law and prophets.' (Compare Mathew 22: 36-40)

After this symposium, Christ emphasised and established that to keep the law is to touch the heart of His father because the heart of the law is to be in deep love with God and man's neighbour. There is a similar incident in Luke 10: 28, where Christ answered the man, 'Do what the law says and live.' Therefore, the theology of St Paul in which he was interpreting the mind of Christ does not mean a different teaching from that which Christ is saying in the Gospels, which gives birth to the Epistles.

Of what need is the circumcision of the flesh since the flesh has no portion in the inheritance of Christ? Of what needs are the principles that forbid a Jew from having things in common with Gentiles, while the Jews are claiming that God is love and the creator of the whole universe including the Gentiles? When one wash his hands and feet and still has his heart filled with all manner of evil, of what good is his washing? This is the fullness of the message of Christ, which St Paul championed. We should all be thankful to God for the liberating ministry of St Paul, which extricates us from fake and manmade observances that make the body look good while keeping the soul in bondage and darkness.

But the people to whom this law was given, even those Pharisees who claimed to be extreme observers of the law, could not keep it because of their rebellious nature. Therefore they added their own and the law became their god, instead of them knowing God through the law. Most of their time was spent in studying the law, looking for law-breakers and punishing them; in fact the Spirit of the Lord is so wise in sending the law to hold the old nature of man in bondage until the day of Christ. In His teaching, Christ exposed their hypocrisy when He said, 'Did not Moses give you the law, and yet none of you keeps the law.' Even with this great hypocrisy, yet this old nature of man full of pride dared to proclaim themselves righteous before God.

In the practical life of a true Christian, observing the commandments of God cannot even make one perfect but the grace of Christ. But without those observances, no one will even get to that level where grace of Christ will manifest itself. This is the practical experience of St Paul himself who sometimes found himself doing those things that he hated; thus he said that his flesh was serving the law of sin, for he truly knew that his old nature was subjected to the holy law. Therefore, he concluded that 'the law itself is indeed holy and the commandment is holy, just and good.' (Romans 7: 12)

To know God in depth, your animal nature must be ruled by the law to the level you will accept defeat to the glory of the law because you cannot keep it; for the law itself is greater than the old nature of man. This is a sort of scenario where one is trying to tame a wild animal into behaving just like a human, which is impossible. This is the scale where God wants you to slide-tackle yourself; lose balance, and fall into the hands of Christ who wants you to depend on Him completely.

The Scripture said, 'For by grace we have been saved through faith, and that not of ourselves, it is the gift of God; not of works, lest anyone should boast.' (Ephesians 2: 8-9)

It is not by work indeed. Yet it's through your efforts by co-operating with the grace that we are saved through the same grace, because nature is only submissive to God when one goes beyond all that is observable to constant communion with God through faith by his good works. To enter this communion is why the commandment must rule our animal nature because if one did not co-operate with the commandment, neither would the grace co-operate with you to save you. If the law truly leads us to Christ, then we must live according to that new man who knew no sin by living like Christ. Anyone who wants to live a life of Christianity must arm himself and get ready to sacrifice: 'for being a Christian must cost you something indeed.' Archbishop Fulton J. Sheen said. Therefore surrender your old nature to the ministry of death so that the grace will abound in your new nature.

To achieve our expected end, which is the salvation of our soul, a Christian must agree that there are two natures of man in us struggling to live. (Compare Romans 7: 23) Therefore, our members which are our body are subjected to the rule of the old tutor meant for the old nature so long as we have these two natures and are still in the flesh. Can you not see this truth! The old nature of man is alive and he wants to live, and play all the games of a living being; walking, seeing, he loves and acts differently, and in all its fullness. But the law stands in his way to cripple, blind and also kill him so that the new man may live. Do you think that the law will find it easy to crush him? Do you think that the old man under the law will easily give up his joy and die? No! For he is spirit and can never die. Therefore, he continues to rebel against his ruler and the ruler in turn refuses to let go. The truth is that both will continue in this war until the new man grows to fullness not needing the law nor living in fear of the old nature, for he has overgrown both as the law and the old nature were left far behind in their everlasting war. This is what the scripture referred to as the death of the law and old man.

This is so because for the righteous requirements of the law to be completed in our soul, we must not work according to the flesh but according to the spirit. All the deeds of the flesh are meant to die through the law of thou shall not's. Thus when St Paul reached that level, he started confessing at the top of his voice, 'I have been crucified with Christ; it is no longer I who lives, (that is the spirit of self) but Christ lives in me.' Because once the old nature ceases to exist or crippled, the final result is Christ living in you and using you as His own. This is that state where a new creation is not under the tutor because the long awaited faith has come, and we know that the life of the new man is only by faith in things he is introduced to yet have not seen. (Compare Galatians 3: 23-25) This is a Christian whose life is joy, peace, longsuffering, kindness, goodness, gentleness and self-control; for his faith has become reality. These are his new life and law, which the fruits of the Holy Spirit achieved through the law and grace.

Christ came to turn the law into life; that is what He gave birth to in man in the baptism, to those who accept Him, to them He assists to live that life to its fullness. We must understand that God did not give the law to save the soul but to introduce the same life to the soul that he lost in the Garden of Eden. Since the soul longs for God after the fall of man, the law appeared as a message of hope for the future life. This is why the heart of the law was the coming of the Messiah, who came not only to redeem but also to give birth to the new life of heaven in man. That new life is what manifested at the fullness of time in the person of Christ Jesus; it is only by accepting Him that we are lifted above the law of sin and death into the consciousness of the divine life.

Confession and meditation

We praise you God our salvation! With law you started the work of our salvation, which grace accomplished.

The Mystic Voice

The children of Adam have struggled so hard against their captor, but cannot break free nor accept their state because the indelible spiritual nature of the man in the Garden of Eden can never be erased from their minds. Most times we wants to do the will of God, but the deep-seated nature against God planted in man stands against us, just as we see St Paul crying for God's deliverance from such a horrible torture, 'The body of death'. (Romans 7: 24)

This is the reason why the old nature of man has no option than to behave according to his inclinations, which He who made him so good in the beginning abhors. As man increases on earth, so he drifts further away from his creator in his deeper zeal to explore the earth, which looks more like home to him because of the nature of the animal that dominates his spirit.

God saw these efforts of the fallen man to return to him and as a merciful father, His heart melted and He took pity on man, remembering what it had taken to create man. (Because of the uniqueness of man, man was not formed along with other animals; rather there was a huge architectural plan before the persons in God could build that great house called man.)

Having announced His new plan of recreation, He started sending the messengers to minister to man; some of these messengers appeared without genealogy on the same mission, not to give man complete fulfilment because that was not their mission but rather as ministers of the shadow of the future event.

After the missions of these great messengers of the ancient world, God called Abraham and started sending prophets through his lineage. But what more did these great eyes that saw the future achieved better than their predecessors? Finding themselves in the old nature of man, even so they ministered to the old nature of man who could not please God. Yet these prophets have fulfilled marvellous work. Christ Himself praised them by saying, 'I have not come to abolish the law and the prophets, but to fulfil it.' He said this because He was the law and the message of the prophets. He approved all their works for He was the one who spoke through the prophets, and the messages of the prophets were law, which was all about doing to people as you would like them to do unto you. You can see that the person who condemned the old man cannot abolish his condemnation simply because He brought grace to the new man. He made it stronger so that the old man who must continue to exist will also continue to be in bondage—for Christ, ministry and death are for the life of the new nature He has created.

When God created man and placed him in the Garden of Eden, He pointed out a certain tree, saying, 'On the day you will eat of this tree, you will surely die.' Not only did physical death follow, but a total condemnation of that nature of man was decreed upon him, which the future ministers unravelled. As I said earlier, God allowed the fallen angels and man whom they had conquered to metamorphose to their fullness of decadence and wickedness before He enforced the message of death of that old nature as decreed long ago in the garden. This He did by sending the prophets; though this prophets were exposed to the Spirit of God, yet their natural inclination was no different from other sons of men so that it would be possible for them to minister death to that nature of man knowing full well how frail is the nature of man and the holy nature of God, because they too learned through their failures.

This death they ministered was the law as contained in the Torah. When God gave it to Moses, He did not mean life to the rebellious inclinations of man, but death. As that nature could not die, probably because there was no new life yet to live as Christ was not yet been given, therefore the law held that nature of man in bondage until the days of Christ. This is what the Scripture later called the Law of Moses—the Ministry Of Death written and engraved on the stones, which was so glorious that even the Israelites could not even look steadily at Moses' face who is the carrier of this holy covenant. (Compare 2 Corinthians 3: 7-8) Thus all the prophets who ministered the law and commandments did not find it easy in their days because their message stood against the old nature of man, and most of them lost their lives because the nature they ministered death to also declared their heads wanted as well—as we can see in the book of Jeremiah who himself suffered greatly for the sake of the word of God.

'I am in derision daily; everyone mocks me. For when I spoke, I cried out; I shouted violence and plunder, because the word of God was made to me a reproach and derision daily.' (Jeremiah 20: 7-8)

This longstanding enmity continues, even in the message of Christ and all the ministers of the good news; for to be a true messenger of God is to be a minister to both the old nature of man and the new nature of man which co-exist in man no matter how holy he claims to be. To the old nature of man, ministry of death to establish the decree of God after the fall of man. To the new nature of man, ministry of life through the salvific blood of Christ.

God uses a man to deliver a family or a kingdom; in the same manner He used the Israelites to deliver the whole world from the bondage and corruptions of the fallen angels through these prophets who acted as His oracle. Because they could understand God better than any man, they were able to hear His voice and pass the message to man. Through their ministry, it was easy for God to judge the fallen angels who were parading as gods of the nations. In the same manner these gods were provoking wars between nations in their battle of control over man, just as they started making wars with the Israelites because they noticed that the Ancient God had special interest in them.

When they could not singlehandedly deal with Israel, they ceased from fighting each other, saying: Let us form an allegiance against Israelites and annihilate them. 'Come let us break their fetters, let us cast off their yoke.' (Psalm 2: 3) For in their wisdom they knew that God had chosen Israel and would use the prophesied fruit of a Virgin to invade them in no distant time because they too understood the message and the mission of the law and the prophets. But was it not in vain that they gathered against the consuming fire and His anointed one? God did not only condemn the old man, He also judged and condemned the wickedness of the gods even as He had done before in heaven. So the war continues on earth in the invisible realm. God with His mighty and strong arm has come to the rescue of man He has created; but in His supreme wisdom, He ministered death first unto the contaminated inclinations of man—using the prophets as His visible hands.

As the children of the covenant continued to prevail against all the furies of their foes, so the invisible Angels of light were binding the gods of these nations in chain to enforce God's law among His holy people. Through their journey to the Promised Land after God with His mighty hand had delivered them from the gods of Egypt, we see the presence of these demons as gods of Amalekites, Jebusites, Gigamites, Medians and so many others. All these nations and their gods were punished severely by the only true God for standing on the way against Israel; Canaanites were destroyed completely, while the Almighty declared everlasting war with the Amalekites. After these great judgements of God, He warned the Israelites against practicing the idolatry of these nations, and not to copy their abominable manner of worship.

You may ask, why did God show the Israelites such great mercy; were they not sinners as many other nations are? Many people have asked this question and many answers have been given. First, we must try our best to desist from defying God about His certain judgements because man is meant to accept all the decrees of loving God who does everything good for love of His creatures. 'God hears the cry of the poor,' the Scripture said. Basically God who is love always helps those people who acknowledge their sins as an offence against Him, even though they cannot help themselves other than to do what they are being compelled to do by man's lower nature. These people always cry for their sins, being filled with the spirit of repentance—for what pleases God most is to be in communion and agreement with Him in whatever He loves or abhors. These are the people about whom Christ was talking in the sermon on the mountain, when He said, 'Blessed are those who test for righteousness, for they shall be filled.'

But those who act in wickedness and hatred of God commit their evil with pride, and most of the time challenge God in His commandments saying, 'Why should He say that?' Some of them even commit the worst sin by denying God's existence in order to justify their sins. Upon these kinds of people He unleashes His threats every day, even to the very base of their existence as Psalm 7: 11 says. This is why the Israelites were delivered and used. In spite of all their sins and weakness, they acknowledged God, while The Consuming Fire consumed some ancient nations and declared war with some. The truth is that it was only Israelites who were worthy of His mercy; although they were as sinful as the rest of the humans, they loved God and cried for His mercy, while the nations under the control of the fallen angels were not only sinful but were rebelliously asking, 'Why should God dare to control man?'

Those who hate Israel because of this everlasting love of God must know that it was not only because of the promise of God to their fathers, but because they suffered so much for the sake of the love of God, and that they cried for deliverance not only for themselves but also for the whole world they represented in those days.

But after all these great deliverances, did they not continue in fornicating with idols because of this deep-rooted nature of evil in man? Was it not the same reason why Abraham sent Hagar and Ishmael away because of the strong idolatry in Hagar's ancestry, which she must not fail to manifest in the near future, which must be a snare to the covenant child Isaac, being a child of an old age?

God is so wise in His counsels; to preserve the future salvation of the world; the bond woman and her child must leave, otherwise the death of Abraham would have given Ishmael control over Isaac, the prince of salvation. This is always a case of the ends justifying the means. In later days that vision of Abraham was fulfilled; even though Ishmael managed to stay in connection to the God of His Father, his descendant later deviated from the true God. So, too, did the future descendants of Esau, because the covenant of the promised salvation continues with Jacob. Even in the later days Israelites on their way back to Abraham's inheritance waged war with the descendants of Ishmael and Esau.

As the Israelites were developing as a nation after entering the Promised Land, so God continued His mission of deliverance with the prophets who helped in making the law the guide for the whole people of Israel, which with time became the state law.

In this Promised Land, did they have rest? No. Because they could not keep the law as their inclinations were so rebellious. You can see that the nature of old man has no remedy—even though God extended their journey into the Promised Land for forty years, so that the generation that rebelled against God might die off in the wilderness. Yet their sons and daughter played idol in the later days in that Promised Land filled with milk and honey. Even their future children confirmed this repetition of the sins of their fathers as it is written in the Psalms. 'For our sin is the same as our fathers.' (Psalm 106: 6)

This is the reason why a man is in bondage until he surrenders his old nature to the commandments of God, so that the new nature may be free in the grace of Christ. Going through the ministry of the prophets and their messages, you will find out that none of them was really talking about the afterlife as a reward for keeping the law, but rather they were still talking about the future deliverance even though they were already in the Promised Land. Their ministry to the old man was based on the well-being of that nature of man on earth if he obeyed the law. When you open the Scripture on all the blessings attached to the law, it's all about increasing your cattle, prevailing against your enemies, the fertility of your land and the fruitfulness of man's endeavours, good health, lending to many nations, and being on the top. (Compare Leviticus 26: 1-13 and Deuteronomy 28: 1-14)

When Moses was giving them final blessings according to their tribes, it was all about earthly blessings and happiness. (Compare Deuteronomy 33) No eternal life in the bosom of the Lord was promised to them because heaven is locked against that nature irrespective of his holiness. Therefore when Christ was teaching, He concluded that the law and the prophets were all about doing good to one another and receiving reward in return. (Compare Matthew 7: 12)

All the missions of both the major and minor prophets were of righteousness to old nature; but being weak, the old nature of man they ministered to was being held in bondage, thereby he was given a message of hope about the coming of the Messiah who would liberate him from that thraldom. Thus the children of Israel spent all their life in praying and supplication to the Lord to send them Christ because they too were in bondage just like the whole world, though they were unaware of that because of the closeness of God in their life.

God in His ministries of the law and the prophets had tried to use so many ways to build the old man, but all those efforts failed. Not that God failed or did not know that it would fail, but being a just God He wanted to use those failures to prove to man that his old nature had failed and therefore bound to the consequences of the judgement not favourable to him. Because God does not have anything to do with spilled oil; rather He creates another for He can do all things. As we can see in the ministry of Moses, he tried so much to accomplish salvation but his people were the worst kind; though they were people who had witnessed the highest glory and the miracles of God, yet they played out the worst idolatry and sexual immorality.

The law that was given to Moses was not just what God figured out; it was the complete life of the fallen man and what

He saw the children of men practising, both the Gentiles and Israelites alike, as at the time when the law was given. The Ten Commandments, the Moral and Ceremonial Laws, the Laws of Sexual Immoralities and the likes. (Compare Leviticus Chapters 18 and 19) All these are covenants made with the old nature because all that which is forbidden is found in our old nature. Thus Moses suffered more because his ministry came face to face with the core nature of man. Many times he interceded for them; they repented today and rebelled tomorrow to the level that their sins made Moses behold the Promised Land from far away but never set his foot on it. With sorrow he departed the world—for there is no pain to the old nature of man that equals the sorrow of dying without testing the fruit of his labour. Yet seeing it was a comfort for Moses because God in His mercy had prepared a better resting place for him who as the humblest of men had suffered so much for the salvation of the world. (Compare Numbers 12: 3)

In the last days of Joshua, did he not go to the level of making a covenant with the children of Israel, that they would continue in serving the living God, making for them a statute and an ordinance in Shechem, and setting a large stone under the oak that was the sanctuary of God as a witness against them, should they depart from the living God. Yet they failed. So that nature continued in that failure in Samuel's and David's days, even to King Solomon in all his wisdom, bearing the witness that the old nature of man is contrary to God by almost dragging the whole nation into pagan worship if not the intervention of God. Hezekiah in his days tried to restore the true worship by going to the extreme of destroying the Moses cross in attempt to crush idolatry but he achieved little. Even in the days of Isaiah, Jeremiah and all the Minor Prophets, it was the same story. Within all these histories of failures, God did not fail to use all manner of punishment; He allowed their enemies to take them captives. Yet that nature did not prove to be any better than the rest of men, because the egg which the fallen angels laid in the depth of man in the Garden of Eden will continue to hatch and manifest itself in different ways that contradict the true origin of man.

··· ··· ···

What was the conclusion of the prophets after all their hard labours to put the old man in the right track until the day of the Lord? Isaiah who was one of the greatest prophets decrees that, 'We are all like unclean thing, and all our righteousness are like filthy rags.'(Isaiah 64:6) Therefore in the day of Habakkuk, in connection to this word he said that, 'the just shall live by faith.'

Can you see that the prophets are connected to the mind of God who programmed them? They condemned the old man they ministered to and even the fruits of the law in him. Can a filthy rag go to heaven? You must believe the spirituality of the Scripture that without surrendering your animal nature to the law; you cannot produce its righteousness which bounds the old man. there is no way a filthy rag will enter heaven; it then means that the filthy rag which is the fruit of the law in the old man must surrender itself to the grace.

These prophets went further to condemn the sacrifices prescribed by the law because it does not lead to eternal life. 'In sacrifice you take no delight, burnt offerings from me you would refuse.' And the prophet Micah asked, 'Shall I come before God with burnt offerings, with a year old lamb? Will the Lord be pleased with the thousands of rams or ten thousands of rivers of oil? Shall the offering of my firstborn cleanse my sins? It is a contrite and humbled heart.'

Yes! It is only the new nature of man who can truly love God with a contrite and humble heart. Make no mistake about this; the righteousness of the new man is not like a filthy rag before God; rather it is holy and perfect to Him who appeared to make man perfect. He lives his life on earth doing good, knowing that his rewards are in heaven. He gives arms, prays and fasts for people secretly; he suffers humiliations in silence and bears wrong-doing patiently. Even when strange things happen to him, he ponders on them and privately offers them to God.

The old man's good deeds are filthy rags simply because he demands rewards for everything good he does; he pays tithes for

God to bless him, he gives arms and proclaims it from the top of the mountain. When he fasts everybody will know, he seeks praises and rewards for everything good he does on earth and even challenges God when he thinks that recognition of his good deeds is delayed, or when God's promises are not yet manifested. Through man's old spirit his righteousness is a filthy rag but through his new spirit created by Christ his righteousness is perfect, holy and acceptable before God.

Note that these filthy rags are fruits of the law in the old man; these filthy rags are the expected standard that God has set for the old man; upon this, grace will descend for our salvation. Then he can become the just man who must live by faith. Amen!

God in the history of dealing with Israel who represents the whole humanity as the firstborn has proved that the nature of old man belongs to the control of the fallen angels of darkness. He sent His Christ through the law and prophets; therefore no man has an excuse not to accept Christ who came that we may have new creation. He bore witness of Him through the law and prophets who appeared as a shadow of the true life.

We are not saying that the ministries of the prophets were in vain. No! It was their ministries that made possible the appearance of the second Adam and Eve for the fulfilment of their efforts. Know you this truth, that without the coming of the incarnate Word of God, the whole blessed works of the prophets would have been indeed a never-realised dream. Because the old man they ministered to has lost its destiny and is always in constant rebellion against God, even when he says yes to Him. This is seen in the manner in which this old nature treats the prophets of God, even up to today, for he hates God to the level of killing His prophets. In the Scripture, it's only a few prophets who died a natural death; even Moses who brought the law would have been stoned to death were it not that God gave him a luminous face which made him more than a mere man, although less than God, for he was a highly mystical prophet of a type never before seen.

'Jerusalem, Jerusalem! You kill the prophets, and you stone those who are sent to you.' (Luke 13: 34)

This is a lamentation and the cry of Christ over the sufferings of His prophets. He continues to pronounce the message of woe upon them, for their fathers killed the prophets and they built and decorated the tombs confirming this evil done by their fathers. The bizarre thing about man's nature is beyond understanding; in the law it is written that false prophets who speak in the name of God what God has not spoken must die. But as the truth has it, these people who profess to love God killed both the good and false prophets because of these multiple personalities in man. The truth is that it is always the populace who joins hands in killing the true prophets, and after the killing, they will say truly he is a prophet, thus they build their tombs and venerate them as Christ has witnessed.

It is a case of history repeating itself, as we see in the nature of this old man even in the history of the church. This was how they crucified Christ: the same people who ate with Him, whom He healed. The same people who said, 'God has visited His people, He has done all things well and welcomed Him as a great king on the day of His triumphant entrance into Jerusalem.' The same people allied with His arch-enemies and killed Him. Even the holy Apostles who were very close to Him, who knew truly that He was the Christ, did not dare to stand with Him before the high priest to bear witness to the truth—that this was Christ, seeing that the counsel of the priests and elders who condemned Him misunderstood His mission and teachings. If they had stood with Him, they may have spared their master that most horrible death.

You may now say, but how would the Scripture have been fulfilled, had Christ not been betrayed by the populace? This is the question we always ask to get over certain difficult puzzles, but we must find ourselves always on the side of truth that, even though the prophecy must be fulfilled, we should try to dwell on the side of the truth to avoid playing a negative parts towards its fulfilment because God must judge all evil, both actions and conspiracies. Of course Christ was destined to die; but also there was a pronouncement of woe to him that betrayed Him.

From the Apostles of the early church to the later, this conspiracy against the prophets continues in the saints even on the higher level. Who was the saint that has not been conspired against, even by the members of the clergy and the religious? In fact the test of sainthood is this necessary persecution within the church. Some of them were even killed or lured into prison by the same comrades who pretended to preach the good news with them, or by members of family. A mystery of that word, 'I did not come to bring peace but sword'.

Father against daughter and brother against brother.' Persecuting the saints, accusing them of blasphemy and being heretic, or being hysterical and ascetical, accusing them of being evil and therefore forbidding them from their active ministries in some cases.

There has never been any saint who was not persecuted both within the church and outside it; because as Christ said it cannot be that a prophet should perish outside of Jerusalem. (Luke 13: 33) And after their deaths, both their friends and those who persecuted them declared them saints even before the mother church proclaimed her judgement. What a horrible nature of man and the mystery of God in purifying His saints! This is truly what was done to the prophets and it is being repeated on the saints of Christ. These negative things are real when people refuse to surrender their animal nature to the law of eternal Christ; they come to Christ with recalcitrance and refuse to let go of themselves thinking that they can please God with their natural inclinations, but the reverse becomes the case—being opposed to the truth, and with their hearts hardened by the deceitfulness of sin, they start to attack the saints. They stand at the gate of heaven and do not go in; neither will they let in people who want to enter. (Compare Mathew 23: 13)

What I am saying is that the royal child suffers so much in the church because she truly want to follow the truth of Christ; they are all gathered there for the sake of Christ but most of them are hidden in the religious cloak to live the same life they pretended to have left to follow Christ. Therefore the evil one who is so rich in that nature uses them to torment the saints of Christ even in His church.

The ministers of good news will continue to suffer; for even though men have known the truth and have received the light of the holy Gospel, yet the old nature of man dominates their entire life and they continue to profess love for God even when their conscience bears witness against them as liars. Thus Christ who knows the depth of man blesses the saints who are persecuted to rejoice, for great reward is waiting for them in heaven, 'For the same was done by their fathers to the prophets.' This spirit that was with the prophets is not death because, in baptism, Christ also pours it out upon us to spread the good news. We must strive to do it with more vigour, having received the authority and message that the prophets never had, lest the world speak well of us as they did the false prophets who were condemned at the left side of Christ. (Compare Luke 6: 26)

I so much wish that I have overcome my old nature, which has nothing good to offer, but because he is equally spirit who is destined to live forever therefore I surrendered him to the holy message of the prophets, so that my new nature will dwell in the power of life unto salvation. Even though sometimes I foolishly look back to him, the voice on the mountain is calling me more strongly. Considering that I have started climbing this mountain, I will proceed further for if this water that runs down from the mountain sustains me, how wonderful it will be when I have persevered to the top of the mountain and can melt into Him who is the fountain of all goodness.

Confession and Meditation

As a new man, my righteousness is no longer a filthy rag but holy and acceptable before God!

The Foudation

When the foundation of a house is not solidly laid, the inhabitant of that house can never have peace of mind all the days he dwells in that house, because the building trembles at every threat of storm and wind. 'Foundation once destroyed, what shall the just man do?' (Psalm 11: 3)

The conception and the birth of man are no different to how other mammals conceive and give birth to their young ones. In breeding their young ones, both wild and domestic animals practise the same thing as man; first, they protect their babies from all possible harm according to their abilities and the capacities of their might. They fend for their babies from day one, until they are capable of hunting, of being independent and taking care of their own needs; some of them will even travel to another territory to begin a new life. So what is the difference between the animals and children of Adam, having seen that their nature has been reduced to the ordinary animal that must live and die just like one?

In human reproduction, man gives birth to what they are, either by will of his flesh or by the will of man. This is the natural birth, which does not make a man higher than the other animals—but baptism, through which another nature is born in man, does. It makes us not only higher beings but it spiritualises man—making him the son of God.

The life of every living being begins from the two parents, male and female who come together during reproduction.

The Destiny of Man

When God poured His Spirit in man after creation, he sent man on a mission of increase, making the spirit in man capable of reproducing exactly his nature. Thus a man can decide to have a baby or not because the power of procreation had already been given to him by God. If it is as we sometimes understand it, that it is God who directly gives children, He would not have allowed young teenagers who have not even known their left from right to conceive, knowing the consequences as the giver of the law He is. He will not give children to people who cannot bring them up in a right manner and with a good foundation. Therefore, it's in man's will to decide when to give birth and also his responsibility to bring him up. God only intervenes in the most difficult cases, when the spirit of barrenness stands against conception. Just as the farmer clear his farmland before planting a seed, marriage is the same for the growing up of a child. We must remember that fruitfulness is a free and natural gift to every created animal, male and female, just like the sun is destined to give light.

In marriage, God has willed the laying of a good foundation for the triumphant destiny of a child. Thus a man and woman will leave their parents and become one, to produce children. God made it so in the beginning; even after the fall, he kept man in that tradition to reduce the wounds already inflicted upon the nature of man through the sin of Adam. This truth is seen in most of the religions and cultures even before the coming of Christ.

To procreate, the old nature of man must show that he is the superior creature of the earth; although he has fallen, yet he retains divine authority over all visible creatures. Therefore, it's most necessary that before procreation, man and woman must be in agreement and in a bond of marriage, as would be father and mother before having children for the benefit of their children, because children are meant to grow better in a family with Mum and Dad by their sides for their protection and better formation. God put in man different breeding and nurturing benefits for a child and a woman has different ones from those of a man. These two must go together if one wants to have the fullness of characteristics meant for a male or female child. The creator did not make one parent to play the role of both parents in bringing up a child, unless certain circumstances occur. There is a personality formation that must be transferred to any growing child of which the lack, in most cases, can cause a great deal of damage to the child; sometimes it may affect that child's sexuality. Whatever a child lacks in the growing process must hurt him in later days. Thus sometimes we see ourselves striving to reconcile ourselves with what we have lacked during our early formation.

There is a natural protection, a kind of mystical transfusion, which can only flow from a parent; when a male child is singlehandedly raised by one parent, he is exposed to many predating elements because each parent not only protects in a physical way, but is also a stronghold in spirit. The birth and formation of a soul starts from the womb; but it continues after birth even into the later years. Together two parents minister to the soul of the child until he becomes adolescent. It takes a complete twelve years for a child to absorb from the parents before separation, and immediately after this circle of years, the puberty stage sets in. In the stages of man's life, we meet people who, most times, are not coincidental in helping in the formation of our being. Therefore for a child to be denied the right of either parent, except for circumstances beyond control, have a serious effect. This protection he never had leaves an empty space in him, which he must seek to fill. This is why the human being is unique among other animals.

This covenant of parenthood we are explaining here is seen in the Scripture when God Himself showed this wisdom by bringing St Joseph into a marriage with Virgin Mary, in order to complete and protect the holy family. Though God Himself was washing over the family and was even in the midst of it, yet He fulfilled this ordinance to make everything in order. God was the father of Jesus Christ who was conceived by the Holy Spirit, yet St Joseph was placed as the husband of Virgin Mary to help to make him a true man with a masculine character though Christ's humanity was only through the Virgin Mary. We must do what God said about raising a child in a complete family, so that He will quickly come to our aid when there is trouble in raising children.

In our generation, man's fake wisdom and ungodliness has let loose one of the enchained spirits whose mission is to trigger what is hidden in man with a view towards destroying marriage. Marriage is under the greatest attack in this age; unless humanity retreats into the truth of our origin, the worst is yet to happen because we are in the age of fulfilments of prophecies. If man will not co-operate with God and loses the battle to save marriage against the arch-enemy of man, what solid ground do we have to stand on in order to raise our children? To maintain a marriage that is not easy, man must be in a solid standing with God who ordained that marriage. If your marriage is shaky, try your best to make it stand and last, for it will not be easy to build it up again if it collapses. Marriage is a cross and the height of self-denial, which survives only by the grace of God.

In the wild life, when a lioness is raising her young ones all by herself without the real father of her cubs, she is in real danger and must lose those cubs to another male lion who must kill them in order to produce children of his own. So to successfully raise her young ones, she must have a male for protection. Is it not more dignified that man, the image of God, should be brought up by the same parents who gave him life?

The spirit in the male and the spirit in the female are completely different both in functions and actions; the male's spirit is more like the sun while the female's spirit is like the moon. Thus the Bible said that a woman must be submissive to the husband, even as the moon is submissive to the sun and suck up its strength. These two spirits complement each other and they come together in procreation; so raising up the child, these two must be together to be able to accomplish their task and to project onto their children what they require to achieve the fullness of human nature. There is a mystical communication between the parents and their children, which helps the children's psychosexuality and balances their morale standards.

Before a tree can bear a fruit, it must wait for the season. Before that season comes, it must have surrendered itself to the rule of nature first by abscission. During this process, it exposes itself to the heat of the sun, after which the new leaves will grow and then will come fruit. The tree does not bear fruit without first having laid a good foundation for their survival. The same wisdom is seen in animals especially those in the wild and sea animals; they all know the right time to breed, and they all keep that law so things may be well for both themselves and their young ones. In the case of the wilder beasts and the birds, which migrate to other regions in searching for pasture during unfavourable conditions, these laws are also kept. They take in and give birth in due season so their young ones will be safe and strong enough during migration. Animals that migrate do not travel in times of full pregnancy to avoid giving birth on the way.

If these animals in the wild can keep these divine laws as prescribed by God for their safety, why should humans, who claim to be the higher animal, refuse to obey this law of oneness and togetherness between man and woman before procreation?

Those who are of the opinion that a newborn baby is free from sin will see how a baby can still bear the consequences of the parents' misdeeds, just as young animals born in the wild to foolish mothers, who miscalculated the fruitful time, quench the hunger of the predators. A man must be convinced that a child shares in everything owned by its parents, both physically and in a spiritual order. Let them plant into their sub-consciousness that the offspring of Adam were never born with the highly spiritual nature which Adam had before his fall; rather they were born as naked as their parents who bore them, feeling both temperature and pain, which Adam and Eve never had in the mystical garden.

Most of the wounds men suffer in their early or latter life began from the womb through parents who want to fulfil their own zeal or disobedience to the commandments of God, who placed blessings and life on the right side and is pleading with man to choose life and not to choose the left side which is death. A good student is not the one who follows his own ideas, but the one who follows the ideas and formula set down by his teacher, or whatever the formula might be which guides what he studies. Even if he invents another formula, it must not contradict what has been.

When God made it that children shall be born by two people who are in the covenant of marriage, He did not do it for His own good, but for the prosperity of the fruits of that marriage. Remember well that anything man can physically do or see, whether positive or negative, belongs to the old nature, which must go in agreement with the commandments meant for that old nature. But the new man's life and blessings are by faith, and faith is not seen, just as the new man born by God in us is not seen; rather it is a spiritual body whose fullness will manifest itself in the future.

God has prescribed principles laid down for all the living things under the sun; outside those principles, there is always a danger. As I said earlier, God is not the one who determines when any creature will procreate; but He made a divine law and a favourable condition when a baby must be born. Man is already in trouble owing to the sin of Adam; how much more trouble occurs when he goes against God by putting the child into more bondage. This is where mothers should be very careful to protect the dignity of the unborn child who, as it were, should be innocent. You should not give into a relationship that will harm your future fruit. In our own understanding as humans, it is absurd that a child who seems to be innocent should suffer for what he did not know; but God who knows the spiritual formation of man knows that a child is a direct fruit of his parents. It's not any child's fault for inheriting something from a parent, but that of the parent who has labelled them through carelessness and negligence of the sacredness of human existence. Once two adults are not in marriage or a serious bond of a relationship with the view of raising a family together, let them stay on their own instead of endangering the destiny of the innocent soul.

Why are there wounds in such a child? Pregnancy should be a joyful thing because a new baby is on the way. But in some cases, instead of joy, it is a cause for sorrow for the family. In some cultures, such children will even be rejected right from the womb with loads of blame being placed upon the mother, and all this hate is because of this new life in the womb. Such culture considers it abnormal for a young lady to have a child without a legal husband. What about the two parents involved? I have seen a case where the expectant mother was crying because she was not yet ready for the pregnancy and the partner was also saying that he did not want the baby. A young baby who was only a few months old had already been declared unwanted by both parents, who should have been happy about their child's arrival. Eventually the baby was born; tell me the future of that baby who has been rejected by both the sources of her existence?

In most cases like this, people choose to abort the child to give themselves freedom, or maybe to prepare for a more suitable time. This is one of the cruellest acts of our generation: depriving a baby of the opportunity to see the goodness of creation. The sin of abortion does not only deprive a child of his life but also deprives Christ, the zealous lover of soul, an opportunity to begot a child through baptism, because the spirit of Christ given to man in baptism cannot procreate irrespective of the man's holiness. The Holy Spirit is always waiting for a child to be born naturally and does not relax until that new born is given a new birth for the salvation of the soul.

Who told you that a day-old baby is not human? Subtract one day or one month from the gestation period, and what you have is a minus from the gestation period. To understand that a few days old is a full human, consider what took place in the incarnation of Christ—Virgin Mary was immediately addressed as the mother of the Lord when her pregnancy was less than three days. Remember she made haste to visit Elizabeth as soon as she heard the good news about the advent of John the Baptist? If Elizabeth called her the mother of a child by inspiration, who told you that you are not a mother? Who told you that you have not just killed your baby? You have just deprived life from a day-old soul taking flesh in your womb.

Once a child is not loved from the womb, the baby's genetic problems have multiplied. Many people have said this and it is true. A child in the womb is a complete human and needs love though his body parts are developing, because the soul of every living being is born first in the womb before it starts taking the flesh of the mother. Everything that is taking place outside is affecting the child as he relies on those actions to form, as it is only from the mother that he receives food, emotions and everything that is projected onto his mother once the mother has accepted it. Thus it is good for expecting mothers to be in the right mood and at peace with themselves and with God the giver of life to be able to deflect all negative arrows for the well-being of the unborn child.

Apart from being in peace with God before child-bearing, people can still inflict a great damage on the sexuality of the unborn child by excessive desire and predetermining the sex of the child without making good calculations to know whether they are most likely to get the particular gender they desire. For example, a pregnant woman who is obsessive about having a female baby may keep saying, 'I want the baby to be a female.' All the projection is 'it must be a girl' even when the baby is already forming as a male, because from the first day of conception, if it is a male soul, it starts that day to form the male body systems and organs. He is forming as a boy inside and outside, but the parents are projecting female characteristics onto him. Because the baby is more receptive, relying on the parents, he accepts these gifts from his gods into his formations. Parents may go to the extent of choosing a female name for him and buying female dresses for him. When people ask them the choice of their baby, they will continue to say, she will be a girl. You can see that the young boy's troubles about sexuality have been established right from the womb in the depth of his being. This baby is now born a boy but part of him feels like a girl and wants to act like one. Even after he is born a boy, the parents do not stop: 'We wish he was a baby girl, that's what we need now.' Having bought females' clothes before his birth, they have no options than to dress him in female baby-wear, thinking that it does not mean anything. When he grows up and starts to live this external nature already sealed in his spirit, people will be against him for what he cannot change and does not have power over, because as it were it is part of his nature.

This same indelible wound on the innocent child continues; when people see a female child who looks a bit masculine, it's always the case to say that she looks like a boy. The same to a young lad who looks more handsome: people tell him that he looks like a girl. It might look as if they are praising or admiring these children but in spiritual terms it is poison and disorder that they are ministering and projecting to them. Believe it, any child in a growing process is receptive and can grow in any direction. Once a growing child start to receive praise about his natural appearance, you who praises them is not helping them, but rather inviting troubles for them, because this is an opportunity for the pride spirit to begin his work. Observe that child's behaviour from that point on; it can never be the same again because she feels so special. This also can boost sexuality damage. I wonder what you expect a girl to do when you continue to tell her that she is masculine or when you tell a young boy that he looks like a girl.

People with such problems did not invite these onto themselves but rather they are victims of the powerful voice, projections and imagination of human beings during their formation stage. Of course human beings have a creative force in them, which can still manipulate people even after birth.

All these things take place because humanity is not aware of their spiritual identity: that man has a creative power to desire and will things, and this will manifest itself. Parents have the right to desire a sex of their choice, but they must not go to the point of projecting their desire to the extent of creating a disorder in their unborn child.

Yet in all these matters, there is hope and good news; so far as Christ is involved, all those natural births do not matter. Whether you were born in or outside marriage, male or female, homosexual or heterosexual, just give yourself to Christ for there is a new birth waiting for all the children of Adam and Eve. Our first birth is the lower birth; and in this lower nature lies discrimination, racism, gender, sexualities; all these make us human and part of the animal family. It does not matter who you are in your first nature, white or black, or who you are in your sexuality; these things do not define your existence, for Christ has died for you to be a supernatural being where all these things do not exist.

... ...

No human being is born with a racial prejudice; either he develops it with time as a result of natural inclinations, or it is implanted into him by the people who brought him up. Most times parents think that they are helping their children to achieve a greater future when they start choosing friends and enemies for them; but it is not always the best thing to do. It is not the best thing for parents to transfer their natural inclinations to a child to behave and see things through their own views and opinions, which may not necessarily be the best. It is a wrong tradition of man to introduce their children to the game of hate and love, telling them whom to avoid or accept. The best thing is to give them a unique identity by teaching them godly principles and good social manners even as the Bible said, 'Train up a child the way he should grow, so that he will not depart from it when he grows up.'

It's very obvious that a child who possesses these qualities will survive in the midst of thorns, lions, wolves and all other negative influences that challenge him daily. As some parts of the world are becoming multicultural, the kind of parents we are talking about will say to their children, 'Have nothing to do with Asian, or white, or black', as the race of such parents may be: 'They are not good, they are racist, and they are thieves.' This is exactly how this child's love for people is destroyed for nothing gets established more quickly in the hearts of children than the message of hate from their loved ones. At the receptive state of man, as we have said, an attitude which is spirit takes a position in his depth once it's projected into him. So it's best to give them a message of love, keep them in check and allow them to flow freely in the world's energy to grow through their own experiences, and you will see that every created human has a unique nature that is different from the parents'. Because imposing a nature on little children makes them replay a life of a past generation; it delays the world's evolvement and the new things our God makes every day—causing a repetition of histories.

When the Messiah was manifested from Nazareth of Galilee, the ruling class refused to humble themselves to His liberating message. Instead they were asking, 'Can anything good come from Nazareth?' Of course it's the highest truth that the salvation of the whole human race came from the most remote area of their days! Not even a prophet was manifested from Galilee because they were like rejected part of Israel. Even in that nation that seems to be so bad, there are good people there; be good yourself so that the goodness of another person may be manifested through the goodness you radiate.

A young man was spreading a racist message, saying that his good father had told him in his growing years not to trust a particular race—for 'there is nothing good about them,' he said. But the funny thing was that the young man was caught the next day stealing from his employer. This is exactly how some parents plant evil in the heart of the innocent child; this kind of seed of hate which is deeply rooted in this man has damaged any mutual love or relationship he might have for any person from that race, because his negative attitude towards them will always provoke a defensive negative attitude from the other, which needs the divine intervention and a kind of death to uproot.

And another said, 'Over my dead body would my daughter marry a man from so and so people.' 'This is what my father told me,' he continues, 'and I will keep that tradition.' In his mind, this is a good tradition as it was handed to him by his father; little did he know that he is holding a tradition which is against Christ's message of love and brotherhood.

It's quite understandable why some parents pass on such messages: maybe because of their past experiences. But the truth is that everybody must not be the same; good and bad people equally abound in every colour and race. We should know that even in the optimum life of every man, there is nature of good and bad existing in him. In a relationship with anybody one should strive to be good oneself, not trying to receive but to give, and one must always be ready to apply the wisdom of forgiveness; for man must not please you, otherwise you will not grow in the knowledge of the truth that no one is good but God.

... ...

When a child begins to hear from his parents that he is the best among other children, he is receiving a step towards failure and having sowed in his spirit a seed of pride that eats like a canker worm. Tell your child to strive to be the best, not that he is the best, because no one inherits greatness but rather it is achieved through hard work and perseverance. Every ugly nature as we are saying has a root; and this is how pride gets rooted in the individual.

Pride is one of the mother sins and vices, the opposite of humility. This is the major sin, which brought down the fallen angels as we know, and who now, finding themselves in the world, established it as a highest homage a man can pay to them. The book of Proverbs says that, 'Pride goes before destruction.' (Proverb 16: 18)

Pride is a spirit and sometimes it can be transferred from parents to their offspring. When a parent has pride and cannot achieve his ambitions according to his mind set, seeing that he may not be able to achieve his selfish aims, he transfers them to his children; even from the womb parents start projecting this spirit into their children, making them kings or queens while they, the parents, are not royals. Most times they do this using the Scripture. It's high time we understand that the Scripture is a message of humility—not the opposite. When the child grows up, having been told that he is the best or was born to rule, he tries every opportunity to live that false glory. God save the nation that he does not find himself on the throne of the nation, where he will become a tyrant—for every other person to him is inferior. Even when his targets fail and he finds himself in lower organisations, his subjects suffer.

Let not this be misunderstood! Of course we should wish our children well, even from the womb, but not to dictate and determine what they will be in the future, which belongs to God through your good efforts. The best thing parents can do is to be in good standing with God and man, and then lay good foundations for their children before birth, so they will find a strong foothold to become the pride of their parents and the nation. I wonder how you expect your child to rule the world with weak foundations; when you, as a parent, have not been good and could not build high edifices where your child would stand tall enough to see the world you wish him to rule. This is not a case of quoting the Scripture on your child as the cases we see around now, because this generation in their selfishness thinks that the Scripture has a mathematical formula they can apply in the way they want. No! For what will be must be. A mango tree will continue to bear mango fruit and can never bear apples. You cannot sow rice and reap potatoes—because a strong house must be rooted on a solid foundation.

The knowledge of the new creation will elevate you to this understanding—that all the words you may be ministering to the child in the womb, philosophically through the mystery of baptism, may not be necessary; it may achieve little or less; because the new man for whom the word of God is meant is not yet born. Unless you are truly born again and know the right word to use, you may be pouring water on rock because most parents want their children to be a top man of the world. Thus St Padre Pio lamented during his ministry that most people who came to him for help never asked to be helped to be a saint but rather they were interested in the material blessings. Which most times enslaves the soul, and we know that this contradicts the message of Christ, which calls for detachment.

This spirit of pride is what destroys the peace and equality of human race. It began from the family and ascends to the top level, even to the governmental systems of the top nations of the world. They know how to preach equality of man but they lack the sense to uproot the root that makes one think he is superior to another.

It is the highest level of the root of pride, superiority and racism to map out a particular continent or region and brand them third-world countries. Thus racism and superiority will not stop unless this disguised evil stops. The first-world countries, by branding some countries third-world, inspire racism and superiority in the hearts of their citizens. May God bring a man after His heart to put an end to this evil!

The world leaders are playing this game because the world system is still operating in the ladder of the old nature of man, which depends on what a man can achieve physically or intellectually and not as a human; they forget that everybody is not gifted equally. Thus they can stand against all manner of migration except highly skilled immigrants and those who will benefit the economy so that the third-world countries will continue to dwindle. They profess to assist the third world, exporting food, medications and basic life amenities to them, but they don't want to accept people from those countries who have entered their country seeking for pasture to better their lives. Why not help them by accepting them as one of you, so they can help their people they left behind? The Scripture is crying, 'But the strangers who dwell among you shall be to you as one born among you, and you shall love them as yourself.' (Leviticus 19: 34) At least accept him because he is a human: the only crime he committed is that he wants to stay among you. This is a pure window-dressing kind of love and it will induce you to believe this truth—that the system still belongs to the old nature who always pretends to love God.

Another root of racism and the worst nature of old man that celebrates and propagates racism is the issue of colour. It is the character of the old man to define people by their colour. Of what use are people's names if it is not enough to identify them unless you also attach their colour or origin? Does the soul of man, which is the true nature of man, have colour? If our leaders cannot stop this, in vain they pretend to fight racism. He is black, brown or white. What is the difference? This must stop now so that the healing process will begin; and future generations will praise us as we are praising the generation who stopped the slave trade.

So far as colour is concerned, no one is white or black. Man started branding himself white to show that he is special and superior to others. We sprang up from the same human stock, in the same manner all men were born, were smiled upon by the same sky and the constellations on equal terms, live and die the same—yet one is called white and another is branded black or brown. Because we all know the meaning of black, let this old system die and decay, for man is not known by his colour but by his name and what he does. When unusual things happen, people refer to the day as a black day; illegal business is branded 'black market'. To establish that calling a race black has something odd about it is when there is inter-marriage between one of African origin and one of European or American origin; the product of the marriage is always branded black in spite of having white origin as well as black. I think the world leaders are deceiving the populace in the pretence of eradicating racism.

As everything has a root and a beginning, so you should understand that all natural disorder has a foundation, and nothing happened by accident. Some people's wounds start from their parents who conceived them, and some wounds take root during the growing years. I want to state these facts but I must tell you to be calm and still! I am not frightening you or trying to impose guilt on any man, but just exposing some roots of our troubles. The Scripture said, 'My people perish for lack of knowledge.' (Hosea 4: 6) By implication, through knowledge deliverance will come just as the cure of every sickness is easy when it is diagnosed. By understanding and applying the principles of Christ in any situation, notwithstanding the depth of it or how magnanimous or ancient it is, freedom will come.

If the sin of Adam and Eve could enslave all the children of men into bondage, what about the parents' sins? Do you think that these have no effects on their offspring? In the understanding of the people of the scripture who started this journey before us, we see this fear of children sometimes suffering for what they do not know. 'Our fathers sinned and are no more, but we bear their iniquities.' (Lamentation 5: 7)

A question was directed to Him: 'Rabbi, who sinned, this man or his parents, that he was born blind?' And Christ answered, 'Neither his father's sin nor his own but to glorify God.' (John 9: 2) This was the same reason St John the Baptist was calling the unrepentant sinners of his days a 'brood of vipers', because they could not do anything better than practising the evil nature that was passed onto them from their parents. Thus the first thing parents should think of is to prepare for the baptism of their child as soon as he or she is born. We are not saying that suffering is always the case of a father's sins. Most times as well suffering is not as a result of sin but the gathering of fallen angels against a man. Thus God always come with the message, 'Do not be afraid!', as eventually He will crush them because He always comes to the aid of man. But the big question is, 'Who has a wound without cause?' (Proverb 23: 29)

In man's growing years a little misdeed or maltreatment can spell torture or damage to the nature of man. Most blessings and troubles of man are rooted in the parents. As we said earlier, parents are the people who decide to bear children. God made everybody fruitful but He does not impose it on anyone to procreate; therefore it is the will of the flesh and blood to reproduce. (Compare John 1: 13)

Every parent reproduces to keep their name and traces on earth as their first mission, which as we have said is a mission of the old nature of man. During this process, the two people in the covenant of marriage extend life, as it were, to their products; they generously bring it out just as one builds a house out of his savings. So no one can claim that God created him directly because God created Adam and Eve and gave them absolute power to increase; and we belong to God through our parents. In the gift of the Ten Commandments, the first three commandments are attributed to God, but in the fourth one God Himself pays homage to parents as a honour to them for using them to fill the earth, knowing too well that to conceive and bear a child is the greatest work He fulfils through man. Therefore He attaches long-lasting blessings to it. 'Honour your Father and Mother—so that your days may be long, and that it may be well with you.' Note that there is a curse for disobeying this commandment which is the reverse of the stated blessings. Parents do not have power over the blessings or the effects of breaking this commandment; it is already judged and decided long before even their own births, as they owe that to their parents as well.

This is another area where the foundation of man is built upon sand when he is not in a good standing with the parents. A wise child must make sure that the hearts of her parents does not grieve in remembering her, but rather to be blessed by their heart whenever they remember her; we owe our parents that honour so long as they live irrespective of the culture of any land which stands against this holy ordinance of the true God of Israel. Parents are the gods we can see; the manner in which we relate to them can build up a man or destroy him. Your parents may be wrong in certain issues, but you may not be right either, because two authorities cannot stand at the same time; therefore you may be the one who is encroaching.

You must not be the one to condemn your parents even when they are wrong; it is the duty of God who judges all, for God will always act through their authority instead of yours so long as they live. Better to endure the injustice and weakness of parents than to suffer the wrath of their anger, which can uproot the foundation of man. We belong to our parents as far as the first nature of man exists because they indeed decided to give us life.

'He who fears the Lord honours his father and serves his parents as rulers. In word and deed honour your parents and be blessed. Even when their mind fails, be considerate with them.' (Compare Sirach 3: 7-13)

During the old age of our parents we must be careful how we handle issues with them; this is when we always think that we are wiser but trust me, your wisdom depends on playing fool before them and continuing to act as the child you will always be to them, until they are no more, so that their hearts will bless you.

In the youthful age of a man, some of us incur more wounds because of disobedience in a quest for freedom. We suffer not only the effects of this later but also those of our mistakes, which we must have made in acting against the advice we were given just because we wanted to do our own thing. We not only drift away at this point from the love of our parents but this is also where we lose the childhood innocence and the true nature of rebellion against God emerges. Thus the Bible said, 'From man's youth the imagination of his heart is evil.' (Genesis 8: 21)

Understand that man has a strong connection with the spirits of his parents and ancestors who set him on this journey; thus it's always in our best interests to put off that old nature and take the new nature of Christ. Otherwise that old ancestral line will keep you forever in the communion that may not be in your favour. Remember what we said about the law and old nature; apply it here, let the nature you inherited from your parents pay homage to them so that your new nature may be able to keep the law of eternal love of Christ alone. (Even if your parents were born again, they still have that old nature that claims you as their son; the new nature in them does not claim the ownership of your new nature because it does not belong to them, but to Christ alone. Thus 'There is no condemnation on those who are in Christ Jesus!' (Romans 8: 1)

In this the ancient text is fulfilled that 'the children will not suffer for the sins of the father.' (Ezekiel 18: 20) But those who are of the old nature will continue to pay for the depth that was owed many years before their birth because the network of the old self and the demons does not mean life for the old nature but death.)

Some parents are idol worshipers or atheists, and the worst of it is when somebody is truly convinced of the existence of God, yet adamantly, through wickedness, decides to belong to occultism and all manner of witchcraft and covens with a view towards worshipping devils. These categories of people know too well that God is the Alfa and Omega but they decide to stand against

Him. The more rooted the parents are in evil practices, the more negative the old nature of their children will be towards anything that has to do with God. Some people were born and dedicated to a particular deity because the nature of man is always to make their offspring belong to wherever they are. When he grows up, he will be going about as a free man without knowing that his final destiny had been predetermined before his birth.

It is always easy to convert the idol worshipper to true God than the atheist because the idol worshiper has a sense of spiritual lords, but the atheist has a stronger demon. Since there is no God according to him, therefore he has made himself god. When two parents are atheist, it is most likely that their offspring will play the same game with them; they are unable to believe because their old nature is completely strange as everything about God sounds so strange to their instinct. It is always easier for the old nature to grow towards God when it is dedicated to God from the formation than when it is completely dedicated to idol and demons of atheism. Yet if the Holy Spirit of God overtakes such a soul, it manifests Himself mightily in such one because such a situation is where He shows His supremacy and Lordship over all spirits. But such a person will experience the purifying heat of the Holy Spirit in the mystery of the loving God dealing with the ugly nature he had.

The occult grand masters and mistresses do not only belong to the darkness alone, they go along with the family. You may not know that money used in bringing you up may have been of the price of blood. Man may not know what his parents were into even before birth; such parents always define everything that belongs to him in the altar of bondage, breeding children with contaminated gifts with money earned in the wrong way even at the price of blood. As a result there may be a cry of blood in the tree of the family. The present suffers while the future will cry. You may not know that you were brought up with money that may have kept somebody in bondage of drug addiction for life. Thus there are untold sufferings of humanity because, unbeknown to us, there may be a cry of blood against the living and there is always retardation and pain for a spirit to cry and stand against the living.

To be a Christian is to be wise through the revelations of God in the Scripture for the Scripture is to educate and to set one free. You need not to go to the best university and be hundred per cent academically equipped before you know the mysteries of the world; open your Scripture, and meditate on it day and night for the beginning of wisdom is the knowledge of God indeed.

This knowledge will induce you to ask questions so you may be free from the effects of unknown gods in our lives. Why am I here? What is my destiny? Is there anything against it? How do I tackle it? Now to achieve the final result and answer, go back in your history. The best way to enjoy the freedom of Christ is to disconnect yourself from all negativities of the past. What you do not know has no excuse to hold you in bondage; rather it enjoys more freedom to grip you tight taking advantage of your ignorance.

... ...

'Nevertheless I have few things against you because you eat things sacrificed to idols.' (Compare Revelation 2: 20)

The eating of food dedicated to idols is another area where our foundation is wounded. This is the reason why a Christian should be careful in eating anything without prayer that sanctifies. When you know that food is dedicated to an idol, I advise you not to dare eat it thinking that you have faith, for this could be putting the Lord to test. If you must eat it, ensure that your faith is firmly rooted in Christ. Food dedicated to the idol is the highest communion of the devil to the old nature of man and is poison to the new nature of Christ. It is a covenant food, which binds the eater to whatever demon the food is sacrificed to. Sometimes we may think that it doesn't really matter because we don't know. Well, this is the game of the devil, to keep his snares and devices out of your knowledge because by knowing that the food is dedicated to demons you will not eat it. If anyone is aware that his food is poisoned, he would not dare to eat it; and the eater of poisoned food dies irrespective of his prior knowledge of the contamination in the food. No wise man will lay a snare and still put up a sign to indicate danger. No! He stays aside waiting for the victim who will fall into it.

Ask questions or keep silent and go hungry, for man shall not live by bread alone.

To retain your Christian inheritance, one must be wise and ready to sacrifice anything to avoid contamination of gods of the world who are in a constant fight to hold a Christian back in bondage. Be as gentle as a lamb, as harmless as a dove, but also you must be as wise as a serpent! Food sacrificed to demons gives the devil the opportunity to step into a soul, and it is thus in all the religions of gods and the so-called traditional religions which are all the branches of gods scattered in the whole world; it is a seal of the covenant to eat the animals and food used in sacrifice. Did you not understand these things? This is why it's always a case of the whole community bringing food together before the deity and everyone eats this food after the celebration. This practice is still retained in some cultures today.

Any sickness that goes beyond the physicality of body and blood may be caused by disorder and it's spiritual: mental sickness, emotional diseases, personality disorder, OCD and many others. All these are wounds acquired or derived at a certain time by whoever is the victim. These can only be healed or remedied by going back to the history of it or where it started and dwelling fully in the mystery of Christ to uproot the root which transmits its poison to the rest of that tree called man. We know that if one want to get rid of any tree, the best thing is to dig deep and uproot it from its foundation, and never again will it germinate once that is done. This is the mission of Christ and Christianity if we can obey and are willing to do what He commanded us to do.

The highest cause of these life-threatening and distressing diseases is a diversion of call or destiny. Sometimes this diversion is done by the parents or by those who, through the fear of the challenges of their destiny or through stubbornness, put off their known mission. There is nothing that devastates a man like missing the track that the creator has mapped out for him. Everybody born into the world has a mission to greatness towards God in spite of all the evil plots of gods of the world, because even in the heart of the deadly fish God kept Jonah alive. If man can turn to God, no matter how horrible his natural inclination may be, God can make him new and separate him from all oldness for He is a merciful God beyond the contemplation of any creature. A diversion of call or destiny can bring untimely death in some cases; if he escapes death, the consequences are always too meagre because, when man misses his mission, he is like a non-existent thing in the eyes of the spirits who depend on him to achieve a particular adventure. Before God, the person is not functioning, just like when a train is out of track. The same way a train is built for the track and cannot run on the road, so are all men uniquely created; when one is not functioning in the track meant for him, there is a tendency towards a kind of stagnancy which calls for unnecessary anxieties. He cannot fit in or adapt to another career other than the one he was destined to, especially when he knows that he is in a wrong circle. Even when people do not know that they miss their mission, anxieties and restlessness will still trouble them because the spirit is not fulfilled. In vain such people try to achieve happiness because the spirit is sick; the only remedy is to allow the spirit a freedom. The more this freedom is denied, the more troubled that man becomes, until he does what he must do or loses control of his faculties to wild angels. This is when compulsive disorders and anxieties take absolute control.

The invisible angels are always around to help man in achieving his mission; but the truth is that you must be on a fertile land to be receptive. You must be a person who recognises that you originated from God and must end up in Him; otherwise all His effort to help you will be in vain because you are dwelling on a dry land where no seed of life can grow. The last thing God will do is to impose Himself on this kind of man because He gave all natural man freewill. But the problem is that man's trouble is so great that he abuses the freewill given to him. But God is merciful, knowing how vulnerable man is on earth; He includes our entire mistakes in all His efforts to help us achieve the purpose we are created to be able to give us eternal life.

There is no torture that can equate with the mental torture of a man who is running away from God when God is chasing him. He knows how weak that particular soul is, and His love keeps the Holy Spirit around to convince him for He never compels any man. Once every door is closed against the grace of God, the person is on his own and is trapped.

This situation brings untold sorrow and torture. The more the person tries to let go the more it increases. No psychological therapy can help to give the person complete joy because he cannot resist that spirit. God Himself is helpless because He loves him and cannot allow him to his own will knowing the fragility of that nature and what is best for him. A good discerner of heart and the exorcist at this point is needed to find the depth of the person, because he is suppressing the Holy Spirit in vain. A psychologist alone cannot help this person because he needs divine intervention to minister God's mercy and the word that sets him free because it is obvious that he is shackled by the demons.

Every human being has greatness in him; some have more greatness than others. If there is a wound in such a person, either natural or caused by his mistakes, the situations above can arise because the mission of the fallen demons is laying snares and waiting for an opportunity which they use to minister their deadly ministry. Sometimes parents can contribute to this problem by not channelling their children in the right direction or exposing them to things that can harm their destiny. The damage may not be noticed at the early stage, but the spirit of that child has started suffering because of missing a direction. In some cases you see a child showing interest in a particular career, but because the parents did not like it, the child became disconnected and the parents have made sure they talked him out of his desire. I am not talking about a child who is trying to copy what he sees on television or with his friends; it must come out of his mind. Thus parents must be wise, generous and selfless to support their child when ambition springs out of his mind even when it is not what they willed for him. On the other hand, when a child goes the wrong way, do not leave him with a choice. With good judgement, bring him back to the right track even when it is against his will. Remember that Virgin Mary took Christ back to Nazareth against His will when He wanted to start early ministry.

We have seen lots of experiences and sufferings in the lives of people who have missed their destiny, and some of them do not even know what is happening to them, especially those who have the oil on their head for serving God on the altar, but with time developed a change of mind because of the influence of peer groups and materialism. It is only a foolish child who lost his childhood dreams because of his friend's ambitions. God always ministers a future way in which a child should go in his innocent stage; it is the duty of the parents to bend down to their children to hear this adventure communicated from their mouths and to place them on that road notwithstanding all the doubts.

In every family, God extends His hand of mercy for the selection of at least one person to live a life of dedication to His service, but the problem is that children nowadays are not exposed by their parents to childhood relationships with God. If this is done, how much less trouble and unnecessary anxiety we would have in our world today, for those children who would have been selected would not have been suffering all manner of troubles in the world now where they find themselves out of track.

... ...

We are always surrounded by the invisible ministers of negative things, which trigger intrusive thoughts, unnecessary anxieties, compulsive behaviour and all horrible things against the truth. This is what St Paul called the powers in the air, ministered by the fallen demons. But once you are on fertile land, it will be easier for you to resist with the assistance of the invisible helpers of man. Bear in mind that anxieties are unavoidable so far as one is human, because it is one of the wounds in the old nature of man and it can only be put in check when one is rooted in Christ. Anyone who thinks that he can live a completely anxiety-free life on earth does not understand what it means to be in the world, neither does he understand the mission of Christ. When a meditation is made in Rev. 12 about the reactions of angels of light when the ancient serpent and its followers were cast out of heaven, one would be able to arm himself with the mysteries of Christ to face all the challenges of man, because man originally owned the earth before the fallen angels overthrew man. Therefore because we are passing through the process of salvation, some anxieties are necessary which Christ helps us to face; but the ones that are not necessary, He takes away.

In rebuilding our foundation, there is every need for man to find himself in the field of neutrality, for that is where Christ wants us to meet us. In that field, God or man does not exist. It is a place where Christ who denied Himself as God is waiting for man who must deny the inclinations and instincts of the old nature to start to walk home with Christ who redeemed him. There, man is granted the grace to resist; because he must not do the things that the external forces that still have access to him project, thus he is a new man grafted in Christ. This is the only place where all the negative things we suffer cannot stand because every connection with the old foundations is done away with, and perseverance, which attracts the mercy of God, has become part of you.

No one would like to put valuable things in the house without good foundation, knowing too well that it's not safe. Thus God Himself does not put His treasure in natural man unless He first rebuilds the foundation of that house well rooted in Christ, the chief corner stone who spiritualised humanity.

Rejoice in this good news! There is a remedy for every damaged nature because with Christ it is always yes. Even in the deadly situations of Job, he said, 'There is always a hope for a tree if it be cut down, that it will sprout again and its tender shoots will not cease.' (Job 14: 7)

The nature of Christ is manifested for all the deadly nature of man, to heal and get all His subjects rooted in Him; the only cost is to rise from your necessary deadly nature and arm yourself with love and trust, ready to do all that He says to you, just as a good wife obeys her husband.

In this healing process, as mentioned earlier, go back to your history through deeper thoughts! Do this by asking your parents, brothers or sisters, or anybody that could be of help; this question if possible should go as far back as when you were still in the womb because it is your life and you have the right to know. It could be that there is something you have not known which can help you to tackle your present situation, bearing in mind that diagnosing sickness is to begin the healing process.

Because some of these wounds may be our mistakes, sins and unforgiving spirit, use what I will call a transport of spirit. Reverse back in your history as far back as you can remember to your infant days; is there any grave thing you have done or any abomination you have committed? Know that ugly things like that need the blood of Jesus pronounced upon them. Have you held anybody in bondage by holding his sins against him? Do you not know that a wrestler holds himself in grip, too, when he grasps his opponent on the ground without releasing him? Set your offender free now and see how far forward you will move. Has the person you offended died long ago without forgiving you, or you can't find him or her anymore? Go and confess that sin; do some kind of penance that can cost you and connect such a person with the blood of Christ for once the two of you are connected in the blood of Christ, all debts are wiped off. Remember that with Christ we are sharing in the ministry of forgiveness. Thus He said, 'Forgive so that you may be forgiven.' When we forgive, God has forgiven.

Is it rooted in disobedience to your parents? Run as fast as you can to meet them alive; make them happy so that their hearts may bless you—for the curse of a parent can uproot a house. Was your call diverted by your mistake or by your parents? If it is still possible, go back to it for today is the day of salvation; if it's late, remain in your present state and fulfil it with your remaining life. You can still serve God wherever you have found yourself though it may be more difficult; do it, accept it as your penance and offer it up to God who accepts every offering with pure heart and good intentions; He considers our frailties as part of His plans even before we existed. Bear in mind that God wants us to forget our pasts, as we cannot change them.

Were you a thief? Restitution is needed if you have repented; if you don't have anything for restitution, confess to the person and offer it to God; it is better to suffer here in the flesh than to suffer in spirit elsewhere. Were you labelled a bastard by the old tradition of man? Let it never even trouble you again as you have been baptised into the new nature of Christ, and the kingdom of God is your destination for even the nature of man born in marriage can never go to heaven without baptism—for all natural births are old and fallen nature can never inherit anything in the kingdom of God. Were you involved in an abortion? You must first of all acknowledge that you are a murderer! For what God hates most is when we cover our sins and with hardened hearts claim that it is not a sin. You should present yourself before Christ in brokenness and cry for your sin just as Mary Magdalene wept before Him; He will treat you in the same manner with His everlasting love: 'Your sins are forgiving you, go and sin no more.'

In any manner our old nature is tormenting us, first we must remember that we have received new life in baptism; but our old nature is still around serving the law. Pay homage to the law with the entirety of the old nature so that the new man may go forward faster, bearing in mind that both old and new nature belong to God and both must act according to the principles laid down for them. The old nature is in everlasting bondage but the new nature has freedom as his eternal inheritance because he is begotten by son of God.

Confession

Jesus Christ! Anointed with Holy Ghost and power is going about doing good, healing the sick, releasing those who are in the bondage of the evil one. Be thou glorified in my history! (Acts 10: 38)

'I am for peace, but when I speak, they are for war.' Psalm 120:7

The Triumph of the True God

Even though the thief and bad tenant have occupied the house and damaged all the property in the house, yet the owner of the house will one day remember his property; he will deal with the wicked occupant and cast him into prison, and there the occupant will pay the price of his wickedness.

He who has set a mission of deliverance by sending the law and the prophets has finally made a way and suddenly found Himself among His people to extend those victories of old to all the children of men up to the ends of the earth. When this Most Ancient Spirit was manifested from the living Ark of the Covenant created by God Himself, the gods and all its princes gathered in vain against Him, having appeared in the most vulnerable form—they thought they could eliminate Him but failed in their efforts because the earth drained away all the poison vomited up by these impostors who destroyed the nature of the old man by posing as gods.

What did they not do to crush this Day Spring from on high? Having prepared all their weapons to challenge Him on His arrival, thinking that He would appear as a warrior, 'He outdid them in foxiness' and appeared as a baby, yet not without glory as the Almighty. He was chased into Egypt, yet He returned back to the Promised Land and spiritualised the way from Egypt as the way of salvation. The gods knew too well that He had arrived because they felt His presence and also they understood the ministries of the law and prophets. They must fight because no wise lord would quietly sit down and wash as his kingdom was taken over by another. Even though the latter might be stronger, the former must make the most noise before he succumbs or is bound by the new king.

The birth of Christ was the manifestation of the holy intention of the Almighty God who left the children of men behind as it were, to purify the root of the Word Incarnate in the children of Jacob.

As we said earlier, Israelites themselves were not free from the manipulations of the fallen angels, but were in fact in bondage as well, even when Christ was ushered in. The difference was that God adopted them to start the work of salvation, which they too were hoping for. In truth the whole law and the prophets were the ministry of hope towards the arrival of Christ the Messiah; therefore they too directly confessed that they were in bondage.

Because of this contradiction that was working in them, we see that they laboured so much for the arrival of the Messiah, yet they became the biggest stumbling block for Him when He arrived. The authority in place that was waiting for Him chased Him out of the land—making life painful for His parents and killing new-born babies in an attempt to destroy Him. This was the extent of ugliness of their nature, in spite of the seal of God they carried on their body, yet they hated and fought God as well as worshipping Him. This is why God will never allow any nature of old man into His rest. It is not a thing of past, for the nature of man continues in this manner of multiple personalities which do not recognise God. A man will pray to God asking for one favour or the other, but when God responds to his request, you will see the same man plunged into more confusion, not recognising the deeds of the Lord because the nature of old man is contrary to the will of God. His prayers are answered, yet he is looking forward to it. For instance, we ask for the meek and humble heart of Jesus; but when humiliations and trials come, which will produce the grace we have asked for, we totally reject them because we do not recognise His voice or the sign of time, for we dwell in the old self and refuse to relent through mortification.

Christ fulfilled three ministries for our salvation: in the spiritual realm of man, in the physical realm of man and in the spiritual realm of the dead. The spiritual realm of man took Him thirty years; the physical realm of man was three years, while the spiritual realm of the dead took Him three days. All these He did in honour of the three persons in Godhead.

In spite of the entire powers of the gods working in the whole populace in the days of His flesh, Christ prevailed and grew up in favour and wisdom before God and man. His mission and ministry was truly a conquering adventure even as it is stated in the law; but not the manner in which it was understood by the Jews, who were expecting Him to be a material warlord. Throughout His days both from His infancy, He was binding many demons and powers in chain, delivering the land from all negative elements of His rivals.

Before accomplishing a deliverance of any kingdom or nation, there must be environmental, ecological and archaeological deliverance; otherwise the minister of the deliverance is ministering in vain. We know that an environment can be infested and when a land is not fertile, there is every tendency that it will never produce healthy tree—or food crops. These He accomplished before He could stand on that land to preach as the Lord of all Spirits; thus people who witnessed His ministry bore witness that He acted with authority. 'And they were astonished at His teaching, for His word was with authority.' (Luke 4: 32)

This hidden ministry of Christ was not known by natural man because he had lost spiritual sensitivity; but Christ, being a new man as Adam was and God at the same time, was able to coexist in the spirit. He reversed back to the days of Adam in the garden and destroyed all the rules of the fallen angels. For a warrior to conquer and establish his dynasty, he must first bind the strong men who are the source of power, otherwise the war will take too long. This is exactly what Christ did to all the principalities and powers that were in control of the world. It was when this work of caging the evil spirits was accomplished that He traced St John the Baptist to the river Jordan for His baptism so that He could work on humanity as well—casting out and binding the demons which had blocked their hearts and infested their souls. If Christ had not conquered the spiritual realm of man, His teachings would not have rested in the few hearts that accepted Him before His death and resurrection.

He descended into the water; and on His coming out the Holy Spirit declared and confirmed the truth of His divinity, calling all men not only to listen to Him but also to follow Him in denial of old nature. Now He is truly a man, a scapegoat and a Lamb of God who takes the sins of the world on Himself. Now He will face the evil spirits that are deeply seated in man—suffering all the punishment that man deserves and also healing man and adopting him.

After His baptism, 'He was led by the Spirit into the wilderness.' Coming out victoriously after His temptations, He was filled with the Holy Spirit and entered the synagogue to begin His teaching ministry. But He must declare who He is before He proceeds with His Messianic ministry because in the heart of the law, the Messiah must be an outstanding figure. With His glorious and domineering presence, the Scroll of the prophet Isaiah was handed over to Him. Opening it, He read:

'The Spirit of the Lord is upon me, for He has anointed me to preach the Gospel to the poor, to heal the broken-hearted, to preach deliverance to captives and recovery of sight to the blind and acceptable year of the Lord.' (Luke 4: 17-21)

The joy of the imminent appearance of the Messiah flooded the minds of everyone in the temple as He was reading out this prophecy in a reverberating voice that was never heard before, like that which Moses heard on Mount Sinai. As He finished and sat down, there was stillness, as everybody was looking at Him as if they had not heard that prophecy before. Then He declared to them that this Scripture was fulfilled that day in their hearing.

Every Jewish man knew that this Scripture could only be fulfilled by the coming of the Messiah, so they could not contain their amazement. 'Who is He making Himself to be?' This was their question, knowing pretty well that He had just claimed to be the long-expected Messiah, although He was an ordinary carpenter from Galilee. He could not be the Messiah because to them the Messiah would have been a warlord who must have fought his way into being recognised and proclaimed as the Messiah. None of the people in the temple were ready to give a second thought to what had taken place in the centre of their hope, except the few disciples of John the Baptist who were in the river when John declared Christ as the Messiah; to them the spiritual insight was given that this was He.

In spite of this first attack on His identity, Christ moved on with His ministry, having accepted some of John the Baptist's disciples as His own; they too were very happy being accepted as His companions. With the glory that radiates from Christ, which made these first followers so complete, they made a request of Him: 'Where do you stay?' Christ did not hesitate to take them home knowing well that their intention was to venerate and pay homage to such a blessed family that had given birth to a long-expected prophet. On arriving they found it was a simple house with His mother, as Joseph had already died. They venerated His mother for being such a holy woman to give birth to Him whom the prophets had 'placed the hope of Israel and the entire world on.' And they stayed the whole day with Him. (John 1: 39)

Through different circumstances in His ministry, Christ continued to choose His disciples until they were completed: the new Israel that the Holy Spirit would use in the later days to reach the ends of the earth. These apostles He formed with both His public and private teachings knowing well that He was not going to be with them for too long. According to the Gospel, we notice that these apostles were formerly ordinary people who had gone about their different businesses, but they left all those things behind as soon as He called them into the ministry of salvation of mankind and they never went back to their respective families or business, bearing in mind that, 'No one who places his hand on the plough and then looks back is worthy for the kingdom of God.' (Luke 9: 62)

This is a strict call of apostolic work; and the apostles who preached it championed it because they were truly formed according to the mind of Christ, who loved them as friends and brothers, to become a new family bonded in one doctrine of love. One who gives into a deep thought about the bond and formation of the apostles would see that it was never the will of Christ to have hundreds of denominations of Christianity as we have today but rather it was the original character of man to do things in his own way which counters the message of love and oneness.

In His three years of ministry, Christ fulfilled the law and the ministries of the prophets and established Himself, being the kingdom of God in person. The kingdom of God is freedom, righteousness and completeness; thus His ministry was deliverance, teaching and healing.

Having dealt with the root of all evil spirits in their spiritual foundations, He faced them in the natures of man. In Luke 4: 33-36, we see the strange event of a man who was one of the worshippers in the synagogue and yet with an unclean demon. Crying out, he said, 'Let us alone! What have we to do with you, Jesus of Nazareth? Have you come to destroy us? I know who you are—the holy one of the Lord!'

You can see that the human beings He had come to save did not recognise Him nor did they acknowledge the hour of the visitation of the Lord they had been waiting for, but the demons did. They knew that He was the Lord and they were so terrified at His glorious presence as the light of the world He was—who shone in the darkness but the darkness could not comprehend it. This story is a typical example of what the nature of man is, even in the presence of God. Imagine if the fiery personality like Christ was not in the temple that day—this man would have been parading around in the synagogue as a true worshipper.

This is still what is taking place today in the house of prayers and church; somebody may be in the first pew in the church and says yes to Christ while he or she is possessed. Thus ministers of today's Gospel are in big trouble if they dare speak about certain types of life people live and still refer themselves as Christians, because many are now possessed by demons of all kinds. The problem facing Christianity today is not directly from people outside but from people who confess Christ but have their hearts fixed in the basic things of the world. They attack the authority of the Scripture and church traditions, not because they are in their right senses but because a particular spirit is at work in them. These things happen when people harden their hearts to live according to their natural disorder even in the presence of God, because they are being driven by the old spirit of man.

The ministry of Christ was a ministry of God in human form, as we can see in all His actions, and in the reaction of the populace in His days who observed in Him as one who acts like God or possessed the power of God. Christ in all His days, being humility Himself, did not directly say in the Scripture that He is God; but He let people confess it through His teachings and works which only God can do. He who denied Himself as God just to save man would not be going about telling people that He is God, but rather His attributes followed Him to bear witness to the truth. This is what the centurion saw in Him when he said to Him, 'Only say a word and my servant shall be healed, for I am a man of authority who commands people to do my wish and it's done.' He had the intuition that, as God, Christ was surrounded by all manner of ministering angels to serve His commands in fulfilment of His mission, God being a shepherd of the people of Israel from of old, as Psalms 23 and 80 said.

In the days of His flesh, Christ also declared Himself as a good shepherd who not only fed and tended His sheep but gave His life for the lives of His sheep. In the parable of the lost sheep, Christ manifested Himself as the same ancient God and shepherd who did not mind the smelly nature and festering wounds of His sheep, but stooped down to soothe them with oil. He did not mind the dungeon they had fallen into; He jumped in too and was referred to as one of them just to get them back into the fold.

During the healing of the paralytic man, there was a manifestation of the divinity of Christ as God who forgives sins. And seeing their faith, He said to him, 'Man, your sins are forgiving you.' In reasoning the Pharisees began to say, 'Who can forgive sin but God alone?' Because the forgiveness of sin belongs to God alone and Christ used this ministry to prove His nature as God though He did not say it directly. His action-speaks-louder-than-words mission was the same, when St John the Baptist sent some of his followers to ask Him about His true identity. But instead of Him saying yes to John's question, which required yes or no, He got up from His position and started to manifest healing: giving sight to the blind, making the lame walk, while the dumb started singing, and numerous people were delivered from the power of darkness. And He sent the followers back to John saying, 'Tell him all that you see.' Making the citation of the Scripture recorded by the prophet Isaiah concerning the days when God will visit His people in flesh, He sat down and continued His teaching. Yet in all this indirect revelation of Himself, they did not recognise the God of the Mountain of Sinai in their midst. (Compare Isaiah 35: 5-6 and Luke 7: 18-22)

... ...

'Your sins are forgiven you.' These are the words of healing that Christ proclaimed upon the same paralytic man, and his healing took place. Does it mean that this man's infirmities were a result of sin? The populace in the days of Christ understood some sicknesses as a result of sin, either sins of the parents or personal sin. When we look into the Scriptural background of this mystery, it's obvious that failings in observing the law most times can bring curses. Many things can be the course of maladies, not necessarily sin; but in the case of this paralytic man, it was sin, thus Christ gave him forgiveness as his healing medicine. In another incident, Christ repeated a similar ministry with a clearer statement about the effects of sin. At the pool of Bethesda, a certain man was there with an infirmity of thirty-eight years; when Jesus saw him, He was filled with pity and He said to him, 'Rise, take your bed and walk.' But afterwards Jesus found him in the temple and said to him, 'See, you have been made well. Sin no more, lest a worst thing come upon you.' (Compare John 5: 1-14)

This is a theology of sin and its temporal consequences to those that dwell in the love of God. To them, it is purification which pulls them closer to God who is holy and called His people to be holy like Him. Note that these two people, though they had been in this pain for a number of years, still loved and sought the face of God who forgives and heals His people even though they may have sinned greatly. They were examples of His children who do not despise the chastening of the Lord, and are not discouraged by being rebuked by Him because He loves them. (Compare Hebrew 12: 5-8)

To those who love Him, He keeps them in His constant care to prevent them from eternal condemnation; He does not hesitate to raise them up from the ground and cleanse them if they fall because He want them to appear before His father in the most perfect state. Those who disregard Him are left as misbegotten, because His love and mystery are not clearly manifested in them; they said, 'He does not see nor punish.' They do all manner of evil and prosper all round according to the basic principles of the world. Thus Psalm 37: 2 said you should not envy them for they are here today and tomorrow are gone. For wrath is well reserved for them.

Even though some people since the law was given suffered as a result of breaking the law, it was also a great truth that many people, both great and small, even in the days of Christ were evil in so many ways against the law of God and yet enjoyed the good health and prosperity which led them more out of the love of God and brought great judgement on them towards the end of their lives to prove the Lordship and greatness of God. Consider Herod; he died the most horrible death when he reached the highest level of evil of exalting himself as god. Worms were ministered into his flesh while he was still alive and he died a miserable and shameful death.

As we said, sin is not necessarily the course of sickness. Sometimes demons can gather against man to bring troubles and sickness as in the life of Job; but God's vindication must surely prevail at last. Thus the Psalm said that 'Many are the trials of the just man, but God will surely deliver him at last.' In Luke 13: 10-16 we see Christ's encounter with the spirit of infirmity. The woman's name is not mentioned, but it is said that she had this sickness for eighteen years; Satan bound her for no stated reason but Christ released her because she was a daughter of Abraham which means that she was at peace with God being addressed by Christ as the daughter of Abraham. In another case of blindness, Christ defended the victim saying, 'Neither this man nor his parents sinned, but that the work of God should be revealed in him.'

This is truly a very difficult mystery to assimilate that things sometimes must go wrong somehow, so that the nature and existence of God will be clearly seen, whether by our mistakes or a natural phenomenon. For man is at very high risk of losing the sense of God when everything goes smoothly because the world is not a permanent home for a true child of God. Thus certain things we experience in life are necessary, though they may be very difficult to put up with, but God allows this to make a name for Himself and also to exalt us into the true knowledge of Himself—without which it is impossible to know who He is, who called Himself Our Father and God.

In His teachings, Jesus used common events of His days to teach and preach the message of the kingdom of God. Most of His messages were cast in parables to the humble hearts alone that can only be patient enough to contemplate the truth of God. We call them parables because we see them as a way of expressing the word, but truly those parables He used in teaching were all events that took place in different parts of the world; for He is the eye who oversees the whole universe. Remember that He has been God since before time; He cannot invent things which have not taken place in the world in order to teach because He is not imagining things but rather speaking the truth about the nature of God and man. For instance, in the parable of the prodigal son, He was telling of a practical event that took place somewhere known only to Him for though the nature of man has been corrupted, yet the goodness of God can still manifest itself in man—for, notwithstanding the corruption in gold, it will still reflect some characteristics of gold.

Any good father who knows what it takes to have a child and watch him grow, bearing all the difficulties of raising a child, will not hesitate to welcome that child back home and still treat him as a son even though he may have embezzled lots of his wealth—inasmuch as he comes back home with a repentant heart and in brokenness. I have seen lots of good parents who battled with the wind and all manner of evil to get their children back on the right track even when those children were not ready to repent, yet those good parents never gave up until their expected result was achieved; how much more so when a lost child suddenly comes back home and knocks at door, even at midnight. In His teaching, Christ asks, 'If you evil fathers know how to give good things to your child, how much more will the father in heaven give good things to those who ask Him?'

Christ did not use this story to compare His love. His love is more highly exalted than that because man who has squandered the wealth and treasures of God in him did not even know how to get back to his father's house; he has lost his identity to his captor and has forgotten his origin. Yet Christ left His kingdom and glory to search for him and when He came to His own, his own did not recognise Him having stayed too long in exile, yet He humbled Himself and started afresh to reintroduce Himself to man as his father and God. Jesus is using this parable to explain the things of the spirit in the manner which human mind can contemplate and comprehend them. The best way of understanding little about His love and mercy is to meditate on His death on the cross even when we are still in sin; and this will expand your understanding that His mercy is greater than that of the merciful father in the prodigal son parable. Note that the prodigal son had repented before his acceptance, but man was still in his faraway country when this merciful father left His glorious kingdom and came for him, denying His divinity to take on humanity. Christ died for us even when we were sinners.

God who manifested Himself in Christ is indeed a father and friend of sinners as the Pharisees and Scribes concluded in Mathew 15: 2. If Christ was seldom found in the midst of sinners, of what purpose is His appearance? This is what I come to understand practically: that a Christian is a sinner who accepted Christ in truth and in spirit and surrendered his miseries to Christ, for Him to begin His work of transformation with our cooperation. In the book of Revelation, He said, 'Behold, I stand at the door and knock, if anyone will hear my voice and will open the door to me, I will come in to him, and I will dine with him, and he with me.' (Revelation 3: 20) No one is good! Not even one. Thus He came and never hesitated to go to any house into which He is welcomed, no matter who dwells in it, for He is the only lover of soul.

Because He was the fullness of man, Christ was subjected to learning things and experiences just like an ordinary man: a sign of contradiction that follows Him as God and Man in one, as the prophet Simeon prophesied at His presentation. We see that throughout His ministry, He spent most of His night in prayer and mystical meetings with His father, who sent Him into the world to answer man, to know and feel the true condition of man and to pay the debts of all men. In these meetings, He presents to His Father all the problems of His brethren, which He learnt through experience. As a representative of man, Christ with His father decide how the new solution will be put in place; then the next day He comes out with new teaching, extending the ministry that used to be God's deeds alone to man and the people of His days marvelled at the kind of miracle they saw Him performing, which had never been seen before—He has given the same power to those who truly believe in Him.

It was a complete negotiation—for even as there was deep counsel within the depth of God, Father, His Word and His Spirit before the creation of man, so there was greater council during man's redemption between the Father, His Son and Holy Spirit through all the days of Christ. The Father is God alone, the Word who took flesh and answered the Son is both the fullness of God and Man; He comes to the Father and says, 'This is how men feel, these are the difficulties they have—this is what we would do for their salvation.' Thus sometimes Christ uses this phrase, 'It has been said, but I said to you.' Bear in mind that Christ is the fruit of the marriage between God and humanity; and as a result of that, He stands in the gap to bring humanity to God and also to bring God to humanity. Know you that God as father cannot suffer but Christ as God man was capable of suffering; all that He obtained for man from His father's throne was not without sacrifice. He suffered so much for man not only for the salvation, but for all the authority He gave to man—transferring His inheritance to man to act like God in so many ways. 'As the father sent me, so I send you.' He established His mission even as it was in His earthly days. Christ Jesus is a new nature indeed because He is the new image of man which we will all have when this exile is over.

He gave man the power of giving new life through the mystery of water and Holy Spirit, when He said, 'Go therefore and make disciples of all nations, baptising them in the name of the father and of the son and of the Holy Spirit.' Forgiving and retaining sins, casting out demons in His name, to bind and to release, exalting man to the level of offering the mystical Lamb of God to God, and most of all knowing the depths of the wickedness of the demons, He allowed Himself to be tabernacled on earth as an everlasting presence till the end of the world. If it were not for Christ in the Eucharistic presence, the demons would have swallowed the whole world in anger after the redemption of man. But He has truly conquered the world; He established His kingdom on earth, dwelt there in flesh and blood, and declared that the gate of hell shall not prevail against her.

All these authorities and gifts obtained by Christ for man was sealed when He died on the cross and poured out His blood on these gifts and all He had obtained for man as an everlasting inheritance. Thus He is the eternal High Priest and Lamb for the offering; and this office will continue until all the elects are made priests to serve God.

This inversion and triumph of God upon the gods of the world is completed when Christ Jesus fulfilled His Messianic ministry, having anointed His apostles with His power and sent them into the whole world. When Christ was still among them teaching, He did not allow them to go beyond the borders of Israel with their teaching because He had not yet paid the price of the sins of the whole human family, but after His sacrifice on the cross and resurrection, He sent them on the mission of new creation to the whole world with the ministry of baptism. He empowered them to teach: 'Whoever listens to you, listens to me.' Even as the Father sent Him, He also sent them, thereby giving them authority over all the flesh and evil spirits.

As we mentioned above about the council, which took place between the persons in God, this was where the work of Holy Spirit was separated from that of the son. It is the work of the Son to establish the new dispensation and, being God in the flesh, He sealed it with His blood to complete the redemption. The work of the Holy Spirit is to spread the Gospel of salvation, to work in us until He convinces us of the truth—banishing the spirit of natural man, which contradicts the eternal truth. Thus Christ always says to them that the Holy Spirit 'will guide you to all knowledge'.

When Christ was commissioning His apostles, He did not fail to tell them to tarry in Jerusalem until the Holy Spirit was given to them which would only come when He ascended back into heaven. This they did after His ascension until the Holy Spirit was poured upon their new life and radicalised their spirits, equipping them with the power of heaven without which no one can wrestle and defeat the deep-rooted gods of the world in our nature. 'He ascended into high and held the captivity captive and distributed all His gifts,' as the Psalm said. These gifts are the Holy Spirit, the third Person and nature of God who fills the earth as the water covers the seabed.

Previously, after the death of Christ, most of the apostles were filled with sorrow and regrets. 'If I had known, I would have continued with my fishing and looked after my family, I would have continued with my tax collection, I would have carried on with my master's business and by now I would have been a man of my own and raising a family; now all my hope is lost. We were hoping that He was the only Messiah who would save us and we have been building our hopes around Him; where is He now?' Even the devil spoke and appeared to them with the voices and faces of Judas Iscariot, making a mockery of them that Jesus was not the Christ.

The apostles suffered so much mostly because, by the mystery of God, their minds could not retain all the truth that had been revealed to them by Christ when He was with them; seeing the horrible way in which He died, they did not remember that He said He would be killed and rise up again on the third day. The tradition declared that they were confused. In a state of dilemma they could not balance the great power of His miracles, the exalted glories, with the kind of humility with which He surrendered Himself to death. All these and more were the darkness that Christ's beloved apostles went through: a torture of a kind that is beyond a certain understanding, unless you have passed through similar experiences secretly supported by the grace of God.

The apostles' fear, doubt, confusions and sorrows at losing Christ were cast away when He rose from death and reminded them what had been said about His death and Resurrection by Himself and by the prophets and Psalms. Even after the Resurrection, and all the miracles He performed in their midst before His ascension, they were still left with shock and sorrow until He replaced Himself by this same presence of God in their midst but in another form who is called the Spirit of truth. Christ was the physical presence of God with them, but the Holy Spirit is God's presence in their spirit. The apostles who used to hide and were afraid of death were filled with boldness, confessing the whole truth they knew about God and all the darkness they had experienced before became a thing of the past. It is good sometimes for Christ to die in our lives so that we may be energised more when He is resurrected again and we find Him.

Even though the apostles were filled with the Holy Spirit, they did not find it easy at all as the fallen angels who are deeply rooted in man raised the cruellest persecution against them even from the heart of the temple. This is a gross contradiction. If Jesus of Nazareth was truly the Messiah and the son of God, why did He suffer persecution from His infancy up to His death and the same persecutions follow His apostles and everything that concerned Him? Why did the holy nation who sacrificed so much for His arrival totally reject Him?

The truth is that He must be God. God has never found it easy to deal with man though He is God who created them. Because a contaminated nature of man is always in conflict with God and God in turn is always too careful in reintroducing Himself to man; man being too delicate, God handles him with patience lest He injure him. Moses whom He used to accomplish deliverance narrowly escaped being stoned to death, though they followed him and pledged allegiance to him—yet it was like when a ram is separated from the flocks of a wild group. We may be saying good things about Moses now because we have seen what he accomplished, but I tell you, the Israelites in his days saw him as a prophet of God yet the nature of demon in them hated him for depriving them of the cucumber they ate in Egypt—preferring bondage to the freedom of a loving God. Just as Christ was persecuted, so too were Moses and all the prophets persecuted, but the big difference is that the prophets displayed the divine power of defence they had over man to extricate themselves from certain situations, as we see in the case of the two families of Dathan and Abiram who were swallowed alive for challenging Moses. (Compare Deuteronomy 11: 6)

But instead of defending Himself, Christ accepted the humiliations and silently said to His Father, 'Do not punish them, rather let their punishments be mine'. For He came to save man, and not to condemn man. We see this when the Samaritans rejected Him and His disciples wanted to command fire to come down from heaven to consume them. But Christ rebuked them. (Compare Luke 11: 54-55)

This is exactly how the prophets before Him proved their mission—for God who spoke in the prophets before Christ did not tolerate rivals until He accomplished His decree. Because of this, the populace in the days of Christ were expecting Him to act in a like manner; because He did not, this makes Him who He claimed to be: a Saviour, everlasting father, lover and the King of the prophets.

One of the major marks of the work of God is difficulty and persecutions; having been what marked the life of Christ, these will not fail to be the portion of the apostles newly equipped with God's fiery spirit. The major work of the Holy Spirit on the newly recreated Apostles was to equip them with all the necessary dynamism to battle with and conquer all the powers of the gods of the universe. Christ had suffered the most horrible death to redeem man and had laid down the foundation of His church; next was to build and spread this good news, which had come down from heaven.

Initially, as we see in the Acts of The Apostle, although Christ established His church as a new covenant in fulfilment of all He had spoken through the prophets and as a continuation of God's salvific ministry, His apostles continued with the established temple worship even as their master did all the days of His life. Because the church, which is the true divine worship, brought down from heaven the message and the hope of the old covenant. The old covenant was a shadow, and the new covenant is the true light; these two were supposed to agree with each other in the physical even as they truly agreed in spirit, until the latter survived the former—for they are both from one God. But the hypocrisy, blindness and veil that covered the Sanhedrin could not allow them to accept the answer to the prayers they had been making since God established a covenant with Abraham; so they rejected the church and all the teachings of the apostles.

When the angel of the Lord released Peter and John from the prison, he did not say to them, 'Go and establish the church since the Jews have rejected Christ.' Rather he commanded them to go to the temple and continue to preach the good news and the word of this life. (Acts 5: 20) This is what they and all the apostles continued to do, irrespective of all the obstacles, sufferings and death they faced all day. After St Paul was converted, he continued to live as a Jew preaching Christ's doctrine among them as the fulfilment of the law they had been waiting for. God had seen the future hardness of their hearts and had spoken concerning the great light that would shine on the Gentiles because of Israel's rejection of the Gospel. Blessed be the wisdom of God! For the children of the kingdom rejected the gospel and that made it possible for the Gentiles to be called the children of God. The king of darkness knew too well that if the apostles were left alone, they would convert the whole Jews; therefore he raised the highest persecution on them, through his nature working in the hearts of natural men.

With this persecution aimed at destroying the apostles and the complete annihilation of the holy name of Jesus, God who makes everything to work for good turned their wickedness into a means of spreading His Gospel to the Gentiles who did not know God. If the persecution did not rise, probably the apostles would have remained and limited their ministry within the borders of Israel as most of them still had the instinct that the Gentiles were not worthy of God. So God who is wise in His counsel allowed them to go through the torture of persecution to spread His victory over the gods of the world. (A mighty ukpaka tree has a stubborn seed that is too hard to crack unless it is exposed to the highest heat of the sun.) This is exactly what persecution has done to the apostles: cracking the seed of the eternal life of the whole world, which Christ deposited in them. As they ran for their lives, the Gospel spread with them to Europe, Africa and Asia—a triumph of the only true God because the more plant seeds are attacked by animals and the wind, the more these adversaries help to carry them to more fertile land and favourable places for growth and survival.

The Holy Spirit worked so marvellously with them; even though they were all scattered they were so united in the Holy Spirit and established the church with the same doctrine of divine worship of breaking of bread as their master commanded them, with Sunday as the divine day of worship because a new man is created. A marvellous thing indeed—worthy of giving more glory to God.

As Christ said, 'A prophet is not acceptable in his own town.' This is what happened to Him and His apostles; they killed Him and chased His apostles away into the Gentile world; and the Gentiles, seeing the wonderful things they did and the richness of the truth they preached, embraced their teachings. In some places, they were even venerated as gods, as people thought that they might be one of the god's incarnate. Truly this is the fulfilment of the old prophecy, 'That those who did not seek God has found Him; I was made manifest to those who did not ask for me', while the children of the kingdom that God had been carrying like a baby were left to their self-seeking righteousness of the old nature.

The whole Gentile world was in total darkness when the light of the Gospel shone upon them, thus they quickly differentiated darkness from light but holy Israel, being under the shadow of the truth, prefers the shadow. We are not saying that it was easy for the apostles in the Gentile world; in fact it was a real tug of war for them to embrace the true God, having been too long with the traditions of the demons that lived among them as gods. This is the same manner in which the Israelites have sacred mountains, days and sites, and the same as the Gentiles have dedicated their entire existence to demons as the astronomical gods, gods of fertilities, love, and harvest—and so many gods even as they still exist today in many cultures. For the church of Christ to penetrate such hydra-headed monsters of the nations shows that God is truth and is excellent in power. All the incantations and divinations against them could not stand because He who sent them on this mission is mighty indeed, shielding them in the blood of the Lamb. They suffered terribly but they prevailed, pulling down all their sacred pillars and trees. We see this continued conflict later in the life of St Boniface, the great apostle of Germany, who cut down the great oak tree and used its timber to construct a temple for the worship of the true God. Those pagan communities waited for him to be struck down by gods, but in vain; they were all converted afterwards. All the apostles acted like Gideon of old who destroyed the altar of Baal to enthrone the God of Israel in the days when the Midianites and Amalekites oppressed the Israelites.

With the holy ministry of Christ, they sanctified and directed to God some of the cultures and traditions they saw among them which were truth but dedicated to the wrong gods. Even though man was corrupted by the fallen angels, yet there were still many good traditions of God retained in old man. These were what the apostles acculturated. But all the abominations of gods were banished and replaced with the righteousness of God. Christianity brought peace, freedom, and truth to the world; she really taught the whole world even as Christ commanded her to do—that the rich, poor, royals, commoners, priests and prophets are all equal in the sight of God. His ministry truly changed darkness into light and those who accepted Him, He made true children of God.

Meditation

All the handwriting and coded signs against man are destroyed in Christ if he is willing to obey.

The Only Choice We Have

Man can predict the weather and get almost accurate results. But can he fathom what the invisible beings hold in store for him? Can he penetrate into the invisible to contribute to the council of the spirits where the destiny of man is defined? The answer is no—for man is left at the mercy of the spirits, both positive and negative, but he who is grafted into the traditions of the eternal God will exist in the authority of His Christ. With Him such person is raised far above all principalities and powers that control the abode of man.

The sense of natural man is totally different and animalistic compared with the spiritual sense, because man is acting and thinking according to the limits of his air space. Be introduced into this truth that the constellations and the planets that are visible to human eyes and intelligence are phantom compared to the invisible kingdoms, territories and planets both within our galaxy and the great beyond. Most times we think that the space is empty; but truly it is occupied by the invisible greater beings. Do not let what your eyes see deceive you or control your understanding—for nothing happens on planet earth by chance. All events take their formation from invisible realities until it is accomplished in our world.

What we are saying here must sound crazy to natural man until Christ, the Head of all principalities and powers, exposes your mystical nature to the invisible realities through His ministry of transformation. Until this is done, natural man cannot see with his inner eye the things that ordinary eyes cannot see, because a natural man is blinded to the things of the spirit, having been trapped in human inclination and intellectual pride. Pray that the grace of God may invade you to put your animal nature in check, for only then will lots of things be made clear to you. Pray also that you may survive the heat that follows, because it's not easy when a spiritual window is opened to a living man.

Man has made scientific and technological advancements but spiritually he is lagging behind, having side-tracked God in his culture; man's spiritual advancement towards God has stopped and man has become contaminated and his spirit addicted to the material things of the world. If the old spirit of man trapped in the flesh could manage to do great scientific exploits, what will happen if he in humility should surrender that knowledge to his higher spirit who is connected to God? But in his pride in the imitation of his master, he denied God, his conscience darkened by the gods of this age. (2 Corinthians 4: 4)

This was what happened to Charles Darwin who invented the theory of evolution, once he made that scientific discovery which is spiritually incorrect and the greatest attack on the cradle of man. He slowly withdrew from going to church, even though he had a good religious wife. In my own understanding and opinion, any knowledge that leads man to the denial of the existence of God should not be accepted by those who believe in God—knowing that such knowledge is from the underworld and aimed at leading people to atheism, just as the people who invented them. The truth of this is that the science of evolution may be truth to a natural man whose spirit is inseparable with his flesh; he is carnally minded. Within the spiritual theology of the existence of man, it is the greatest fallacy and the decay of the eternal truth of God in the heart of man. To believe it is a crime in the spirit, because man was not an animal before the fall of Adam. He was more of the spirit that he did not realise that he had flesh until he sinned and fell down to the planet of the animals and was struggling in vain to step up until Christ came.

It is a crime indeed and a contradiction, when Christ, your Lord and master, said that, 'God made them male and female from the beginning'; and one who claimed to be Christ savant says otherwise. Remember so well that He said, 'The servant cannot be greater than his master.'

Man was a spirit; man is a spirit and will continue to be a spirit when his exile in the planet of animals is over. Man fell from a greater realm to a lower realm, not the other way round. Did the Bible not say that God created man in His own image and likeness? How do you think that God made man in His image only to procreate like other animals, which were not created in the image of God, but rather were just formed by the spoken word? Was man created by spoken word like other animals? If God did not create man with His spoken word but in a unique manner after deeper counsel within Himself, then we must accept this truth: that the animal nature as we have it now was as a result of the fall of man, not the original nature of man but his hidden nature that manifested itself when he found himself in the material world. Therefore man did not metamorphose from lower to higher, but rather from higher to lower, so that he may become a true spiritual man created and born out of the spirit of God Himself without anything earthly found in him when his exile is over in the fullness of time. This is what Christ has accomplished in giving us new spiritual creation.

The reason why God allowed man into the territory of scientific knowledge was to go beyond those discoveries that are earthly minded into the search of the Supreme Being who created and fixed the planets. But instead man chooses the way of rebellion, thinking that he is wise. No human intelligence, eloquence or science can fathom the mystery of God or the foundation He laid in the creation of the world and man who is His greatest visible attributes. The Scripture has said it all: 'For as the heavens are higher than the earth, so are my ways higher than your ways, and my thoughts than your thoughts.' (Isaiah 55: 9)

The greatest aberration of human intelligence is to dare to humanise heaven, comparing spiritual things with the glory of the natural man who is reduced to animal instinct: the glory of the animal planet trying to define the universe, of which he is just a little dot in one of the kingdoms called planet.

What would they have done if they were exposed to a little bit of what the spirits of the saints of Christ were made to see? What we called planets is called kingdoms in the spirit. There are hundreds of kingdoms created by God. You will cry for the deceit of some of our scientific findings when your mystical eyes gaze beyond unapproachable light. Yes! The saints were exposed to the mystical consciousness of the eternal truth, which is kept out of the most learned and wise men of all ages. This is what St Paul was shown in 2 Corinthians 12: 1-5.

St Thomas Aquinas, one of the greatest philosophers, was also exposed to a deeper mystery when he was writing his Summer Theologica. His vision during the mass in December 1273 moved him to stop and leave the work unfinished. He said, 'All I have written seems to me like a straw in comparison to what I have seen and the mystery revealed to me. Yet some of the scientists who have not gone beyond the first heaven claimed to know more and rejected the existence of God. Their pride has deprived them of the knowledge beyond the visible because a natural man has the visible constellations as his limit.'

The beatific experience is one of the secret of the saints, thus they were able to turn their backs on the fake treasures of the world, having been introduced to the reality of the true light which illuminates the world. Pray son of man! That your inner eyes may behold this truth; otherwise the intellectual bravado of the natural man will toss you around and put your precious soul at the greatest risk. If one's joy and freedom do not go beyond the worldly treasures, one may lose one's soul.

The mysteries and the knowledge about God is hidden, released only to the humbles. As I said of the Apostles, though God is invisible beyond the contemplation of the prophets, He is a consuming fire to the old nature and His glory transforms Moses' face after a meeting with the Lord to the extent that the children of Israel could not look at his face. Yet these apostles believed and accepted Christ the fruit of Virgin Mary's womb as God who visited His people. Christ rejoiced in spirit praising His Father for hiding these things from the wise and prudent and revealed them to babes. (Compare Luke 10: 21.) Because notwithstanding the wisdom of the most learned, without Christ, all their exploits will remain only for the benefit of the animal nature of man which has no place in eternity.

The syndrome core of this thesis is that man must acknowledge and accept Christ; otherwise one's knowledge will lead one astray—for having great knowledge without Christ will always lead to utter foolishness, just as the Bible said that it is only a fool who says there is no God.

In the Gospel of John Chapter 3, Christ said that He was not sent to condemn the world, but that the world through Him might be saved. Through all His teaching, Christ operated within the context of this above citation: giving freedom to the captive, healing all manner of sickness, setting free those who were condemned by the law of Moses as we see in the case of the woman caught in the act of adultery, while those who had been struck dead by the spirit of death were revived. Truly He did all things well even as the populace confessed; for He never considered the unworthiness of any sick person before He extended His healing and his friendly hands to them. He who extended His hand to man also wanted man to extend his own hand back to Him, responding to His call to new life so the mission of Christ might be fulfilled in one's life.

... ...

Answering a Christian name or Christian nation has less to do with Christ unless one is committed to the core truth of Christ who was manifested for freedom of those who believe in Him. He continued to say that not believing in Him is already a condemnation upon a man. Why? Because without Him man is old nature, condemned in the spirit of Adam, and as a result he can do nothing good, as the Scripture says.

Know you that not knowing Christ is getting stuck to the core nature of man whose whole imagination is evil from birth, and he must remain as such because that new nature that is born through water and spirit by the invocation of the Holy Trinitarian name of God is not found in him; therefore he remains animal nature and dies the same. The manner of our understanding of the concept of following Christ should not just be a member of His church, just as we have different types of religion that preach the right way of living; rather following Him is a total new nature of man being born in you—a unique and exalted life far above all that is called the way of life—for life has no way of it, so to speak, rather than one living the true life which is in Christ Jesus.

People always say, 'I have found the way of life', maybe because some religions define their teaching as a way of life. But remember what you are being introduced into: that there is no way of life the old nature of man can find, neither can he find any true identity of self than losing his old nature and taking on the new nature of Christ, which is the true image of God in which the true man was created. This is the product of the new covenant and fulfilment of the promise which He made in Jeremiah 31:31-34. 'Behold the days are coming when I will make a new covenant with the house of Israel and Judah—for they all shall know me from the least of them to the greatest of them, says the Lord.'

This is the apogee of this mystery, when the fullness of growth is completed through the mystery of Christ. Souls will be able to live solely in the truth of God firmly re-established in the fertile garden to bear fruits, having grown high above the standard of the natural man. This is a state in which he does not need a teacher because he is connected directly to the Holy Spirit who begot him; no longer is he living, for Christ is living in him. Taking back that position he had lost in the garden, nearest to the angels of light, doing everything in union with them including feeding on the bread of the angels that is Christ Jesus. Angels of heaven and the earthly children of God are united in adoration.

We are not saying something new or imagined here, but rather we are declaring the eternal truth dictated in the spirit that has been prophesied and hoped for. This was the foreknowledge of King David when he prophesied in the Psalms that, 'In guilt I was born, a sinner was I conceived'. (Psalm 51: 7)

We know that he was not born out of marriage as their understanding has it even in the day of Christ—that anybody born out of marriage has no place in the family of God. When Christ referred them as the children of the devil, they were making a jest of Him and nearly stoned Him to death, defending the nobility of their birth: 'We were not born of fornication; we have one father—God.' (John 8: 41)

David was born into a family of a devout Jews, yet he prophesied this new birth we are proclaiming, acknowledging that human nature has been contaminated from Adam and Eve on. He who confessed to God that he was born in sin was also crying for cleansing, probably for a rebirth, knowing that God can do all things even as he confessed in the Psalms.

It is a grace of God and light of the Holy Spirit to understand the mystery of Christ; His nature and the nature He bestowed on all the believers through His holy baptism. In the Gospel of John it is said:

'But as many as received Him, to them He gave the right to become children of God, even to those who believe in His name: who were born, not of blood, nor of the will of flesh, nor of the will of man, but of God.' (John 1: 12-13)

This is where the Holy Spirit defined the nature of Christ and the new mystical creation of man. This is what sums up the mission of Christ as God who came to recreate man. It takes the Holy Spirit for one's spirit to be open to the understanding and acceptance of this verse as it is. This is a clear statement about the new nature received in baptism; they were not born of blood or the will of the flesh. This means that this new nature is not the product of sensuality and sexual intercourse between male and female or the desire of the flesh. Not of the will of man—which means not by natural order of procreation, the way all of us were born; the natural birth is out of question in this matter. In other words, it does not matter, for this new creation is born of God through water and spirit. It is being nurtured by God, hears and obeys only His voice. Because the nature of God is not male or female, this new nature is also neither male nor female, therefore he stays virgin all the days he may dwell in the temple called man and cannot procreate because his procreative mystery is only through water and the spirit, while his animal nature procreates. Thus in Christ's mystical teaching, He said that the resurrected nature neither marry nor be given in marriage but will be just like the Angels in heaven. What a mystery of righteousness God has bestowed on the new nature of man, who can only experience the resurrection of the just with the fullness of the spiritual body.

This is the greatest mystery—that through water and spirit, new life is created within the old man. Once one is grafted into the whole mystery of Christ, there is a new nature in him and he must strive for its growth, because that human nature given birth by two parents through sexual intercourse cannot fulfil the law of God; and by implication it has a different direction in which to grow, being an animal nature of man. Human nature having been contaminated, we were born with all manner of contradictory inclinations: deep-seated inclinations that oppose God in different ways.

God, knowing all these things that we cannot control, sent His son to come and die the death of that old nature who has been condemned to death in His justice, so that the new nature of human may grow. You must accept this truth that God is so marvellous in His mysteries. When the recalcitrant angels whose presence in heaven caused great trouble were cast out of heaven, the holy angels were crying on their descent to earth, knowing too well their destructive mission on earth against the sons of men. But Almighty God who can do all things allowed them to do their worst in contaminating the nature of man of the dust so that He can do His best by creating the new nature of man, not made with dust but with the bread of heaven. The fallen angels thought they had destroyed man and established themselves as gods; little did they know that the animal nature into which they had dragged man was to be the beginning of man's true creation.

Now fear not—for all natural inclinations do not matter, whether one is born a slave or free; even races, sexuality or colour do not count because there is a new nature of Christ waiting for you. A unique nature which everyone who has received baptism instantly has, which is identical within all who have received it: it is love, a divine nature born out of God Himself which is meant to spend eternity with Christ. Cry no more! For you cannot help yourself nor change that which grew up with you right from your mother's womb. Come to Christ and surrender that ancient man to that ancient testimony of Mount Sinai which ministers death; let both of them stay behind so that the new spirit you have received in Christ will drag your soul forward with Christ to bear fruits that leads to eternal life.

You may say now that many people are still in bondage of their natural disorder even after they have been baptised into Christ. The reason is that this is your lower nature, as we have discussed in the new creation; and it's a spirit on its own that also wants to live life in its fullness. Human nature being more of animal and a system we are used to before grafting into Christ must not be easy to put off, but a continuous effort is what God needs from you and you will see His grace pouring out on you to reach your expected end. In heaven, when you look back after this battle is over, your soul fully exorcised and possessed by the spirit of God, you will see the multitude of demons cast out of your soul at different stages of your life and will forever thank Him who has marvellously redeemed us to God. Know this truth: that His grace will not come unless one moved forward with Christ—rooted in the devotion to the Fullness of Grace of Luke 1: 28.

Most times, even when we are pressed down, His grace will secretly support us and push us forward until we completely lose our strength, to prove that we can do nothing without him. It is then that His super abundance grace will manifest—for God wants you to slide-tackle yourself and fall into the hands of a loving father who cares for your soul.

It is said in the Epistle of John that anyone born of God must defeat the devil. This is a true saying because the spirit that entered into man after baptism is a fresh breath just as He poured into the moulded image of Adam, to combat and rescue the soul of man from bondage of the old spirit. Once one can respond faithfully to the Gospel of Christ, that new nature is unstoppable until it fulfils its mission, which is the salvation of our soul. That spirit is full of light because it does not connect to the flesh; though it dwells in man, its actions is only on man's soul and it reports directly to the Holy spirit who aids him in this mission of rescue. When this spirit is active in man through his cooperation in the saving grace of Christ, the old nature does not have a basis on which to operate because the soul is occupied with the freshness of the Holy Spirit. It is only when this spirit is dormant that man becomes truly human, fulfilling all the lust of the flesh which is triggered in his old nature.

We are all born with wounds of original sin that have the destiny of death; thus we must all accept Christ for the destiny of life. I used to wonder why we have all manner of wild and natural disorders, but now I wonder no more and I condemn no more—for truly in sin we were conceived and born into sin, so no one indeed is good; otherwise Christ appeared in vain. The old nature of man is so bad that the law could not even exalt it but rather griped it on the floor until the day of Christ. (Compare Romans 8: 3)

When you see people condemning people, it means they have not known Christ, or themselves, because this knowledge will transform and change the concept of your understanding towards the nature of man, who was more of the spirit in the beginning and later became more of the flesh. This is why sexual immorality became one of the sins that offends the Spirit of God and pulls man down, because the spirit we received in baptism is pure: a type of virgin spirit which will eventually take us to heaven to live like angels who never engage in sexual activities. That nature of Christ in us has no connection with the natural instinct, but rather is divine and angelic.

This is the depth of man: that man was truly a spirit and this is why Christ appeared to restore all things. To know this truth, man, having been introduced into the mystery of Christ in baptism, must imitate the apostles who first followed Christ. How would you know the root of a man you just met on the road without getting close to him and become his friend? Did the apostles not meet Christ on the way and yet followed Him to His home, perhaps for better knowledge of His identity? How do you think you can know the truth of Christianity without deeper humility in studying its history? Knowing that by so doing one will be able to extricate oneself from all the false teachings, doctrines and politicians who flagged themselves up as if they speak the truth while they are introducing a different gospel to sooth their own preferred way of life.

These political blusterers with fake eloquence introduce the doctrines of man into the mystery of faith: disregarding the mystery of self-denial, even though from the ancient days God manifested Himself as a spirit and demanded true worship in the spirit and truth; yet they prefer to use the holy Gospel for the benefit of old nature of man while their spiritual nature is lost.

What are we saying? That a man who met a beautiful woman on the road who displayed a virtue worthy of being his wife does not fail to extend their friendship to her home, not only to seek her hand in marriage, but also to become part of her family. This is what every Christian who wants to inherit eternal life must do, irrespective of the denominations he may have found himself as a result of politics and disobedience; otherwise he might lose the faith of the apostles by confessing a different thing that the apostles never confessed. As a Christian you have met a beautiful faith which started a long journey many years before any of us were born; to know that faith, one must follow that faith back to where it started, just as this young man we described above did because of the love he has for a woman, so you will unite with the grand church fathers in one confession and get your spirituality rooted in the same foundation which the Holy Spirit has started with them—for to be a Christian is to be in communion with the

Christian grand masters—for disconnection in the physical has a gross consequence, and how much more a disconnection in spirit. To be a good historian, one must connect with the past histories.

The worst thing that happened to Christianity is false doctrine and deviation from the foundation. This is the worst attack of the gods of the world when they saw that the persecution of the apostles they provoked did not hinder the mission of the apostles, but rather helped in spreading it; they deployed their agents and evil men to spread the false message, men who are bound in the old instinct of man—who do not know that Christ and Virgin Mary were the new Adam and Eve whose natures were completely different from that of fallen Adam and Eve. But Christ who is the good shepherd knows what He was saying when He said that He is a good shepherd, and that His sheep must always follow Him and not a stranger. (John 10: 4-5)

Do not be wise in your own eyes, no matter how awkward you might think that the ancient practices are; hide in humility and practise it for it is life. Close your eyes and let your soul guide you. Were it not that the apostles were humble and so foolish in the eyes of the populace in their days to believe that God manifested Himself in the flesh, they would not have been exalted by Christ and we would not have had this salvation. But they endured all the cajoling of the wise and learned and the Rabbis who classed the followers of Christ as an accursed crowd who did not know the law. (John 7: 49)

Most times we see ourselves blaming the Jews for not believing in the divinity of Christ but the truth is that we would have done worse than that had we found ourselves in their position. How can someone whose parents you knew, who you saw born and who grew up among you suddenly claim that he who sees him has seen God? To believe such a claim one must be a highest fool who has the Holy Spirit as his teacher because the Bible exegesis sometimes also becomes addicted to the greatness of God that they forget that greatness and humility are both the attributes of God who only stand as a mighty giant to the natural man, but as a father and lover to all who denied the worldly wisdom to follow Him.

...   .

Most times people thought that they could live the type of life as they have read about in the Scripture or in the lives of the early Christians and the Saints, with the same experience of the wave of the Holy Spirit. In vain the spider sits patiently waiting for food without first building its web and stays still hoping for a catch. In vain the seed tries to grow on the dry land without water and fertile earth.

The ancient Christians operated in the theology of the new creation in Christ Jesus, understanding that there is a new man in them after baptism that needs nurturing and taking care of in order to grow. All the Apostles and the church fathers operated in the highest definition of self-denial before this new nature in them could conquer their old nature and spread the Gospel of life. Most of them lived more of a vegetarian life—avoiding certain foods and sometimes meat according to their diverse callings. This is the root of and the connection to why some Christian churches avoid eating meat on some days in communion with these apostolic traditions. It does not say that meat is bad, but it is food to the old nature of man, which makes him more earthly. Thus in the Old Testament, the Law forbids the eating of certain animals in order to make man's soul tameable and to separate himself from the spirit of flesh.

In the New Testament, Christ sanctified all food but the Holy Spirit who spread the church guided them to the knowledge that the flesh and blood does not give to the spirit, rather it takes away, and makes man truly a natural man with all manner of concupiscence of the flesh to live more of his animal nature. But the new spirit has a new food entirely and does not feed on the same food as the old man does which kept him in the bondage of the flesh. 'Man does not live by bread alone but by every word that proceed from the mouth of God.' (Here, Christ is talking about the spiritual nature of man whose life does not depend on material things at all.)

Therefore this apostles inspired by the Holy Spirit kept to the minimum the intake of food, especially the food that goes beyond the flesh to the spirit. These are the reasons why we could not experience God and the action of the Holy Spirit in our time to do marvels as they did who were indeed mystical Christians. One cannot neglect the principles of the spirit and still want to operate in the invisible because to be Christian is to live more of the spiritual life though we are trapped in the flesh. All the virtue our holy faith introduced us into can never be carnally acquired but only through the spirit; thus sometimes it hurts to keep to the commandments of Christ which is Eternal life because out of ignorance we nurture two natures the same time. All the promises that were meant to follow all the believers depend on one's deep roots in the spiritual principles.

Why did Peter's shadow raise the dead, and St Paul's apron emanate miracles? Do you think it was just because of their faith in Christ alone? It was because they also practised all that He commanded them to do which defined faith; both those things He whispered in their ears which His Holy Spirit still whispers to the ears of those faithful who are willing to obey Christ and whatever His church is teaching.

Consider St John the Baptist who spent all his life feeding on the locust and wild honey; having been freed from the effects of original sin from his mother's womb, yet the Holy Spirit prescribed him a type of food in order to keep his spirit up to fulfil his mission in the salvation of the world. Virgin Mary the mother of Christ was said to have fed with only bread, fish and water all the days of her life; but she never ate meat. Thus she could be able to keep her spirit united with God who truly saved her. Though these two great souls have grace in abundance, yet it is not without mortifications and self-denials that they were enabled to fulfil their destiny. It is a true saying that Virgin Mary fears sin as serpent, or as a natural man fears death. Therefore the only option for her was mortification. Yes! The natural man fears death because that is the end of his freedom, as he does not want to use his days on earth to earn eternal life.

Before one can be a true follower of Christ in truth and spirit as He commanded, he must first understand the true nature of Christ, what He preached and how the apostles who first followed Him practised His teachings; though we are weak, we would become strong when we look into the lives of these saints of Christ because it is a transformation and power we need—seeing their weaknesses and power of God which only manifested themselves in greatest weakness. Going back to the history in the lives of the saints is the most powerful devotion we need in this contemporary time when there are lots of false messages and wolves in sheep's clothing as messengers of good news. Because when one reverses back in history and comes back to the present moment, it would be easier for him to decide to follow Christ or most of the new doctrines which have no place in Christ and God.

I used to think that some people may be exempted for their ignorance in following the false teachers, but the Scripture is saying clearly, 'My people perish for lack of knowledge'. When Christ was handling the same issue, He said, 'If a blind man leads a blind man, both will fall into a pit'. (Mathew 15: 14)

In the practical reality of being blind, I have never seen a blind man who chooses to walk with a blind man as his guide; rather he waits patiently for one with sound eyes to lead his way. But these people who are blind in the truth of God choose to run with blind prophets who see only darkness even though it is very clear that they are impostors. This is why Christ proclaimed Himself as a good Shepherd, who calls His own sheep by name and leads them out; the sheep hear His voice and follow Him recognising His voice. Yet they will by no means follow a stranger, but must flee from him—for they do not know the voice of a stranger. This is a natural blessing; even in the lives of human beings; a baby always recognises her mother's voice and will always cry looking in the direction she believes her mother to be, hoping the mother will hear her and run to her aid. Consider also baby animals in the wild; even among the thousands of herds of animals, who look so similar, their young ones instinctively have a unique image and scent of their mothers. If this unique knowledge is in the wild animals, how could one excuse or go blind regarding the truth of his origin and be deceived?

Jesus went further to tell some of His listeners that they do not believe in Him because they are not of His sheep: 'My sheep hears my voice and they follow me.' Christ's sheep are not special predestined people, as some think, for Christ died for everyone; but people who love and long for God no matter where the gods of the world have condemned and caged them. They long for His deliverance. Thus the Psalm said that, 'He looked down from heaven to the earth that He might hear the groans of the prisoners and set free those who are condemned to die.' (Psalm 102: 20-21) These are the sheep of Christ and none of them will be lost as long as they continue to cry from that pit of death and most of all listen to hear the voice of that great Shepherd who goes about looking for His own; they must hear and recognise the voice of He whom they have been waiting for.

In a relationship with God, God must be taken as He is, loved and adored even as He prescribed for us, and His commandments must be loved better than life we have. Any man who exists in this code is the one who belongs to Him as a sheep. If we are truly the sheep, we must eat the food He has prepared for us, and stay within the territory He mapped out for us. Christ loves us as sheep and does not want us to cross over to the goats' side. When a good shepherd is strict with his animals, it shows that he loves them and does not want them to feed on certain grass knowing too well that it will go ill for them. So if by mistake one of the sheep oversteps and crosses the border to the side of goats, the good shepherd does not hesitate to look after it and bring it home, but it must get ready to go through the healing process as for many days it has been in the strange place eating forbidden foods and being bitten by all manner of poisonous insects. If the good shepherd fails to do this, the result will be that the contaminated sheep will transfer its effects to the rest of the flock.

This is our Christ—a good Shepherd to His people! In the Gospel, He regarded some people as the goats because they refused to be under His Lordship that He may heal them, considering it the best option to be on their own, going into territories infested with all manner of poisonous reptiles whose bites bring death, eating food that their bodies crave which is forbidden by heaven because it brings death to the soul of man.

During the earthly life of Christ, Mary Magdalene as a lost sheep was a harlot; yet later she became one of the great saints. She was in bondage and was crying in her heart for freedom that only God could give; she loved God and knew that what she was doing was wrong but could not help herself to stop. Deep down inside her she needed salvation—for generally salvation does not come to people who do not look forward to it. Thus the spirit of repentance embraced her when she heard Christ spoke. Probably she may have been one of those who enjoyed the miracle of multiplication of bread and fish; did we not read in the Gospel how she was weeping at the feet of the merciful Christ who forgave all her sins and set her free? This is the kind of mind that Christ wants His people to have: loving God above your natural inclinations because Christ does not come to the assistance of people who do not first of all hate whatever sin they commit even though they are trapped in it. To them He does not fail to give blessings and the salvation they crave.

One of His sayings in the Beatitudes is attributed to such people because He loves them so dearly. 'Blessed are those who hunger and thirst for righteousness, for they shall be filled.' This was the same situation in which St Paul found himself when he was Saul. Most times people talks about St Paul as somebody who was really bad before his conversion: but it's not so.

Saul was one of the people who loved God even more than some of the Disciples of Christ. But he misunderstood the mission of His Christ—thinking that Christ and His followers had a mission to destroy the Law and the Prophets, therefore like the soldier of God of Moses he was, he determined to root out Christianity to uphold the law of God. According to the law, he was fighting a just war, and persecution of the Christians was justified because of his misunderstanding of the law. To the Jews, Christ was crucified because He was a false prophet and God did not defend Him; therefore His followers must not live or be allowed to spread their error freely. To them Christ was not the Son of God; if He were, God would not have allowed Him to be crucified and His affirmed Resurrection was propaganda. So Saul was fighting for God, against God. Before his conversion, Paul was a man who kept the law to his highest ability, longing for the coming of the Messiah. These were what Christ, who looks to the heart, saw and came to his aid—making him one of the greatest Apostles because of the greatness of his love and faith in God of his fathers.

When a man hears the voice of God and cannot follow Him, it means that he has no love of God in him. Though love of God and His principles most times clashes with the natural inclinations of man, yet His children love Him, surrendering to His commandments that transform—until they begin to think and behave like Him, loving all that He loves and abhorring all that He abhors. It is called having one will with God even when our lower man is saying a different thing. Many people fear the truth because they do not want to be hurt by its transmuting force; therefore they remained in bondage of their lower nature—choosing to have the gods as their shepherds instead of the only true God who gave His life for His sheep.

In following Christ the truth, man must get ready because the truth He is must hurt you, but truly it is the beginning of your healing. It is an exalted truth that the old nature of man begins to die as soon as man understands that Christ has begotten him: that is to say that a new life from baptism has started growing in him. He is the Truth and Life, and the spirit that controls the old nature of man is the lie and death; and these two cannot agree. Did you not hear what St Clement 1 said: 'This world and the world to come are enemies, and we must not be friend to both at the same time.'

Christ called Himself the Truth and the Life, because the gods who had been ruling man had lied to man. From the Garden of Eden, man has been deceived and made to believe and act like flesh and blood while he was a spiritual being from the day he was created with dust and raised to a spiritual level with the breath of God who is spirit. So He appeared to tell man this truth that is so hard to believe and live because man has dwelled too long in the strange kingdom. To those who believe in Him—life everlasting; but to those who do not believe in Him—eternal condemnation. For upon this greatest truth the judgement has been predetermined. If any man is following Christ and has never been hurt by that great Truth—I mean in your old man, know you that you have not started following Him in truth and in spirit—such a fellow is still in the spirit of old self; and the spirit giving birth in you through baptism has not even seen broad daylight. Know you that if that new spirit does not grow, neither would your soul bear any fruit of eternal life; thus you could not feel the pain of the death of your old man—for you can only feel its death when the new spirit is growing, just like the old seed is dying when the new seed begins to form. This is the testimony of the saints and we must believe and accept it as the truth that saves: that following Christ is the death of our animal nature and sin that springs out of it as its tradition.

Forgive me if I have offended you; but am I not the most pitied fellow? Yes. The mysteries in this book are the hardest truth with which I have had to battle so far, against lots of forces both in the air and within myself, to write. I have offended myself so greatly, because there is no manner in which one will tell the truth about God without hurting his old nature, unless he has no truth in himself. Everybody who needs everlasting life must strive to know this truth that sets free, in spite of how hard or offensive it may sound. Know you that if truth does not beat you down mercilessly, you cannot accept it and reconcile with the divine spirit.

Is it the best thing to endanger our souls because we are afraid of the truth? No! Therefore, it is holy advice to you who want life of the Gospel to run away from the feel good gospel message which makes one a stranger in the mysteries of God.

In John Chapter 3: 19 Christ said, 'Him the light has come into the world, and men love darkness rather than light, because their deeds were evil.' The simple truth is that no one in his right senses would choose darkness rather than light; it is just that the nature of man craves for darkness instead of light. To natural man, darkness is light because his glory has been taking away and replaced with the shadows of the world; so in him dwells the darkness and his nature feels better in darkness doing his own thing. We all used to belong to this darkness; it's just that some people have greater darkness based on their foundation, thus men are grouped as sheep and goats.

In this context the sheep will eventually end up in heaven, but the goats will not, even though both eat grass. Yes! Even though everyman sins every day, the righteous cry every day for his sin, and God who hears every groaning wipes away their tears and will eventually grant them the fullness of salvation which they love and crave—while the wicked will sin and grow worse and worse without repenting, deceiving and being deceived. Blessed are those whose spirit is crying every day for the sins they commit! But not so are the wicked who are hardened by the deceitfulness of sins, crossing the borderline given to man by God who is love. As if crossing this line is not enough for them, they start to erase it, asking why such a line should be drawn.

In praise of the most sacred heart of Jesus, He is called the zealous lover of soul. This is what the depth of God is: a Lover! His principles and commandments laid down for man are out of love. The eternal truth is that God is all good; He created man to subdue the world, but instead man failed. What has He done wrong? Did He not give man enough strength, creating him just a little lower than the angels? It is not His fault that man failed, but because man chose to listen to the stranger he never knew since he knew God as his Creator and Father. Yet in all that man has brought to himself, He in His mercy denied Himself His nature as God and fell down into the captivity and death of man to redeem man. So to hate God and His THOU SHALL NOT'S is the greatest mistake any man could make. We must come to terms with the fact that the present nature of man is not what God intended for man from the beginning; and no matter how comfortable man is or how hard he is trying to adapt to the state in which he found himself, God can never be satisfied until He returns man to his formal glory—putting all things under his footstool as it used to be.

By the way, what about our state laws? Are we all comfortable with these all the time? No! But they are enforced for the upkeep of a peaceful society. Without laws, man runs the risk of becoming wilder than animals, so these are good. Even so the precepts of the Lord are good and worthy of all veneration to keep man of the earth very close to his origin.

The choice we face is that man is at the mercy of God and must follow God who knows the way; in Him is the fullness of redemption, because He is merciful. He is God and Man; having experienced all the weakness of man, He knows too well how to administer justice and mercy to the one of His precious creatures called man. Let all the wisdom of man give way; let His own stand. Let no man claim right before the presence of God, but rather let them claim the right of mercy—for mercy is the only right that is justified before Him no matter how miserable or sinful a man may be, though He may bear a bit longer with man but He cannot change His highest attribute which is mercy.

Prayer and Meditation-

Oh Lord! Help us as a seed sown in the earth to die and grow a new man that will inherit your kingdom. As that man in the Gospel who has nothing with which to pay experienced your mercy, even so we solely depend on your mercy for we have nothing absolutely with which to pay.

The entirety of the Gospel of Christ is a raised SWORD against the negativities of our lower nature; you must raise it for liberation of your precious soul!

The Destiny of Life is Optional

Remember the voice of the eternal spirit who said, 'The only way back to the heavenly paradise is self-denial'? Why not ask for the grace to suffer the death and the decay of the nature that you are denying? For salvation is free to the spiritual nature of man but it is indeed very costly—for it will cost you the worldly traditions of your lower nature.

Truly on earth, man is in exile. We are from very far away, not in any way to be compared with being in exile in a worldly sense, but the kind that takes a deeper understanding of where we used to be in order to be able to seek and get back to our original home. As an exiled spiritual being, man must long for the day of freedom, for it's not a good omen for a spirit to be trapped in the flesh.

It is very clear to the soul that it's trapped in the body—for many things he does not want to do, he does, and the same with the things he wants to do which he cannot. All these he cries for, and the voice of the most ancient spirit in mercy says, 'Seek me and live!' (Amos 5: 4)

Only in seeking Him lies the freedom of man; otherwise he will be trapped forever in his encasement which must decay and such man will still live to suffer the effects of the decay because the soul trapped therein is immortal.

We do not truly know our spiritual existence because we all have left home long ago. Just like the prodigal son who left his father's home having stayed too long on his own, the pigs' food began to look good to him; so it's man's case on earth. We always seek the things our flesh thirsts, thinking that it's all that matters without knowing that it's all about what is available for us since we have left our true state.

The story about the fall of man as stated in the book of Genesis must continue to be folklore to a natural man until he decides to wake up from his deep slumber and fight to get back to where he had fallen because Christ has come. God is calling all men to emulate the prodigal son in remembering the kingdom he had left for slavery so that returning will be possible. To do this, we must acknowledge and accept that the image of God is imprinted on man's heart. As the coin that bears the image of Caesar was given to Caesar, so man who has the image of God must dedicate himself to God.

It is truly condemnation and a complete separation from God for man to reject Christ. One may say 'I have God', but the truth is that no one can know God without the nature of Christ in him. As we have said before, the offspring of Adam was banished from the divine presence of God, thus Christ the new Adam appeared to beget the new offspring for God which Adam could not do. When a child of Adam accepts Christ, he accepts the spirit of eternal life that Adam had lost, and through the spirit will call God 'father' which the offspring of Adam cannot for he is a slave who cannot remain forever. You must come out from every creed you confess which is outside Christ, or better still include Christ in your creed to divinise it—for the old nature of man cannot know God until he accepts the new nature of man which is in Christ.

Consider His virgin birth through which God has reconciled Himself to man even as the angels proclaimed in their song when He was born. After His ministry and crucifixion, there was a great mystery, proclaimed by the inscription on His cross as 'JESUS THE KING OF THE JEW'. This was written in Hebrew, Latin and Greek. Hebrew represents the people of God, Latin symbolises the power of man, and Greek represents world knowledge. A Jew spiritually means he whom God is with. (Compare Zechariah

8: 23) Therefore this Jew must come from these identities that represent the world.

... ...

My child, I am the Lord your God, who brought you out of the land of Egypt, out of the house of bondage. You shall have no other gods before me. Keep all my commandments and worship me who made you, so that it shall be well with you. This is the summary of the cry of Exodus 20: 1-17. God want man to keep his precept to be happy on earth and inherit back that lost eternal life.

When Christ was on earth, He re-established this fact—that without Him, man can do nothing. Not Him as a prophet or a righteous man, but Him as the new Adam and the living God. Most times we have this mentality of God as a Being; and we forget that His attributes are clearer to us as no one has seen His form nor has anyone known His infinite greatness, being the Life, the Truth and the Light.

When a child is born into the world, these attributes are what he or she needs: being alive, dwelling in the light and going in the direction of the truth, just as the new growing plant traces the direction of the sun even when it is planted under shade. When a seed germinates in the confined space without the sun, it pushes forward towards the sunbeam; there is a tendency towards unhealthy growth or even death when it fails to prevail. The same is true of the life of every man born under the sun because he must respond to the creation call to adore the Lord of creation who manifested Himself not only through His prophets, but also in His natural laws and finally in the last days manifested in His son. Dwelling in this truth is the advance of growth—for the Scripture says that Christ is the true light of every man who comes into the world. (John 1: 9)

What is the truth? This is the question that Pilate put to Christ when He said that He was born to bear witness to the truth. 'Those who are of the truth listen to my voice,' Christ concluded. How peaceful the world would have been if all parents should bring up their children in the way of the truth. The nature and the knowledge of God grows within a human person as he develops because human beings are naturally religious beings; thus you cannot see a city without a temple or shrine dedicated to higher beings, either to true God or false gods. It is so because of the nature of God retained by man even though he had fallen; as this nature hides in the depth of man, he continues to search and has no rest with any other or within himself until he finds God and rests back in Him, just as St Augustine said.

After the fall of man, his punishment was not only that he was debased as an animal, but more that God whose presence lights up the nature of man is hidden completely from him; therefore his soul continues in search for God. (Even though the Gentiles do not know God, yet they continue to venerate Him having been surrounded by demons who took the position of God; they offer to them homage which is meant for the creator.) This God saw and sent His Law to His first born, Israel; that through it His nature will come back to man in Christ Jesus, and that every tribe may be blessed in Him. (Compare Psalm 72: 17)

We know that God is spirit and a spirit has a presence whether it is good or evil. So as we said God is a spirit; to those who connect to Him, He gave His presence and planted His word in their spirit. On the other side, those who could not connect to Him are those who the princes of the world, the gods of this age, have occupied, darkening their hearts and filling them with their presence so that they can never see beyond it. They are the same unfortunate first group on the wayside in the Christ parable where the devil comes and snatches away what was sown in their hearts. This group of people are always in a far greater number even in the days of Christ. With them the evil one establishes his kingdom and spread his errors; they are the world he rules as he is called 'the ruler of the world' in the Gospel.

Do not think that our world would have been the way it is if our children were exposed to the presence of Christ in the early ministries. Even though not all of them will experience Him in the same measure, the few He will choose among them will be used to put each generation on check and evil would not have dominated the way it is now—for with Him one can chase hundreds. But our technology, which is the fruit and pride of the old nature of man, has taken most of our children and many destinies, and calls have been destroyed or diverted towards the glories of the world. We spend only a little time with God while we spend most of our life on earth searching for a knowledge that will one day decay, and building houses and empires which exist today and tomorrow are no more. In this, man's soul is exposed to the everlasting shame because he prefers to preserve his body, which is not even his property but was given to him so he might adapt to where he found himself. Be that wise man who did not remain in the posh house offered to him during a visit, for there is no place like home.

As we have traced the human origin from the depth of God, to the earth, to the Garden of Eden and finally back to the earth from where his physical attributes began, one can now realise that man can do absolutely nothing without his loving maker. Even if out of stubbornness man decides to live his life without God, he will not be complete because he is meant to be a higher being which he can only attain through connecting himself to God. And the spirit says, 'In vain a natural man claims to be a higher being without the creator.' Therefore, it is right and just for man to strive to get back to where he truly belongs. By the virtue of the death of Christ Jesus, it is everyman's right to inherit salvation given freely by the creator Himself even when we do not merit it. This salvation comes only through Christ and His church. No other creed, institution or any faith has divinity to recreate and redirect the destiny of the fallen man. 'There is no other name that is given through which man will be saved.'

Christ is for all men. It is very sad that many religions did not acknowledge Him; even those who acknowledged Him did not do this as God made man He is. Even some Christian denominations, out of pride, doubt and false doctrine, did not accept Christ as God.

Why should a believer be held in such utter darkness even when the Scripture bears unclouded witness to this? Are they not awestruck with the very beginning of the Gospel of John, which strikes like the thunderbolt—proclaiming the consubstantiality, the divinity and the immortality of the Eternal Word of God who took the Virgin's flesh to become man? Did they not see that the Gospel account of John Chapters one and three is the mystical account of the second creation of the supernatural man within the natural man, even as Genesis Chapter one was of the creation of the spiritual Adam who later became animal Adam?

In the book of Ezekiel 34: 11&16 The Lord God said, 'Truly, I myself will search for my sheep and seek them out. As a shepherd seeks out his flock on the day he is among his scattered sheep, so will I seek out my sheep and deliver them from all the places where they were scattered. I will seek what was lost and bring back what was driven away, bind up the broken and strengthen what was sick.' This is Him among us in the fulfilment of this prophecy, the ancient Lord of the Eden Garden—healing humanity and bringing them back to that holy paradise whence they were driven away. You must not shut the door against Him.

As I said earlier, the nature of man is rebellious to anything divine. It's not a surprising thing to Christ, thus He came in flesh to be able to practise the highest level of self-denial and patience in convincing man to follow Him back to God. He did everything possible to be able to achieve this, even being among sinners, and was identified as one of them. Yes! He was a sinner for our sake; and that's where our love for Him should spring. Since God could become man to save man, there is no level to which a man should not descend to do the same for the sake of his fellow men who may be weaker or of a more wounded nature. But it must be with a clear conscience and deep humility to identify oneself with them, otherwise converting people will be near impossible, and God will not have an option other than to push you down to humble you.

When God calls a man to officiate as His minister, it is not from a high level, but from the lowest level to His altar: not to be proud but to represent and speak for his people. 'For every high priest taken from among men is appointed for men in things pertaining to God, that he may offer both gifts and sacrifices for sins. He shows compassion on those who are ignorant and going astray, since he is also beset by weakness.' (Hebrew 5: 1-2)

God did not call us into this new life only that we may enjoy His kingdom, but to help in building and furthering His kingdom. By loving not only the brethren in the church, but also by extending that love and light of Christ to them that are still in the shadow of death, knowing that it was the same place we were when Christ found us. When one who is filled with pride and self-righteousness follows Christ without a compassionate heart for the conversion of his fellow men who he thinks he is better off, God being a merciful father who wants all men to be saved will cast such a fellow down into miseries, which will make him to realise there is no difference between him and a miserable sinner despite His grace. Having stayed in their midst, he will accept his weak nature and identify himself with his mates before God allows him closer again. Coming back with humility, he also comes with the spirit of love and intercession—pleading for the salvation of his brethren from among those whom God has called him for their sake.

When God gave salvation to a criminal, it was not for his sake alone, but so that he could appear before God with the rest. He must go back into the world to testify how God has transformed him from darkness to light. No one knows the gravity of sin and the magnitude of darkness better than he who has been in darkness, for he enlightens his comrades much more easily. In such a way God is magnified and the doors of salvation are open to those overshadowed by darkness without hope. This is the kind of mentality ministers should have and things will become easy for us to achieve the eternal life that Christ has earned for all humanity.

One of the problems we face is that some of the clergy and ministers of religion sometimes seem to forget that there is not much difference between them and the people they minister to. Were they not sinners taken from among sinners, exalted by grace to minister mercy and to intercede, and not in any way to condemn those whom Christ has died for? We all possess the wounded nature of Adam, which can do horrible things; the difference is that a true Christian is concealed under the shadow of the Almighty and through Him is able to control his rebellious nature. But those without Christ are in the womb of the spirit of the world, fulfilling all the laws that control their nature. The basic fact is that notwithstanding the righteousness of any man, there is a deep-rooted nature of sin in him; being in the presence of God suppresses it. But outside the grace, what he sees or hears can trigger that nature which must act contrary to God. Therefore every preacher must preach with humility, bearing in mind that he is not better than those he ministers to. Also when a clergy member falls, his flocks should treat him with love knowing that he is just as weak as anyone else. Let us speak no more against the ministers, for they have the greatest temptation in daring to fix our spiritual nature.

Being a true Christian is just like engaging in serious battle with man's deep-seated nature of sin, which is very difficult even when one is a true Christian. By implication, without Christ man is just natural and must act it. Even though God chased man out of His garden, He still loves man and He wants him to seek His face to find the way back home. When man rejects God, he loses the sense of morality and must live according to the principles of the spirit, which controls the fallen nature of Adam—to fulfil the lust of his flesh and senses which are natural and the tradition of the animal kingdom where we found ourselves.

To grasp the full meaning of the teachings of Christ especially when He established His doctrines as contrary to the world, one must understand the principles of the world with the mind of the Scripture. It is called the spirit of the world. It is the complete opposite to the spirit of God because its economy is being controlled by the arch-enemy of God and man, who rules the spirit of a natural man. On this context Christ based the saying that He did not come to bring peace in the world, but rather division. (Compare Luke 12: 51)

Christ is a divine nature of man thus He was called a sign of contradiction. This is the reason why a natural man must continue to contradict the doctrine of Christ until the nature of Christ is born and grows up in him; then he ceases to contradict. Because the divine nature is incarnated in a natural man who now lives as a new man and those doctrines that were strange become truth to him because it is the life of heaven of which its citizen he has become. He will now believe and confess with St John, 'if anyone loves the world, the love of the father is not in him.' (1 John 2: 15)

Out of this Christ Jesus given to humanity, there is no salvation! The ruling spirits of the world must control him and consequentially the natural man has no option than to live out the wounded nature he was born with. A true Christian must allow the Holy Spirit to convince him that every child born into the world not only inherits sin but is born and shaped in iniquity. Formed according to the spirit of the world to adapt on earth—thus baptism comes in to super-naturalize that child to live as a heavenly being.

By saying no to Christ, man is left with the option of living a life that characterises the lust of the flesh and eyes and the pride of life that St John also said is not of God.

... ...

These things we see going on in our world today about sexual orientations, the right to live them and all manner of things which are clashing the heads of the religions and politicians are all human nature deeply rooted in the natural man, and must be his right and life unless he is by the grace of God able to deny himself living the new nature of Christ which is optional. No one has the right to dictate for his fellow humans on how to live his animal nature. Christ Himself did not condemn anybody and forbids His followers from judging. He did not impose His doctrine on anyone; rather He stands by the door and is knocking at it; whoever opens the door for Him, He comes in and blesses him and eats with him whether he is homosexual, heterosexual or asexual in his animal nature. We should always imitate Christ who, though He was God, did not impose His pure nature on anyone but rather acted as if He were pleading. He declared at the top of His voice, 'God did not send His son into the world to condemn the world, but that the world through Him might be saved.' (John 3: 17, 12: 47)

This will induce he who thinks that he is holy to thank God more for what he is not, and cry for what other people are. Do not judge or condemn them for many of them cry silently for what they do which they could not resist and they always say, 'I wish I could be like this good person.' Why do you not also cry to God and ask Him to change them to be like you, if you are truly holy as you claim?

Are we encouraging a natural man? Certainly very far from that! But we respect every human culture and orientation. We appreciate it since it is what we have at the moment and it is also a stepping-stone in understanding that only God is holy, and also to understand what God want us to know about being human. Of course Christ said, 'He who is unjust in what is least is unjust also in much.' (Luke 16: 10)

How would you know and accept the divine nature if you have not known what it means to be a human? All our natural inclinations should be seen as a platform and as solid ground we must stand upon to be able to know God.

We must understand very clearly that all the offspring of Adam have no inheritance in the kingdom of Christ and His God. But every natural human being has the right to live his life and enjoy everything just like everyone else if he so chooses.

Since fornication and premarital sex are no longer seen as sins by the populace, how dare the same people stand against homosexuals? What do you want them to do, seeing that the heterosexuals are living their animal nature without minding the principles of godliness? Are they not all the same before Him who is holy? For sexuality and all manner of natural life exists only in Adam's nature of man, which has nothing to do with the nature of Christ neither can it inherit anything of the kingdom of light. Learn first how to cry and sort out your ugly nature by taking care of the planks in your eyes, to be able to see more clearly as the Lord said. Or have you not seen in the Scripture that 'you are inexcusable whoever you are who judge, for in whatever you judge another you condemn yourself; for you who judge practice the same thing.' (Romans 2: 1)

Let us lift our mind above all these characters of the old nature that will eventually head down to oblivion, and gaze on Christ and the purpose of His manifestation. Our kerygma is a total call for the universal repentance and acceptance of Christ!

Homosexuality cannot be considered a choice or a personal sin, but rather part of being human and an orientation one found oneself: a kind of disorder which we all have in diverse ways. Of course no one is free from disorder; and God did not create anyone to be homosexual, disabled or with all manners of mental syndromes. It is just how the person was formed and born, as we all are the product of the contaminated nature of Adam with different wounds. Let our understanding be elevated that God is no longer creating but rather He is watching His works as they display their procreative circles as He eternally made them from the beginning.

The issue of homosexuality in our days is just been over-exaggerated by the world of today as if it's a new thing. It is one of the satanic strategies to spring up what is hidden in man, because a subject becomes important when much emphasis is projected towards it. It's not a new thing but the nature of man! Those who said, 'it's not' do not really understand the basic mind of the Scripture concerning the natural man. Trying to defend the uniqueness of the natural man, they stand against the mind of God who knows that man in the flesh can do anything, even the most horrible thing that offends. This nature has been there with the fallen man, even in the days of Abraham and Lot. Was it not there as the character of the natural man when God was giving Moses the moral code? Thus God did not fail to mention it. (Compare Leviticus 20: 13)

Accept this liberating truth you who follow Christ; do not be worried because your old nature is not meant to be good if you are truly a child of Christ. The old nature of man is a thief, drunkard, murderer, and a bastard; he may be a homosexual, and may not elude practising bestiality or even the worst; so that Christ may see more reason to reborn and look after him if only he can deny that nature, to transfer you into His marvellous kingdom of light. God is not even interested in those moral codes of do not do this or that because the old man has been judged and condemned. Yes! God has left the old man behind with the law to deal with him because Christ has come; He is interested in the offspring of Christ who is created for heavenly inheritance. He knew that the old nature of man cannot please Him since he left the Garden of Eden; therefore He imposed a burden of the law upon him just to tame him till the fullness of time. His desire after Christ cried on the cross, 'It is finished!' is that man should give himself to Christ who paid the debt of the old nature, so that Christ will bestow upon him a new nature that is divine, a spirit that helps the soul deny whatever disorder he has in his lower nature.

This new nature does not need to keep any law but to live a life of heaven with the instinct of the nature of Christ who knew no sin. Thus the Bible is saying, 'Look unto Christ, the author and the finisher of our faith.' (Hebrew 12: 2)

Take your mind completely out of the old nature and his deeds and follow Christ if you can! Let every encouragement be given, and prayers and sacrifice be made for anyone who has made up his mind to follow Christ even if he is still patronising his old nature, for we all equally have disorder. You may not know that the prize of making heaven is equal to every human born by a woman; that is the reason why you are busy looking at another person's wound. Let us follow Christ in truth and the spirit; He knows how to deal with us; after all Christ did not die for the angels but rather for the natural man and whatever disorder and handwriting were coded against him. He wants sinners to follow Him and not the saints. How dare you condemn those for whom Christ has died, even when he is still in sin?

According to human anthropology, history and the Scripture, homosexuality is a deep-rooted nature of man spiritually traced to the nature of Adam. However, it is a wounded nature of man that directly attacks procreation, thus those who are so unfortunate to be born with it suffer much mental torture, deprivation and cruelty from people as if they are directly the cause of their feelings. Nobody knows how painful a situation is unless one is able to fix himself somehow in such a situation, after which he must have a change of approach and understand the teaching of Christ when He says 'Do not judge!'

Some people are of the naive opinion that marriage can heal homosexuality, because they are not sufficiently spiritual to know that human nature is gravely wounded, mistakenly thinking that Christ came to heal the nature of Adam. Christ came to born new spiritual children, not to heal the old nature that has been banished from entering heaven.

To get over the addiction which one may have got into in his adult stage is as hard as death, and how much more so the natural instinct which lives and grows within. We have seen that some of the marriages that break down are rooted in this, because the two people involved cannot be soul mates. For a man with such inclination to enter into marriage is like a mockery of marriage, unless he has decided to die to that nature and clearly defines the situation to the other half before the marriage, because it's a kind of self-denial in which the other partner will suffer much because they can never be intimate. Otherwise both he and those who pushed them into the marriage will be guilty and responsible for that would be doomed marriage and its consequences on the affected children.

Must everyone marry? Don't get into things because it's how the majority of the populace sees it. Eventually you will get stuck in it and will not be fulfilled, because not everybody is meant to marry. If you are not drawn into marriage, do not engage in it, otherwise you will suffer. Enter into the great mystery of Christ and follow Him with all your heart. He has a message of love that is satisfying waiting for you.

Our existence in the world is far beyond getting a good job, having a marriage and having children. We will understand when we grow above the worldly mentality and evolve more spiritually that increase means more than raising a family. Christ Himself and most of the saints did not marry to establish a better understanding that increase does not only mean bearing children. Who has increase more and better in the world than Christ and those who followed Him closely though they never married? We felt the pain of not being called into marriage because of the wrong mentality of the world setting. Let us strive for the indwelling of the spirit of Christ in us so that we may balance our animal nature and live an exalted life either in marriage or single life.

Let those who suffer more in their sexuality run to Christ who is so merciful and has a solution to every human problem. He has an abundance of grace and He gives this according to the wound each man may have. There is nothing like Christ changing a man with such an inclination to heterosexuality; what He does is to give grace for such person to be able to cling to the new nature received in baptism which has nothing to do with the natural law of sexuality for it is divine. Unfortunately our world has been sexualised which makes this divine life seem impossible. It is the nature that will be like the angel in the last day. As we have said, sexuality exists within the nature we all inherited from our parents and it will remain so far as natural life is concerned. When one who is homosexual in his lower nature wants to follow Christ, through much prayer and sacrifice, grace will be given to him for self-denial either in marriage or single life—which truly speaking is not an easy adventure. Following Christ in the nature of Adam is not possible; neither can He change that nature to suit Him. The nature of Adam must step aside if you want to follow Christ; but if that nature must live, it must live whoever he was born. Even married people who do not have a separate altar of divine love set aside in their heart cannot by any means please God who demands the complete love of individual souls.

Let every man see his problem as the reason why Christ appeared—for man knew that he needed a Messiah, thus the whole humanity in the voice of the holy Israel prayed fervently to God to send the Messiah who has come to set all men free from all manner of captivity. Now, it is not the case of your sins or your ugly nature, but your love, struggles and perseverance in following

Christ. It is very obvious that the sins of this generation are far greater than that of old, but Christ has come and felt as we feels. He is standing between the gap, healing our wounded humanity which He accepted out of love; He has not given up on you unless out of despair you let go of this hand of the zealous lover of soul, who humbled Himself and took human nature in our wounds, suffering our darkness both in our sexualities and all the evil spirits working in human nature, thus He dealt torturously with all kind of demons.

This mystery is what the Scripture celebrated when it said 'For in that He Himself has suffered, being tempted, He is able to aid those who are tempted. (Hebrews 2: 18) Understand well what this means—all these things you may be suffering now hit on Christ like rock and shattered into pieces so that he may save you today if only you could give yourself to Him now. As we were born and live with different disorders, even so Christ calls us and gives us unique nature to live above our first nature. Forget who you are in your lower nature; fix your mind on He who took your old nature to Himself and died its death that you may live the higher nature which Christ has given you freely. Of course you must bear in mind that this is the hallmark of self-denial! He who wants to live above the contaminations of Adam's nature must exist in the mystery of death decreed by Moses and exalted by Christ.

...   .

It's very obvious that we all differ in DNA molecules, as we all differ in our natural instincts and inclinations. But the new nature has one unique identity characterised by the agape type of love; he is created in the flesh so that he may practise the final destination of his soul in the flesh, so that the kingdom of God will not look strange to him in the world beyond. Blessed are those that fixed their eyes on Christ while on this great journey of the soul. Happy are they who live their animal nature in the right manner before God and spiritual man.

It is said in the spirit that a stranger will never enter heaven—for it must be people who practice heavenly tradition in flesh that would recognise the way to heaven in the spiritual journey of their soul when they depart the flesh. That connection will take them back into God because they existed in the eternal life of Christ on earth and were able to immolate their animal nature. The saints of Christ were born with all manner of natural inclinations that clashed with the divine doctrines, but through the nature of Christ in them, they lived above it.

Just as men of Nineveh will arise at the judgement and condemn the generations that ignore penance, the queen of south will do the same to those that reject the wisdom of heaven made manifest in Christ. Even so the glorified saints of heaven will arise to condemn man whoever he may be who justifies himself to live his ingrained nature against the eternal life, for they too had all manner of natural instincts worse than ours, but they submitted their human nature to the great commandment of God and went forward as sons and daughters in the nature of Christ. If one does not practise the teachings of Christ on earth, in the spirit the gate of heaven will look very strange to him that he would have no option than to choose the gate of that master whose doctrines he lived on earth.

It is only through grace that we know God, and this grace comes through no other way than our sincerity in acknowledgement of our natural weakness before Christ—for the deepest love of God is manifested in the most miserable nature of man when in humility he trusts and cries to God. So for the grace of God to work, natural disorder in man is necessary. Though this natural man's character may not be necessarily sinful, it can never agree with God; man is bound to know that God is holy and merciful. Therefore we need not to be ashamed of our lower nature, nor should anyone suffer hate and abuse from their fellow humans who should love them simply because of their orientations; for this is how it's meant to be.

One great truth I realised in the lives of the saints, both in the Scripture and the church history, is that God does not use people who seems to be good, but rather those who have more complications and are in total darkness regarding natural life as He knows the depth of every being. In this mystery He displays His excellent greatness as the Divine Alchemist. Have this great truth in your mind that it is the will of Christ that you should forget who you were completely that you may know Him.

There are lots of testimonies of this great truth that Christ is a great lover who treats humans not as sinners or servants, but in just the same manner that a good husband loves and takes care of his wife. This holy relationship is possible because in Him is the combination of the divinity and humanity. On this platform, His humanity accepts and heals us just like the good shepherd; He soothes our wounds, healing us and taking us into His divinity, which is one with His father. Here the mystery of becoming one with God and the heavenly people is fulfilled.

Man can do absolutely nothing without God in the spiritual sense. When He appeared, He simply called man to repentance, declaring that the kingdom of God was at hand. After His ministry and death, the only kingdom He left was His church with her ministry of recreation. There is no other place the new life is other than in His church where man is reborn, renamed and set on a journey towards eternal life. This kingdom of God is within man because that nature born in baptism is a divine nature and the offspring of the Holy Spirit who can only establish the principles of godliness around him.

Any man born out of the spirit of Adam who needs salvation must follow Christ. The best way to do this is to trust His ministers and look beyond them to see He who gave His life as ransom for many. Man has no right to hate Christ because it's a capital crime against oneself; such a person refuses life and remains in the darkness. Consider the kind of His death for the whole world; the Jews condemned Him and the Gentiles crucified Him. It is a great mystery that both the Jews and the Gentiles united perfectly to put Christ to death; so that the whole world, both the Jews and the Gentiles who believe in Him, may be saved. Yes! Both spiritual races must have salvation through His holy blood.

Sometimes we see that many people deviate from following God out of their quest for knowledge or academics prowess and success. Because of his proud and self-acclaimed wisdom, man calls himself the intellectual; he began to question the eternal truth, comparing the divine and spiritual things with the physical and human knowledge, which can never agree. Even when a religious leader dares to apply his academic intelligence to the things of spirit, he becomes a destroyer of the kingdom he is trying to establish. This is the case where spiritual insights of God revealed are regarded as delusion or mental pictures of imagination, and a person who is so unfortunate to be under their guide is enveloped in many clouds of darkness.

Intellectual wisdom is good but we must lay it aside when it comes to things of the spirit, otherwise a grave error will occur. This is the reason why most of the people who come close to Christ have been the common people who are not wise in the eyes of the world because they are far more enriched than the philosophical ideas of the learned. Of course the populace in the days of Christ were more confused about the wisdom of the apostles, seeing that they had not acquired any formal teachings of the law as the scribes and the Pharisees, only that they were with Christ. What have you read or known which made you deny the existence of God? You must have just studied a branch of knowledge. Maybe you are a doctor who knows only how to manipulate the human anatomy, or an astrologer who knows very well how to gaze into the galactic systems. But have you existed in the world of the mystics who sometimes exist beyond human senses, and other branches of learning which are so vast? One should not conclude that God is not; because not withstanding what you studied, your wisdom is still limited.

Remember the popular saying that a tree does not make a forest; different types of tree must grow around it, and yet it must attract all manners of animals—with the birds of the sky celebrating it, declaring it a forest with their beautiful songs.

When riches increase, many people drift away because riches of the world also have powers and forces that are being manipulated by he who captured the natural man. Thence that wise man prayed, 'that I may not be rich and deny God'. (Compare Proverb 30: 9)

It takes an extra grace of God to serve God faithfully if He calls us to Him when one is well loaded with the riches of the world. There are riches of the world and the riches of heaven and these two do not agree even as the tradition of the heaven and earth do not agree because they are being given to different natures of man. As we possess the two natures of man in us, old and new, even so God blesses these two natures separately; remember we bear the visible nature of Adam, but also there is the invisible nature of Christ growing in us, which will come to its fullness when that great separation is due. The natural man, He blesses with being happy in the world. The supernatural man, He enriches with the effusions of the divine grace to live the tradition of heaven in flesh so that he may inherit heaven.

Riches of the world are the blessings of God that He created in the world for its inhabitants: gold, silver and all the mineral resources of the earth, all the blessings that radiate from the stars of the heavens. All these are gifts for natural man. Men are gifted in many ways, with different kinds of natural talents and skills to build and beautify our world and make it a happy place to our capability. The bitter truth is that all these natural talents of man are meant for his worldly glories and therefore are subjected to the manipulations of the devils that also laid claims to the treasures of the world because they defeated and subjected the natural man to their rules.

Though man had fallen and deviated from the original plan of God, yet his nature of Adam is blessed to be fruitful but for the glory of the earth. Everything we do which does not contradict is blessed so that the fruits of those works will help us to save our souls by keeping us in the right spirit to seek for the true happiness. Make no mistake! No natural talent will take one to heaven; neither will it condemn anyone unless you lose its purpose, which is for the edification of our lives. Just as the keeping of the law cannot save a natural man, even so all his material achievements do not make up his salvation. Natural talents are good; strive for them and achieve them for God enjoys seeing us prosper physically and spiritually. Dethroned from the spiritual nature, yet it pleases Him that man should display wonderful skills showing that he is a product of the Wisdom Himself.

These natural talents have their tragedy and sometimes make the possessor live a miserable life with a tragic end if one has no regard for godliness. The spirit of old nature which possesses this gift is under bondage, therefore one can easily be puffed up with pride, thinking that he is better than all men; thus one sells his soul completely to the devil and the talent becomes one's god. Hence most of the talented men of the world are far from the truth of God; that which is supposed to bring blessings becomes a curse.

I will conclude that this is too complex, we praise our talented stars for things they do which we cannot, and it is good to do so. But the misery of natural man is so vast that praise sometimes drifts him away to destruction, unless he is deeply rooted in God. Many may not accept this, but the truth stands that all the worldly blessings do not come directly from heaven as we think, but natural man from the day of Adam has been blessed already to prosper on earth and that does not follow him beyond. Just as He created everything good and empowered them to prosper all-round, so we have been made to prosper freely. Explore and delve into the treasures of the world and prosper scientifically, intellectually and otherwise; be wealthy and enjoy life but do not fail to seek for the real treasure of heaven, which can only be acquired by those who love God and look beyond material things.

Blessings of God on the nature of Christ in us are the divine grace, which is called the gifts of the Holy Spirit. When a natural man with the riches of the world lacks these gifts of the Holy Spirit, his talents are bound to control him. But not so with the new creature, for he knows that the glories of the world are fading away with time. If any man calls himself born again but Christ has not liberated him from the slavery of his wealth, let him not fail to cry for deliverance bearing in mind that money itself is god according to the Gospel. A Christian may have an abundance of wealth, but there must be liberation from the attachment to it.

This is the grace which separates one from his wealth, even though it belongs to him yet he handles it as a stranger it is to his divine nature—bearing in mind all the time that his wealth is a good servant who wants to become the master at the slightest chance.

One of the greatest bondage of the natural man is a quest for riches; in it he forgets that there is God and that our life here on earth is temporal and that we will leave soon and everything will be left behind. We must live beyond the standard of that man of the Old Testament, to whom the law was given to banish him from living. God has a standard because heaven is another realm with a different tradition, and to get there Christ wants us on His nature.

Most times even those who profess to be Christians may not have known Christ or have excavated the mystery of our salvation because we still base our relationship with God on our animal nature and always busy labouring on our old nature, which can never inherit eternal life after death. Such person lives his entire life for the glory of the world, and forgets that Christ was manifested to give us a second birth, making us priests to serve His God.

Who will set us free from this quagmire if not He who chased us away? How can He do this if we cannot humble ourselves with the psalmist and pray that the Lord will make us know the shortness of our days that we may gain the wisdom of heart?

We long for the leader who will dethrone money and introduce true equality for everyman. Those who seem to be less important but do the hardest jobs with minimum wages need to be reconsidered and respected, because our system would not survive without such people. The world system favours the talented people while the less talented are neglected simply because money rules. If the rule of money can be dethroned, we would see how peaceful and lovely the world would become, because everyone would be happy to do what he or she loves and be more creative, not jumping into a profession they have no passion for simply because of money. If this happens, new job opportunities will be created because human potential will abound out of the happiness each man derives from the work he loves to do. For working is part of living and should bring happiness and joy—just as a Trappist monk derives joy and happiness in being alone with his God, which another may find difficult to grasp. This is part of the teaching of Christ in the parable of the workers in the vineyard. We read that the landowner paid all of them equally even those who worked only one hour along with those who bore the heat of the whole day. He did not pay them according to the hours they covered, or their intelligence; rather he paid them according to their zeal. For even though the last labourers put in only an hour, he paid them a day's wages because they had been waiting all day to find a job. I long for this kind of world—wondering when it will be, because once money is dethroned, pride, anxiety and all manner of troubles will be things of the past.

…   …   …

If man will humble himself and meditate deeply in the mystery of the fall of man and our salvation, we would find out that God is truly our creator, father and lover. Of course no father can be that angry with his son especially if he shows remorse. Man's condition on the planet earth is not the best nor is it the first plan of God. To hate Him because of troubles one experiences in the world is the greatest darkness and the tragedy of man. Natural man in his ignorance committed the worst crime against love and God—allying with the arch-enemy of his position in the created order to fight his maker and God. He is acting as if God is a sadist who does not want man to enjoy life. In blind covenant he bound himself to his greatest enemy posing as his friend while seducing him to destruction, while his greatest lover was seen as the enemy.

God in human form is calling us to Himself; He loves everybody no matter who you are because He accepted the same nature in His humanity in order to heal us, especially now that He still has the wounds in His body that our ugly nature had inflicted on Him. As a high priest, He purifies and offers us back to God. Though it's not easy to follow Him because of the nature we found ourselves in, we should strive for this, for He is the only happiness and complete rest waiting for us at last. It is the hardest thing to do in the mystery of our salvation—striving in the flesh to return to the spiritual nature—but that's the choice we face without any option for He is ever with us.

Having been sent out of the Garden of Eden into the world, man became a seed sown by God into the earth to die gradually and produce fresh seed worthy of being called the sons of God. For us to understand our mission on earth, we should meditate on the seed sown in the ground, and how it dies and decayed before the new one is produced. 'For the body is sown in corruption and it's raised in incorruption. It's sown in dishonour and rose in glory. It's sown in weakness and it's raised in power. It is sown in natural body and it's raised in spiritual body.' (1 Corinthians 15: 42-44)

It is the kerygma of the church and the entire chronicles of the Scripture that corruption and natural man who exists within the flesh and blood is not able to possess the kingdom of God. Therefore you earth-man must follow Christ irrespective of the nature of old man you bear; it is very clear that rejecting Christ is standing against the destiny of life unto salvation because the destiny of the natural man is to inherit corruption in its fullness unless he follows Christ, which is the reverse of the destiny.

Hear you the word of God oh you creature and holy image of God, seek Him and live! Even if you don't want to listen to the preachers of the good news, be calm within you and hear the voice of Him who descended to your level to reason with you. The voice of Christ in these last days is calling for conversion. This great task is laid in the hands of all Christians and men of good will; but how can we achieve this? Is it through eloquence or by preaching by the streets? Yes, all these are good and encouraging. But the core foundation in the conversion of soul is sacrifice, offering much prayer, mortifications and fasting in secret for the souls who are yet to know Christ. This is more efficacious and helps to strengthen the voice of your preaching and call to repentance; otherwise you may be pouring water on the rock—'giving what is holy to the dogs and casting of pearls before swine. Of course they must trample them under their feet, and turn and tear you in pieces'. (Mathew 7: 6)

What our world of today needs are the true Christians with the hearts of sacrifice to offer to God for the conversion of sinners in the imitation of Christ who practiced the same during His ministry. To be a good labourer in the vineyard of the Lord, one should be able to fix oneself in the position of whomever one is trying to convert and ask: how would I have welcomed this message if I had been without Christ? This will help one to strategize the best way to harvest for the Lord more fruitfully with love. Many people have different religious orientations; even in the Christian nation, many people were born of parents who place no value on Christian principles and brought up their children in this manner. You can see that many people are not responsible for what they believe or not, but rather this is caused by the kind of life given to them by their parents. So sacrifice is greatly needed before preaching so that Christ Himself will go before us to convert even through our shadows if necessary.

Meditation

The greatest truth is that all the animal instincts cease as soon as man dies; our soul who is spirit survives. What would you tell the creator if you have allowed your animal nature to deprive your soul of her divinity?

Entering into His Rest

The destiny that awaits the sown seed after death and decay is to produce a fresh seed. How happy the farmer is when he harvests his seeds, separating the good ones from the bad ones and the weeds. He puts them in his barns, with his heart full of joy because all his efforts are crowned with success.

Man as a great seed sown by the Lord faces the same destiny when this battle is over. He has stayed too long in this field of growth, and his Lord is so desperate to harvest and place him back in that garden from where he was sown into the field to produce a new man. God, angels and man will be happy together again—entering into rest as one family. Man will be so happy because in spite of the poisonous venoms from the tares he met in that great field called the world, he triumphed and proved that it is the hand of the Almighty God that has planted him. God's own kind of happiness is also unimaginable; He will be happy as a father whose lost child returned after many years of wondering, just like a good shepherd in the Scripture who found his lost sheep. If it were possible to say that God can grow old, we would say that man would be the pride and joy of His old age after all that great work we have put Him through; but He is a spirit.

After the creations in the book of Genesis, God truly rested; but this rest was like a temporary one, for after the fall of man, there has never been rest for this great ancestor who lost His child to the enemy. And Christ proclaimed, 'My father is still working until now, and I have been working.' (John 5: 17)

Who is that loving father who will have peace all the rest of his life if one of his children got enslaved in the hand of an enemy? It was all huge and a master plan of God to redeem man. In the same way He said, 'Let us make man in our own image and likeness.' And a serious meeting was held within His persons before man's creation, in the same manner in which He spoke again after the fall of man and the great battle that cleansed heavenly places from the fallen angels.

Not only that, God begin a new and longer work within Himself more than He did before the creation of man; the new angels and powers were also manifested. Man has gone down to the earth with the wicked enemy who never meant him well; but God did not leave him even one moment. He sent His seven Spirits into the world as recorded in Revelation 5: 6.

These spirits of God Himself were the great force that work in the depth of man to remind him that he left a place and found himself in exile; thus man always fixes his eyes on heaven calling on God even if his senses are giving him a different signal. These spirits also put the fear of man on the fallen angels themselves who hold man, just as we see in the zoo that even though a lion and other wild animals are held in captive, the zoo attendant fears them knowing that their strength is still within them.

God despatched His powerful angels on the four cardinal points of the universe, as we can see some of these angels in action in the book of Revelation. This He did because these fallen legions would have had control over the constellations against man. In the seas, though, some of these demons have taken their place; God placed His angel in charge through which 'He gave the seas their bound so that water should not transgress his commandments: Ruling it in its pride and stilling the surging of its waves. You set limits they might not pass lest they return to cover the earth.' (Compare Psalms 87: 10, 104: 9 and Proverb 8: 29)

Otherwise the enemy's power can stir up the sea to cover the earth. Finally seeing that the fallen angels have sown the seed of all manner of wickedness in the heart of man to commit various evils and bring sickness and death to their soma, in mercy He despatched millions of angels. Some of them work as guardian angels, and the rest are responsible for peace on earth, teaching, healing, wisdom, purity, intercessors and war-faring angels. Even on earth, the angels of heaven continue their war with the fallen angels and it will continue for as long as man is still in earth exile. Oh, the love of God for man!

Take a very good look at yourself and tell me why God would not love you since He dared to die for you, His creature. How dare you think that He does not love you?

We see the few evidences of this war in the book of Daniel where a lower angel was withstood for number of days until the archangel Michael descended to aid him. (Compare Daniel 10: 13) The similar act of deliverance took place in the book of Tobit where the archangel Raphael came to fight and eventually chained one of the fallen angels in the mythical graveyard and delivered a young lady they held in bondage. (Compare Tobit Chapter 8) Truly God is merciful as we can see how His mercy has been following man around to ensure his final salvation.

Sending His prophets and assigning angels to aid them is a proof of His continuous work that they accomplished excellently but not without difficulties and obstacles—for nothing good comes to man on earth easily without the angels of God fighting for it. There is always war in the spirit for the sake of man even for his happiness on earth and final salvation of his soul. Most times in the Scripture we see something which is supposed to catch our attention, to make us pause and ask some question, but because of our carelessness and slowness to understand the spiritual voice of the Scripture we overlook it. In the parable of the sower, we see that some seed falls by the wayside and the demons snatch them away, so they don't understand it.

Did it not trigger in you an alert to ask what is going on? How and why should God send His word to man with the intention of saving the soul and the evil one dares to take it away? This will induce us to always find ourselves on fertile land to be able to accept the salvation of Christ without unnecessary struggle. Once the spirit of God is not rooted in man's heart, the evil one, through the old spirit of man, can take away whatever good is deposited in man's soul. Thus sometimes we have a vision or revelation in the dream and forget. You must have this mentality that he who dares to defy the angels of God in the presence of God is not a mere spirit; but always rejoice because you are the sons and daughters of God who is the Almighty.

It is the will of God who gives life after death to give man rest after all his works as his final destiny. Entering into His rest is doing His will, which delivers from multitude of evils, as we are made to know that anything that resists the will of God in our nature is evil spirit. To do the will of God is only easy when one surrenders himself to the Holy Spirit through the Gospel of Christ, then this Holy Spirit will begin the gradual work of revolution in one's soul through the new spirit given in baptism. The Supreme Spirit will now take the soul through a journey that starts with reasoning together with the soul. If the soul is ready to make a covenant with the Holy Spirit at this point, he will go very far because the deeper love of God will be poured in his spirit. This soul, who used to do his own will, will now enter into deep thought—what I will call the foundational teaching of the Holy Spirit.

'Who am I?' begins the dialogue. 'Where am I from, did God create me out of His own will without any mutual agreement between us, did He not fashion my chemistry and decide the number of days I will live? He knows my strength and weaknesses as well as my natural inclinations. If He had not made me, I would not have been. I just found myself existing without knowing when it starts, "naked I come, and naked I go". Therefore if I must live peaceably and fruitfully, I must exist in the will of He who made me.'

Having considered all these facts and being ready to sacrifice, the spirit will now start manifesting His will, which demands sacrifice: a mystery of self-denial because His will contradicts human ways. Remember what He said to Peter: 'you think the way man thinks, not as God thinks'. When this truth dwells in one's heart, it becomes easy for us, having known that His will and love are better than what we know as life.

... ...

For the soul of any man to reach heaven without Christ Jesus is like when one decided to travel on foot a journey that takes an aeroplane twenty-four hours. How is it possible? How can he possibly cross the seas and rivers that surrounded the landmark that leads to his destination? Definitely he cannot avoid walking through the forests, some of which are occupied by wild animals that can prey on humans. Who would defend him against these wild animals or carry him across the seas? Who will feed him and strengthen him? Thus the Psalmist was crying, 'Who shall climb the mountain of the Lord'. Climbing the mountain of the Lord is not an easy adventure even when one is righteous because of the narrowness of it. Though Moses was righteous, it was not easy for the children of Israel, thus God Himself walked with them with His angels around them defending and feeding them with the mystical bread; yet that old nature could not make it to the physical place of rest, not to talk about the spiritual.

This is what Christ is doing with whoever believes in Him. He walks along with him defending him with His mystical wounds with which he redeemed him, which marks such a person as Christ's own. Nothing terrifies the demons on our way back to God like a candidate who is grafted into the mystery of Christ—for the blood of Christ speaks for him in any territory he came across. No child of Adam is allowed a passage in those spiritual territories, no matter the creed he professes or the prophet he invokes, except the children of the new covenant, the product of Christ and Virgin Mary. The prophets before Christ and such like who claimed to be after the death of Christ were also not allowed because they too needed a redeemer. Because Christ is the way, the truth and only life for no human whoever comes into the world can go to God except through Christ who is the life of everyone who came into the world.

The price of man's redemption is so great that God Himself came down to carry the whole lot, as the Scripture said that the chastisement for our peace was upon Christ. (Isaiah 53: 5) His father laid it upon Him because Christ decided to lay down His life for the guilty and banished children of Eve in order to create them anew, which He completed by His death and resurrection and had every judgement committed into His hand.

The mystery of this thesis is so crucial! Everyone is called to look into it. Let theologians and philosophers excavate it. Let the preachers and the singers spread this eternal truth whispered by the Holy Spirit who is so much in love with man and wants him to come to the full knowledge of the truth. Even the atheists are not excluded to this great truth of the new nature in Christ and the final destiny of man.

Truly the kerygma of the apostles and the teaching of the church in the mystery of baptism is that there is new creation. Our spirit is not born again but rather a new spirit is created and given in baptism. Our old nature is the spirit which was passed to us from Adam through natural birth, while the new nature is equally a spirit, but of Christ who is spiritual man. These two can never agree for they are two different natures of man with different destinies. If our spirit is born again as some people preach, then it means that nobody would ever sin after baptism; but the reverse is the case for the first nature that is earthly and a sinner lives. In him dwells the instinct of sin for he is the nature that had fallen and is contaminated; yet he must live because there is a mission that he must fulfil—for the gift and call of God is irrevocable.

To this first nature was given the mission of increase and the birth of a soul which he must fulfil before the spirit from Christ comes to liberate the soul. Based on the nature of spirits, once a spirit is defiled, there is nothing like purification or rebirth for that spirit; it must face the condemnation that follows. Thus God cast away the fallen angels and the spirit of man they defiled, for they are spirits and by the implication know the truth.

Why are we so slow in understanding? Was Christ, whose nature we have given to marriage or sensuality? Was His mother not the ever virgin as confessed and held by the church? When Christ was confronted by the Sadducees about resurrection, did He not tell them that 'the resurrected nature of man neither marry nor is giving in marriage, but will be like the angels in heaven'. (Mark 12: 25)

The mystery remains that the old spirit of man controls the soul during intercourse and birth, and every other thing the soul can achieve on the earth for his well-being; but the spirit of Christ is responsible for helping the soul to detach from earthly things and labour for the kingdom of God. With Christ Jesus, humanity is a Divine Generation; they are no longer natural but spiritual to inherit the kingdom that was meant for spiritual Adam.

There are lots of differences between these two spirits according to their source. The natural man gathers and builds higher edifices not caring about anything beyond his geographical existence; having left the life in that garden for many millenniums and become completely earthly, he is addicted only to the tradition of the world. But the new spirit connects the soul back to God, opening his eyes to the mystery of Christ to labour so hard to acquire for himself the treasures of heaven so that he may return to his heavenly home. Because the truth exists in such a soul that he is a stranger in the world.

We must always remember that Adam the giver of the first nature was sinful, but Christ the giver of the later spirit is sinless. Thus the Scripture said that whoever has been born of God does not sin, for His seed remains in him. (1 John 3: 9) Yes! This is this new man who is meant for heavenly inheritance; he is a new nature who knows nothing but the life and character of Christ who gave it. This is the nature of soul when it dies completely to the spirit of the world; and it becomes holy and perfect just as Christ called us in the Gospel to be just as the father in heaven is perfect. Did the scripture not say that the law of God is not difficult for the children of God? Simply because the new nature has the same will with God no matter the pressure of his human instinct—for he overcomes the world being born of God. (Compare John 5: 4)

... ...

Our true life begins as soon as our soul departs the body; all the feelings and human instincts disappear, because a separation has taken place between the soul and the flesh. And the soul will follow whatever spirit he obeyed on earth for his reward and for continuation of his life. Of course the souls of the just will enter into His rest—for that was the purpose of the manifestation of Christ.

'They shall never enter my rest.' This was the same statement that follows the old nature of man even as God said to the children of Israel after proving to them the decadence of the old nature of man. He tried by all means to tame them so that they may have rest but did not prevail. Even their children that entered the Promised Land never had a complete rest because God used that to symbolise the future event that would take place in the days of Christ. The Scripture said, 'If Joshua had given them rest, then God will not afterwards have spoken of another day' (Hebrew 4: 8) because there was no rest as the attitude of rebellion continues even the worst with their children; their labour and suffering continues. Therefore it is a convincing infallible truth that Christ Jesus was manifested to create new man, which must enter into His rest.

To enter into this rest is to be completely free from suffering and labour that must take place beyond. It is the final destiny of the new man to become spiritual priests to serve God when perfection is achieved through the ministry of Christ and perseverance in prayer. At this level you will be able to endure sufferings—being able to offer everything named suffering and persecution to Christ, the only High priest, who in turn offers them to God for the salvation of souls. For until a Christian reaches this level of feeling less pain to whatever may come his way on the narrow way that leads to life, he may not achieve more in fulfilling his duty as one who is participating in the priesthood of Christ. Because salvation is given to us so that we, too, may be able to win at least a soul to make heavenly beings happy. Of what purpose is it for us to be proud of being Christians if we are not yet ready to fulfil our spiritual duties as priests, thereby being able to save our soul and others? You must know that your sacrifice is needed for salvation of souls—for somebody known alone to God must have offered costly sacrifice united to the crucified Christ for us to be called a Christian, and we must do the same, 'offering ourselves as a living sacrifice holy and acceptable to God'. (Romans 12: 1)

To be able to understand who we are as priests, one must reverse back to the law and the prophets and study well with the Holy Spirit what priesthood represents in the old covenant and what their duty was. Consider that even as the levitical priests have something to offer, so Christ Himself offered not external sacrifice but Himself which is His humanity. Yes! He redeemed us with His humanity and recreated us with His divinity. In the garden of Gethsemane, His nature as God was completely hidden so that His humanity could pay the price of sin to its fullness. There in the garden it was not His divinity that struggled with the will of God but rather His humanity. His humanity that yielded completely to the will of God and suffered mentally, emotionally and in the flesh, was the nature that He sacrificed as a high priest for the sins of the world. Therefore it is a true saying that the Word of God used the flesh and blood of Virgin Mary, which He created and took during the incarnation to sacrifice for our redemption. This same flesh having dwelled in it, He told His followers to feed on it for their eternal life because through it He intended to get rooted in the depths of our being. Archbishop Fulton Sheen in his contemplative mind testified that, 'the Word of God took the flesh of the Virgin Mary that He might give us the bread of life'. What a mystery of the new mystical creation of man fulfilled in Christ?

Let us consider also that the prehistoric Christ who was manifested is not only called the Messiah, but also a High Priest. Not just a priest as of old but a high priest unto endless life because He offered Himself, accepted all our abominations as His own, was convicted for this and died because 'the soul who sins shall die'. (Ezekiel 18: 19) In Him we all died. This He did, 'washing us from our sins in His own blood to make us kings and priests to serve His God and Father'. (Revelation 1: 6) So if He died to make us priests, we must strive to know how to offer sacrifice—entering into the heart of Christ to offer the sufferings of humanity from any stock where he may have chosen us to serve Him.

This stock means the various darkness from where we were called. Whatever inclination you are struggling with as a Christian, offer yourself to Christ along with other people whose daily life is of such character because they are not in Christ; this is what it means to be a spiritual priest. Know exactly who you used to be or would have been if not for Christ; then stand before Christ for them and refer to them as your brothers even as Christ referred the whole humanity as His brethren before His father.

To exist in this mystery is not reality until God willingly allows us to mystically, mentally and physically feel what other people suffer. When these strange things are over, one will have no option than to embrace such people and identify yourself with them before God. This is the mystery of Christ in His manifestation—calling us brethren because our sins are His own. Therefore upon Christ was the whole anger of God against the soul of man; sin was condemned in Him. Thank God for Jesus who took the condemnations of the children of Adam and Eve on Himself!

We are saying that heaven is not meant for people who are automatically saints or predestined in some certain sense of understanding. The saints of heaven were all sinners who were taken from all classes of darkness. But they were exalted in the mystery of total self-denial, recognising that there are two natures of man in them controlled by the spirit of the world and the spirit of Christ.

This is the deepest secret of the saints: knowing that the nature of Adam and Christ exist in them. Therefore they denied the negative nature of Adam in them. They too suffered with tears the constant threats of their old nature which they were denying, but the gifts of the Holy Spirit were their consolation, which was not without dryness—for to live the life of the spirit in the flesh is truly the death and the decay of the nature of Adam. The Scripture said, 'The men of Nineveh will rise in judgement with this generation and condemn it, because they repented at the preaching of Jonah'. (Mathew 12: 41) Even so the saints who were born with the worst inclinations will rise up on the last day to condemn whoever that refused to let go of the ugly things of his lower nature and follow Christ.

Do you think that the saints have no wounds in their instincts and orientations? Whoever you are reading this book, the saints of heaven were just like you in any way you may have wounds in your genetic codes, heredity, sexuality or otherwise. When the Scripture said that on the last day people will gather before the Lord from all tribes, languages, people and nations, it means also from all manner of sinful natures and traditions of man—for the saints were truly transferred from the kingdom of darkness to His marvellous light. Indeed no one will have any excuse on the last day; the poor and all manner of disabled people will proclaim very loudly, 'Even with all my troubles I loved and served God on exiled earth faithfully'.

To enter into the rest of God is truly with the cross through the narrow way; there is no other way. If the journey to greatness and achievement of great destiny in the physical world could be tough, how dare one think that returning to the glorious kingdom of God will be easy? A Christian should always consider some of the harder sayings of Christ to be able to work out his salvation. How could one strive to enter heaven and yet be thrown away on the last day?

Truly it makes me tremble, especially nowadays when the culture of the world is humanising heaven in total denial of the basic truth.

They want to return man to the UR of Chaldean from where God called Abraham and made Himself known to him. As we said briefly before, it was a place where the whole compendium of God was folklore and fairy tales. The spirit of error has been circulated as part of our curriculum in the hearts of the future generation. If they are left alone to make everyone believe that man originated from ape, of what need is it to believe that God is a creator and lover who kept Adam in His presence before his fall? The motive of the spirit of evolution theory is to convince man that he is a common animal and by implication bring more disconnection between God and man. This is what the world order based all their arguments on, thereby returning man to where he was when Abraham found God.

It makes my heart shed tears when most of the new world set-ups are only how to progress in this life without thinking about the soul that has been given eternal destiny to survive the flesh. Are we not most foolish as the Scripture said: 'If our hope in Christ Jesus is only in this life, then we are of all men most pitiable.' (1 Corinthians 15: 19)

Foreseeing all these things Christ said, 'Do not think that I came to bring peace upon earth. I came not to bring peace but sword.' (Mathew 10: 34) His Gospel is truly a divine inversion into the heart of man to liberate man from the death that follows the nature of Adam. But the strong spirit of man possessed by the fallen angels could not let go; and it became truly a tug of war, which confirms His words in the Psalms: 'I am for peace, but when I speak, it brings fighting.' (Psalm 120: 7)

It is truly by the grace of God that we can fight this war, uniting with the nature of Christ in us to liberate our precious soul from the spirit that lives strongly in our flesh. The poison of our old nature is so cancerous that one must study the nature of his old man very well—knowing his character, always keeping his soul above it, beating it down and stabbing it really hard whenever it dares to release its poison. One must ensure that he is rooted in the doctrine of heaven, otherwise you will not be able to deal with this poison of the old nature through which the devil rules.

... ...

Of course the soul of man is truly the tabernacle of God if he is willing to obey. If our eyes are open to see how the angels of God follows man, minding him in all that he does, we would understand that God wanted to dwell in us indeed. But it is very hard because He cannot impose Himself on us unless we make ourselves available. And making ourselves available is not easy unless we wrestle hard with the unwelcome guests who dwell in the depth of man so that we will sense the love of God.

The paradise of God is the final destiny of man when Christ must have dwelled in man on earth and completed the work of salvation of our individual souls. Yes! The fullness of our salvation is not yet completed as long as we are still in the world and in the flesh, for we are yet sinners when Christ died for us. Christ's presence in the soul tolerates no rival. He gradually takes away everything negative that runs through Adam so that the soul will be truly new and Christ's nature.

By the eternal truth of the decree of heaven, the product of Adam will by no means return to paradise. This is the reason why Christ was manifested. If human nature was good and could merit heaven, then Christ appeared in vain! In vain did He suffer the most horrible manner of sufferings and death on the cross: 'Christ was wounded for our transgressions, bruised for our iniquities; the chastisement for our peace was upon Him.' (Isaiah 53: 5) He suffered all the consequences of the love covenant between God and man, which was broken in Adam. As the new Adam, He begets new children on the earth by establishing His church as a new kingdom and world to breed them and returns them to the true presence of His father beyond the paradise where Adam and Eve was, because His offspring are one with Him and God.

The mystery and the nature of the product of Christ is that they are no longer that nature of Adam that was made of dust; rather they are a new kind of species made of the bread of heaven. Adam was made of dust but his soul was that breath of God that made him a living being. During the incarnation of Christ, the new nature of man was manifested which, as we have said earlier, is the product of a mystical marriage between God and man to liberate the souls of men by creating new spirit for the souls. In this new nature of heavenly man the new man was created because the man of the earth has been cast out with his spirit condemned in the flesh. This Christ Jesus, though referred as the second Adam, is far above Adam both in prominence and excellence, because He is ontologically divine without anything earthly found in Him.

As John the Baptist bears witness, 'He who comes from heaven is above all'. With His spirit He recreated man; in the mystery of His mystical flesh and blood He liberates and refreshes man's soul. The soul of the old man has flesh made of earth as his covering, while the soul of the new man is the flesh and blood of Christ. This is truly the nature of the new man created for the glory of God—for the old things have truly passed away.

Turn now and take a good look at yourself in the mirror, or better still look at the face of any human around you. What you see now is an angel. Yes! Man is a missing angel who found himself in the flesh. Look into those eyes made of glassy sea. Though he is in animal nature yet he does not have a look of an earthly creature; he is truly in a strange planet and vessel. If this missing angel would follow Him who came from heaven in search for him, his final destiny will be freedom from flesh into his angelic inheritance in heaven. For the Virgin Mary who is the mother of the new creations is truly the Queen of the angels. Therefore we the children are going back to our angelic nature when this long battle is completed, to inherit our eternal destiny in the presence of God.

Confession and Meditation

Man was created by God and redeemed by God in a new creation fulfilled in Christ.

Some Biblical Substructure of this Book

The ground network and the resources of this book are based on the mystical truth from the heart of the Scripture. Of course the Scripture is the mother book and one of the most ancient writings that has survived through all ages. The supreme revelation of the most ancient spirit that speaks to all ages, having contained the very beginning and the end of all human family from our spiritual world to the material world where we found ourselves. Since the Scripture did not contain the whole truth ministered by Christ during the days of His flesh, the Holy Spirit still uses it to bring out some of the teachings of Christ, which are still hanging in the air. For it is impossible that His words will hang without being written down and communicated to every living, for the time is very near.

It is the only ancient book that is highly venerated and that triumphed and found its way on from all the books of antiquities: a salvation and covenant kept by the eternal God for those who desire to return to that great paradise we lost with Adam and Eve. Other ancient books which dared to compete with it did not stand the test of time and ended up as mythologics, being the false glories of the fallen angels who posed as gods to enslave humanity. Yes! There is only one God; and His testimony as contained in the

Scriptures is eternal life, which the natural man had lost. To obey the Scripture is to return to this eternal life.

1. Man was created by God in the beginning. His early conception was from one of the kingdoms created by God which we called the planet earth. On Earth God formed him and made him a living being. (Genesis 1: 27-29)
2. Man was spiritualised and exalted with the breath of God. Being as glorious as the image of God, man was raised to the spiritual realm called The Garden of Eden to dwell in the midst of heavenly spirits and live as one family in adoring Him who is Infinite. (Genesis 2: 7-8, 15)
3. The sin of man and his fall back to where he started his existence to till the ground and live the fullness of his animal nature since his spirit has been contaminated and can no longer withstand the glory of God. Just like a seed, God threw him into the earthly field to die and be regenerated as a new man. (Genesis 3: 6-7, 23. Isaiah 5: 1-5. John 12: 24-25)
4. Condemnation of the natural man. God went further to declare that this old nature of man will never enter His rest. (Genesis 3: 16-19. Psalm 95: 11)
5. There are truly gods in our world of today even as there were in the Biblical histories. Thus we see some ancient practices rising up again. The hidden natures of man are also rising because of the hidden devotions to these gods, which the true message of Christ held in bondage for quite a long time. Therefore it is right to say that humanity is returning to where they were before Christ. (Exodus 20: 3. 1 Samuel 5: 2. Exodus 12: 12. 1 Corinthians 10: 20. Psalm 96: 5)
6. God promised a redeemer, and the plan for the new nature of man began. (Genesis 3: 15. Isaiah 7: 14, 11: 1-2, 43: 19. Ezekiel 36:25-28. Micah 5: 3. Luke 1: 31, 2:7. John 1: 12-13, 3: 5. Galatians 4: 4) Peter concluded that we are

redeemed with the incorruptible. This redeemed stand is recreated in the ancient text. (I Peter 1: 24)
7. The old nature of man with the spirit of fallen Adam is not free and will continue to be a slave so that the soul will be free in the new spirit of Christ. The whole levitical law was imposed on the lower nature of man. The law is directly against the inclination of the natural man, and thereby condemned his inclinations as sinful. (Exodus 20: 1-17. Leviticus 18: 1-30. Romans 7: 1-25.)
8. The old things sometimes refuse to go because we get stuck in our old nature. Therefore the soul pays double homage to the law and grace until he learns how to die in his lower man and live for Christ alone. (Romans 6: 1-23)
9. In Adam and Eve, God created the whole humanity. After creating everything in Genesis, He saw that they are good; He made them capable of procreating and regenerating themselves. He is resting as all His works displays the wisdom of God. We all have the ability to procreate and do whatever we purpose. We are responsible for whatever our children are because they are our fruits. Children receive whatever the parents project onto them, especially when they are forming in the womb. God is not responsible for any disabilities or disorders in human nature because the first man He made was perfect. (Genesis 1. 2: 1, 11: 6. John 1: 13)
10. All the blessings of God to the old nature are based on fulfilment of the requirements of law. Paying tithes is also part of law holding the natural man in bondage since he is no longer a son but a slave. If the old nature of man is truly a son, why must he pay tithes? What must a child pay his father in order to gain his inheritance if not loyalty? The father's properties belong to the son. If all that the father has belongs to you as a Christian, why should you pay tithes to have them? The tithing principle for Christians should be to give generously to the church and to give to whomever asks you, as commanded by

Christ in the gospel to share all we have with people who do not have. The apostles and the kerygma of the early church did not lay emphasis on tithes because the offspring of Christ is completely free. To ask for the grace to share whatever you have is the greatest tithe required by Christ. (Leviticus 26: 1-46. Deuteronomy 28: 1-68. Psalm 51: 16-17. Malachi 3: 10. Micah 6: 6-7. Mathew 5: 42. Acts 4: 32)

11. A Christian is a new creation, and an old thing has passed away if we are willing to let go the old man in us. (Ezekiel 36: 26. Isaiah 44: 3. Joel 2: 28. John 3: 5. 2 Corinthians 5: 17. Ephesians 4: 24. Colossians 3: 9-10)

12. A new creation is freed from the law and from condemnations. New creations are sons and daughters of God through the mystical creation they have in Christ; for both the father, Christ and those begotten by Christ are one. In truth all the offspring of Christ are freed from the law because the law was given to rule the seeds of Adam and Eve. (Romans 7: 6, 8: 1. Galatian 5: 1. Ephesians 1: 5. Colossians 2: 10)

13. Adam and Christ were two different natures of man; the former is natural and earthly while the latter is spiritual and divine. What the ancient church called the immaculate conception of the Blessed Virgin Mary is one of the greatest mysteries fulfilled by God towards the salvation of the fallen man. Though Christ was a complete human, He did not share the fallen nature of Adam. This is the kerygma of the apostles even as seen in the epistles because God prepared a body for Him that was not of the will of flesh nor of this creation. Christ Himself confirmed this infallible truth when He said that the ruler of this world is coming and he has nothing in Him. (John 1: 1, 14. John 14: 30. Romans 5: 12-21. 1 Corinthians 15: 44-49. Hebrew 9: 11, 10: 5)

14. Through the eyes of heaven, human nature is so wounded, having fallen down to the animal nature which cannot obey

the laws of God. (Ecclesiastes 7: 20. Psalm 14: 2-3. Isaiah 53: 6. Romans 3: 10, 8: 7. Luke 18: 18-19. John 15: 5)

15. Christ loves every man, for with Him there is no disorder or ugliness. He is ready to stand in the position of all your disorders and handwriting against you if you will give Him a chance. Upon Him was laid the whole sins of the world. (Isaiah 53: 4-5. Mathew 11: 28. John 1: 29. 3: 15-17)

16. The planet earth is not our home; rather we are pilgrims on the earth. We are meant to inherit the kingdom of God prepared for us before the world began. (Psalm 119: 19. 2 Corinthians 5: 20. Philippians 3: 20. Hebrew 13: 14. 1 Peter 2: 11. Mathew 25: 34. Ephesians 1: 4. Revelation 21: 7)

Other book by the author.

THE NEW CREATION

HEART OF THE CHURCH AND SCRIPTURE

DANIEL OBIKWELU